£9.99

KT-223-037

Dictionary of
Economics

A & C Black • London

www.acblack.com

First published in Great Britain in 2003
Reprinted 2006

A & C Black Publishers Ltd
38 Soho Square, London W1D 3HB

© P. H. Collin 2003

A CIP record for this book is available from the British Library

ISBN-10: 0 7136 8203 5
ISBN-13: 978 0 7136 8203 8

Text Production and Proofreading
Heather Bateman, Katy McAdam

A & C Black uses paper produced with elemental chlorine-free pulp,
harvested from managed sustainable forests.

Text typeset by A & C Black
Printed in Italy by Legoprint

Preface

Economics is the basis of our daily lives, even if we do not always realise it. Whether it is an explanation of how firms work, or people vote, or customers buy, or governments subsidise, economists have examined evidence and produced theories which can be checked against practice.

This book aims to cover the main aspects of the study of economics which students will need to learn when studying for examinations at various levels. The book will also be useful for the general reader who comes across these terms in the financial pages of newspapers as well as in specialist magazines.

The dictionary gives succinct explanations of the 3,000 most frequently found terms. It also covers the many abbreviations which are often used in writing on economic subjects. Entries are also given for prominent economists, from Jeremy Bentham to John Rawls, with short biographies and references to their theoretical works.

Where necessary cross-references are given so that the reader can refer to other comparable entries.

I am grateful to the following for their valuable comments on the text: Barbara Docherty, Lesley Brown and Jill Garner.

Specialist dictionaries

Dictionary of Accounting	0 7475 6991 6
Dictionary of Aviation	0 7475 7219 4
Dictionary of Banking and Finance	0 7136 7739 2
Dictionary of Business	0 7475 6980 0
Dictionary of Computing	0 7475 6622 4
Dictionary of Environment and Ecology	0 7475 7201 1
Dictionary of Human Resources and Personnel Management	0 7136 8142 X
Dictionary of ICT	0 7475 6990 8
Dictionary of Information and Library Management	0 7136 7591 8
Dictionary of Law	0 7475 6636 4
Dictionary of Leisure, Travel and Tourism	0 7475 7222 4
Dictionary of Marketing	0 7475 6621 6
Dictionary of Media Studies	0 7136 7593 4
Dictionary of Medical Terms	0 7136 7603 5
Dictionary of Military Terms	0 7475 7477 4
Dictionary of Nursing	0 7475 6634 8
Dictionary of Politics and Government	0 7475 7220 8
Dictionary of Science and Technology	0 7475 6620 8

Easier English™ titles

Easier English Basic Dictionary	0 7475 6644 5
Easier English Basic Synonyms	0 7475 6979 7
Easier English Dictionary: Handy Pocket Edition	0 7475 6625 9
Easier English Intermediate Dictionary	0 7475 6989 4
Easier English Student Dictionary	0 7475 6624 0
English Thesaurus for Students	1 9016 5931 3

Check Your English Vocabulary workbooks

Academic English	0 7475 6691 7
Business	0 7475 6626 7
Computing	1 9016 5928 3
Human Resources	0 7475 6997 5
Law	0 7136 7592 6
Leisure, Travel and Tourism	0 7475 6996 7
FCE +	0 7475 6981 9
IELTS	0 7136 7604 3
PET	0 7475 6627 5
TOEFL®	0 7475 6984 3
TOEIC	0 7136 7508 X

Visit our website for full details of all our books: **www.acblack.com**

A

A, AA, AAA *noun* letters indicating that a share or bond or bank has a certain rating for reliability. The AAA rating (called the triple A rating) is given by Standard & Poor's or by Moody's Investors Service, and indicates a very high level of reliability for a corporate or municipal bond in the USA.

ability to pay theory *noun* the theory of taxation that the level of taxation should be related to the taxpayer's ability to pay. Taxpayers with higher incomes pay tax at a higher rate than those on low incomes. This is the basis of progressive taxation. Many taxes, such as VAT, fuel tax, or sales tax, are not linked to the purchaser's ability to pay and are therefore regressive taxation.

abscissa *noun* the horizontal value on a graph. The vertical value is the y-value or ordinate. Also called **x-value** (NOTE: The plural is **abscissae** or **abscissas**.)

absolute advantage, absolute cost advantage *noun* a situation in which a country, or sometimes a person or company, is more efficient at producing something than its competitors (i.e. its output per input unit is higher). This gives an advantage to established firms which can keep costs low in comparison to new entrants.

absolute value *noun* the size or value of a number regardless of its sign. The absolute value of –62.34 is 62.34.

absorption costing, absorption pricing *noun* the fixing of the price of a product to include both the direct costs of production and a part of the overhead costs which are absorbed as well. Absorption costing follows three stages: allocation of actual overhead costs directly to the cost centre to which they relate; apportionment, by which common overhead costs are divided between various cost centres in proportion to the estimated benefit to each cost centre; absorption, by which the total costs are charged to each unit of production.

ACAS *abbreviation* Advisory, Conciliation and Arbitration Service

accelerated depreciation *noun* a system of depreciation which reduces the value of assets at a high rate in the early years to encourage companies to invest in new equipment, because of the tax advantages. This applied in the UK until 1984: companies could depreciate new equipment at 100% in the first year. The system still applies in the USA where a 5-year tax depreciation can be applied (instead of the usual 20-years) to certain types of equipment.

acceleration principle *noun* same as **accelerator principle**

accelerator coefficient *noun* a calculation by which the value of an investment increases with an increase in output

accelerator-multiplier model *noun* an economic model which incorporates both the accelerator and multiplier effect: if government investment expenditure increases this will lead to an increase in consumer demand which itself leads to an increase in output which in turn will lead to a further increase in investment. Also called **multiplier-accelerator model**

accelerator principle *noun* the principle that a change in consumer demand will have an even greater percentage change on the demand for capital goods, so that firms produce more of a commodity when demand is rising and less when demand is falling. This has the effect of exaggerating booms and depressions in the economy. Also called **acceleration principle**

acceptance *noun* the act of signing a bill of exchange to show that you agree to pay it

acceptance bank *noun US* same as **accepting house**

accepting house, acceptance house *noun* a firm, usually a merchant bank, which accepts bills of exchange (i.e. promises to pay them) and is paid a commission for this

accommodating monetary policy, accommodatory monetary policy *noun* a policy which allows money supply to increase as the demand for money increases

account *noun* STOCK EXCHANGE the period during which shares are traded for credit, and at the end of which the shares bought must be paid for. On the London Stock Exchange, the account period is three business days from the day of trade. (NOTE: On the London Stock Exchange, there are twenty-four accounts during the year, each running usually for ten working days.)

account day *noun* the day on which shares which have been bought must be paid for. On the London Stock Exchange the account period is three business days from the day of trade. Also called **settlement day**

accounting entity *noun* same as **accounting unit**

accounting period *noun* the period usually covered by a company's accounts. The balance sheet shows the state of the company's affairs at the end of the accounting period, while the profit-and-loss account shows the changes which have taken place since the end of the previous period.

accounting unit *noun* any unit which takes part in financial transactions which are recorded in a set of accounts. It can be a department, a sole trader, a Plc or some other unit.

accruals, accrued expenses, accrued liabilities *plural noun* liabilities which are recorded, although payment has not yet been made (this refers to liabilities such as rent, rates, etc.)

acid test ratio *noun* same as **liquidity ratio**

acquisition *noun* the takeover of a company. The results and cash flows of the acquired company are brought into the group accounts only from the date of acquisition: the figures for the previous period for the reporting entity should not be adjusted. The difference between the fair value of the net identifiable assets acquired and the fair value of the purchase consideration is goodwill.

ACT *abbreviation* Advance Corporation Tax

activity indicator *noun* an indicator such as industrial production, capacity utilisation, and volume of retail sales, which shows at what stage of the business cycle the economy is

activity rate *noun* the percentage of the population of working age who are actually in active employment. Also called **economic activity rate, labour force participation rate**

actual growth *noun* the final actual result of growth in the Harrod-Domar model

actuary *noun* a person employed by an insurance company or other organisation to calculate the risk involved in an insurance, and therefore the premiums payable by persons taking out insurance

adaptive expectations *noun* the theory that behaviour changes because of what people expect will happen: so workers ask for more pay because they believe inflation will rise, and this increase in pay actually fuels an increase in inflation; similarly economists will exaggerate their inflation forecasts to take into account errors they made in previous forecasts. Such adaptive expectations always exaggerate upward or downward trends. ♦ **expectations lag**

ADB *abbreviation* **1.** African Development Bank **2.** Asian Development Bank

adjustable peg regime, adjustable peg system *noun* a system in which a currency is pegged to another, but with the possibility of adjusting the exchange rate from time to time

administered price *noun US* same as **recommended retail price**

administration *noun* the appointment by a court of a person to manage the affairs of a company which is in difficulties

ADR *abbreviation* American depositary receipt

ad valorem tax *noun* a tax (such as VAT) which is calculated according to the value of the goods or services taxed. Compare **specific tax**

advance *noun* an amount of money paid as a loan or as a part of a payment to be made later ■ *adjective* paid as a loan or as a part of a payment to be made later ∎ *verb* to pay an amount of money to someone as a loan or as a part of a payment to be made later

Advance Corporation Tax *noun* a tax (abolished in 1999) which was paid by a company in advance of its main corporation tax payments. It was paid when dividends were paid to shareholders and was deducted from the main tax payment when that fell due. It appeared on the tax voucher attached to a dividend warrant. Abbreviation **ACT**

adverse selection *noun* the theory that bad quality goods will be more likely to be sold than good, because some traders want to get rid of products and buyers are not capable of judging if the quality or price is too low. This applies in many commercial spheres, such as the stock market or insurance, as well as in general trading. Three factors come into play: (i) the variable quality of similar products on the market; (ii) the fact that buyers and sellers do not possess the same information about the product (usually the seller knows more than the buyer); (iii) sellers are more likely to want to get rid of bad quality products than good quality products. Also called **lemon problem**

adverse supply shock *noun* shock caused to an economy by a sudden stoppage in the supply of raw materials or other inputs. An example would be the reduction in supply of oil caused by a war.

advertising *noun* the business of announcing that something is for sale or of trying to persuade customers to buy a product or service. Heavy advertising will stimulate sales, but the cost will be borne eventually by the customer.

Advisory, Conciliation and Arbitration Service *noun* a government service founded in 1974 which offers facilities for companies and representatives of their workforce to meet and try to solve disputes about matters such as employees' rights or union recognition. Abbreviation **ACAS**

AE *abbreviation* aggregate expenditure

African Development Bank *noun* a bank set up by African countries to provide long-term loans to help agricultural development and improvement of the infrastructure. The bank now has non-African members. Abbreviation **ADB**

age-earnings profile *noun* a graph showing the earnings of workers at different ages and in different industries

agency shop *noun US* a contract arrangement making it mandatory for workers who refuse to join a union to pay the union a fee

agent *noun* **1.** a person who represents a company or another person in an area **2.** *US* the chief local official of a trade union

agglomeration economies *plural noun* economies which firms achieve by being located in large urban areas

aggregate concentration *noun* the proportion of production which is in the hands of a few large companies

aggregate demand *noun* the total demand for goods and services from all sectors of the economy (from individuals, companies, the government and exporters) during a given period

aggregate demand curve *noun* a curve showing aggregate demand at all price levels, from a small demand at high prices to a large demand for lower-priced goods and services

aggregate expenditure *noun* the total domestic expenditure during a given period divided according to four sectors: households (consumer expenditure), businesses (investment expenditure), government expenditure and foreign purchasers (i.e. exports minus imports). It forms the gross domestic product. Abbreviation **AE**

aggregate output *noun* a method of calculating the national income by adding the total value added at each stage of production in manufacturing industry, service industry and agriculture, together with property income from abroad

aggregate supply *noun* the total production of goods and services available to meet the aggregate demand during a given period

aggregate supply curve *noun* a curve showing the quantity supplied at each price level; in the long term, supply pushes up prices

AGM *abbreviation* Annual General Meeting

agricultural sector *noun* the sector of an economy formed by agriculture, forestry and fishing

aid *noun* help given to a business or region by a government

AIM *abbreviation* Alternative Investment Market

alienation *noun* worker dissatisfaction, the lack of a sense of fulfilment when a worker cannot see any positive result of his or her work

allocative efficiency *noun* the action of satisfying as far as is possible customer demands for goods and services by pricing them at a price which is near to the production cost while still allowing a margin to the producer. If a market is allocatively efficient it produces the right amount of goods at the right prices for the right customers.

Alternative Investment Market *noun* a London stock market, regulated by the London Stock Exchange, dealing in shares in smaller companies which are not listed on the main London Stock Exchange. The AIM is a way in which smaller companies can sell shares to the investing public without going to the expense of obtaining a full share listing. Abbreviation **AIM**

alternative technology *noun* the use of methods to produce energy which are different and less polluting than the usual ways (i.e. using wind power, tidal power or solar power, as opposed to traditional or nuclear power)

American Depositary Receipt *noun* a document issued by an American bank to US citizens, making them unregistered shareholders of companies in foreign countries. The document allows them to receive dividends from their investments, and ADRs can themselves be bought or sold. Buying and selling ADRs is easier for American investors than buying or selling the actual shares themselves, as it avoids stamp duty and can be carried out in dollars without incurring exchange costs. Abbreviation **ADR**

amortisation, amortising *noun* **1.** the repayment of the principal of a loan or putting money aside regularly over a period of time in order to repay it in due course **2.** the act of depreciating or writing down the capital value of an asset over a period of time in a company's accounts

analysis of variance *noun* a method of testing if real differences exist between sections of a population which is being sampled

Andean Pact *noun* a trading agreement signed in 1969 and now formed of Bolivia, Columbia. Ecuador, Peru and Venezuela. Tariffs between the member countries are reduced and a system of preferences towards other members of the group introduced.

annual allowance *noun* an allowance against tax which is calculated each year, such as annual depreciation of assets

Annual General Meeting *noun* an annual meeting of all shareholders of a company, when the company's financial situation is presented by and discussed with the directors, when the accounts for the past year are approved and when dividends are declared and audited. Abbreviation **AGM** (NOTE: The US term is **annual meeting** or **annual stockholders' meeting**.)

Annual Percentage Rate *noun* a rate of interest (such as on a hire-purchase agreement) shown on an annual compound basis, including fees and charges. As hire purchase agreements quote a flat rate of interest covering the whole amount borrowed or a monthly repayment figure, the Consumer Credit Act, 1974, forces lenders to show the APR on documentation concerning hire purchase agreements, so as to give an accurate figure of the real rate of interest as opposed to the nominal rate. The APR includes various fees charged (such as the valuation of a house for mortgage); it may also vary according to the sum borrowed – a credit card company will quote a lower APR if the borrower's credit limit is low. Abbreviation **APR**

annual report and accounts *noun* the report from the directors on the company's financial situation at the end of a year, together with the balance sheet, profit and loss account, statement of source and application of funds, and the auditor's report, all prepared for the shareholders of the company each year

annuity *noun* an amount of money paid each year to a retired person, usually in return for a lump-sum payment. The value of the annuity depends on how long the person lives, as it usually cannot be passed on to another person. Annuities are fixed payments, and lose their value with inflation, whereas a pension can be index-linked. When people retire, they are required by law to purchase a compulsory purchase annuity with the funds accumulated in their pension fund. This gives them a taxable income for the rest of their life, but usually it is a fixed income which does not change with inflation. Also called **perpetuity**

anticipated inflation *noun* the rate of inflation which most people think will exist at some time in the future

anti-dumping action *noun* action which a country takes to protect itself against dumping

anti-dumping duty *noun* a tax imposed by a country on imported goods, to increase their price to a position where they do not offer unfair competition to locally-produced goods, especially where the price of the goods imported includes a subsidy from the government in the country of origin. Also called **countervailing duty**

anti-globalisation movement *noun* an umbrella organisation for several hundred groups of people with different aims: preservation of natural resources, anti-exploitation of native peoples, etc. Unfortunately, the movement also contains extreme left-wing groups who use the movement as a cover for extremist and violent protests. Abbreviation **AGM**

anti-trust laws, legislation *plural noun* laws in the USA which prevent the formation of monopolies or price fixing and so encourage competition

APACS *noun* an organisation set up in 1985 by British banks and building societies to manage the networks by which money is transferred between bank accounts on behalf of customers (CHAPS and BACS). Full form **Association for Payment Clearing Services**

APC *abbreviation* average propensity to consume

APM *abbreviation* average propensity to import

APP *abbreviation* average physical product

applied economics *noun* the application of economic theories to the real world, formulated by economists as advice to planners

appreciation *noun* the increase in value of an asset. Also called **capital appreciation**

appropriate technology *noun* technology which is suited to the local environment, usually involving skills or materials which are easily available locally. In many parts of world, devices to help the local population cultivate the land can be made out of simple pipes or pieces of metal. Expensive tractors may not only be unsuitable for the terrain involved, but also use fuel which costs more than the crops produced.

appropriation account *noun* a part of a profit and loss account which shows how each part of the profit has been dealt with (such as how much has been given to the shareholders as dividends, how much is being put into the reserves or what proportion of the profits comes from subsidiary companies)

APR *abbreviation* Annual Percentage Rate

a priori *adverb* on the basis of ideas or assumptions, not of real examples

APS *abbreviation* average propensity to save

arbitrage *noun* the making of a profit from the difference in value of various assets. Means include: selling foreign currencies or commodities on one market and buying on another at almost the same time to profit from different exchange rates; buying currencies forward and selling them forward at a later date, to benefit from a difference in prices; buying a security and selling another security to the same buyer with the intention of forcing up the value of both securities.

arbitrageur, arbitrager *noun* a person whose business is risk arbitrage. Arbitrageurs buy shares in companies which are potential takeover targets, either to force up the price of the shares before the takeover bid, or simply as a position while waiting for the takeover bid to take place. They also sell shares in the company which is expected to make the takeover bid, since one of the consequences of a takeover bid is usually that the price of the target company rises while that of the bidding company falls. Arbitrageurs may then sell the shares in the target company at a profit, either to one of the parties making the takeover bid, or back to the company itself.

arbitration *noun* the settlement of a dispute by the two parties concerned, using an arbitrator (an outside person chosen by both sides)

arc elasticity *noun* a reasonably accurate method of measuring the proportional change in one variable compared with a proportionate change in another

arithmetic average *noun* a number calculated by adding together several figures and dividing by the number of figures added

arithmetic progression *noun* a sequence of numbers with a constant difference between them, such as 2, 5, 8, 11. Compare **geometric progression**

Arrow, Kenneth (1921–) American economist, winner of the Nobel Prize for Economics in 1972, particularly interested in the questions of decision-making. He showed that a series of acceptable choices by individuals in a group will inevitably lead to the choice of one individual being dominant.

Arrow's impossibility theorem *noun* the theory that in a group of two or more it may happen that it becomes impossible to get a result from majority voting which accurately reflects the preferences of individuals in the group. Either the result goes against the majority preference or it is possible for a single individual to make the final decision.

articles of partnership *plural noun* same as **partnership agreement**

ASEAN *abbreviation* Association of Southeast Asian Nations

A shares *plural noun* ordinary shares with limited voting rights or no right to vote at all. A company may be set up with two classes of share: A shares, which are available to the general investor, and B shares which are only bought by certain individuals, such as the founder and his or her family. Such division of shares is becoming less usual nowadays.

Asian Development Bank *noun* a bank set up by various Asian countries, with other outside members, to assist countries in the region with money and technical advice. Abbreviation **ADB**

asset *noun* a thing which belongs to company or person, and which has a value. A company's balance sheet will show assets in various forms such as current assets, fixed assets and intangible assets. An individual's assets will include items such as his or her house, car, and clothes.

asset-backed securities *plural noun* shares which are backed by the security of assets

assets revaluation reserve *noun* an amount of money from profits not paid as dividend, but kept back by a company to be used when the company's assets are revalued

asset stripping *noun* the buying of a company at a lower price than its asset value, and then selling its assets

assisted area *noun* area of a country which is given aid by the government to under European Union legislation. They have unemployment levels higher than the norm in the European Union and the aid is aimed at increasing employment are given to companies, sole traders or partnerships for capital expenditure (not general jobs which otherwise would be at risk. Currently the areas are being reduced because Britain's unemployment level is lower than the European Union average.

Association of Southeast Asian Nations *noun* an organisation formed originally in 1967 to promote economic growth, social and educational development and general stability in Southeast Asia. The current members are: Brunei, Indonesia, Laos, Malaysia, Myanmar, Philippines, Singapore, Thailand and Vietnam. Abbreviation **ASEAN**

assurance *noun* an agreement that in return for regular payments, a company will pay compensation for loss of life, or will make a payment if the insured person lives to a certain age. Also called **life assurance, life insurance**

asymmetric information *noun* a situation which exists in all countries where all the consumers, suppliers and producers do not have the same information on which to base their decisions

ATM *abbreviation* automated telling machine

atomistic competition *noun* same as **perfect competition**

auction *noun* a method of selling goods in which people offer bids, and the item is sold to the person who makes the highest offer. Another form is the Dutch auction where the seller names a high price and gradually reduces it until someone makes a bid. ■ *verb* to sell goods at auction

audit *noun* the examination of the books and accounts of a company ■ *verb* to examine the books and accounts of a company

auditor *noun* a person, firm or partnership which audits books and accounts. Audits can be external, that is independent from the company, or internal, that is members of staff who examine a company's internal controls. External auditors are appointed by the company's directors and voted by the AGM. In the USA, audited accounts are only required by corporations which are registered with the SEC, but in the UK all limited companies must provide audited annual accounts if they exceed the size criteria for audit exemption.

auditors' qualification *noun* a form of words in a report from the auditors of a company's accounts, stating that in their opinion the accounts are not a true reflection of the company's financial position and profit or loss for the year. Also called **qualification of accounts**

auditors' report *noun* a report written by a company's auditors after they have examined the accounts of the company (if they are satisfied, the report certifies that, in the opinion of the auditors, the accounts give a true and fair view of the company's financial position)

Austrian school *noun* a school of economic study at the University of Vienna during the later part of the 19th century under Menger, which emphasised the concept of utility – i.e. the pleasure derived by the consumer from the product, as opposed to the value concepts of production and supply. Later Austrian economists developed the theory of interest and capital.

authorised capital *noun* the maximum capital which is permitted by a company's articles of association

autocorrelation *noun* same as **serial correlation**

automated teller machine *noun* a machine which gives out cash when a special card is inserted and special instructions given. Abbreviation **ATM**

automatic stabilisers *plural noun* changes in government spending or in government tax revenue which are not caused by policy decisions, but by events such as the rise in unemployment during a recession which increases government spending on benefits, and at the same time decreases taxation revenue. Also called **built-in stabilisers**

automation *noun* the use of machines to do work with very little supervision by people

autonomous consumption, autonomous expenditure *noun* national consumption expenditure which does not vary with national income, but which represents expenditure which is necessary to maintain a basic standard of living even when personal incomes are zero. It is not related to the GDP, but can have an effect on the economy.

autonomous investment *noun* investment which is not related to increases or decreases in national income or in ouput, but which may be due to factors such as changes in government policy or the response to new inventions

AVC *abbreviation* average variable cost

average *noun* the sharing of the cost of damage or loss of a ship between the insurers and the owners ■ *adjective* representing the total number divided by the number of units ■ *verb* to reach or calculate an average figure

average cost *noun* the total cost of production divided by the number of units produced

average cost pricing *noun* the setting of a price which is equivalent to the average cost of the product, so covering marginal costs and fixed costs and allowing the producer to break even

average fixed costs *plural noun* costs calculated by dividing the total fixed costs by the number of units produced. The cost per unit falls with the number of units produced.

average income per capita *noun* same as **per capita income**

average physical product, **average product** *noun* the average output per unit of variable input, such as the average output per worker. Abbreviation **APP**

average price level *noun* the average price of a particular product in a country at a particular time. Also called **price level**

average product *noun* same as **average physical product**

average propensity to consume *noun* the proportion of total disposable income (per individual, per household or national) which is spent. Abbreviation **APC**

average propensity to import *noun* the proportion of total disposable income (per individual, per household or national) which is spent on imports. Abbreviation **APM**

average propensity to save *noun* the proportion of total disposable income (per individual, per household or national) which represents income used for savings as opposed to expenditure. Abbreviation **APS**

average rate of tax *noun* a figure calculated by dividing the total income tax paid by a person by his or her total income. Compare **marginal rate of tax**

average revenue *noun* the revenue from one unit of product sold, calculated as the total revenue divided by the number of units sold. It is the same as the average price.

average revenue product *noun* the revenue derived from each unit of variable input

average total cost *noun* the total cost per unit, calculated by dividing the total costs by the number of units produced. It is the sum of average fixed cost and average variable cost.

average variable cost *noun* the variable cost per unit, calculated by dividing the variable costs by the number of units produced. Initially the cost falls with the number of units produced but then rises as more units are produced – it forms a U-shaped curve. Abbreviation **AVC**

avoidable cost *noun* same as **prime cost**

axiom *noun* a basic assumption which forms a theory; normally axioms cannot be proved by must be taken on trust

axis *noun* one of the vertical (y-axis) or horizontal (x-axis) lines which join at zero and against which a graph is plotted

B

back door *noun* financing by the Bank of England which increases money supply by selling Treasury bills. This is opposed to front door where discount houses which run short of cash ask the Bank to make them short-term loans which it does at a high interest rate.

back-to-back loan *noun* a loan from one company to another in one currency arranged against a loan from the second company to the first in another currency. Back-to-back loans are used by international companies to get round exchange controls. Also called **parallel loan**

backwardation *noun* the difference between the spot and futures prices, as when the spot price of a commodity or currency is higher than the futures price (NOTE: The opposite is **forwardation**.)

backward-bending supply curve *noun* a curve which shows that when the price of goods or services rises, so the quantity offered for sale falls. Also called **backward-sloping supply curve, labour supply curve**

backward integration *noun* a situation in which a company joins with another which is at an earlier stage in the production or distribution line, as when a supermarket purchases a milk company. Also called **vertical integration** (NOTE: The opposite is **forward integration**.)

backward-sloping labour supply curve *noun* same as **backward-bending supply curve**

BACS *abbreviation* Bankers Automated Clearing Services

bad debt *noun* a debt which will never be paid (usually because the debtor has gone out of business) and which has to be written off in the accounts

bad debt provision *noun* money put aside in accounts to cover potential bad debts, which are likely to have to be written off. The bad debt provision is deducted from trade debtors for balance sheet presentation. The change in the provision from one year to the next together with any bad debts written off is the charge for bad debts in the profit and loss account.

bad money drives out good Gresham's law, that where two forms of money with the same denomination exist in the same market, the form with the higher metal value will be driven out of circulation when people hoard it and use the lower-rated form to spend (as when paper money and coins of the same denomination exist in the same market)

Bagehot, Walter (1826–1877) British economist and political theorist who wrote in particular on the money markets and the nature of government

balanced budget *noun* a budget where expenditure and revenue are equal. This is the ideal situation, though Keynes said that governments should aim to run a deficit during a depression to encourage economic activity, and a surplus during a boom in order to cool down economic activity.

balanced budget multiplier *noun* the percentage change in GDP caused by a change in government spending which must be matched by an equivalent change in tax revenue

balanced growth *noun* a situation in which all sectors of an economy grow at the same constant rate. Compare **steady-state growth**

balance of payments *noun* a statement of the international financial position of a country, showing transactions which have taken place over a certain period, usually one financial quarter. It includes invisible as well as visible trade; all trade and movements of money between the residents of a country and other countries worldwide, including export sales and import purchases which when added must produce a balance. A balance-of-payments deficit occurs when a country imports more than it exports and so pays out more in foreign currency than it earns; this is also called a trade deficit. A balance-of-payments surplus occurs when a country sells more to other countries than it buys from them. Abbreviation **BOP**

balance of payments deficit *noun* same as **trade deficit**

balance of trade *noun* the international trading position of a country in merchandise, excluding invisible trade. If exports are greater than imports there is a balance of trade surplus (or favourable balance of trade). Also called **trade balance**

balance sheet *noun* a statement of the financial position of a company at a particular time, such as the end of the financial year or the end of a quarter, showing the company's assets and liabilities. The balance sheet shows the state of a company's finances at a certain date. The profit and loss account shows the movements which have taken place since the last balance sheet, i.e. since the end of the previous accounting period. A balance sheet must balance, with the basic equation that assets (i.e. what the company owns, including money owed to the company) must equal liabilities (i.e. what the company owes to its creditors) plus capital (i.e. what it owes to its shareholders). A balance sheet can be drawn up either in the horizontal form, with liabilities and capital on the left-hand side of the page (in the USA, it is the reverse) or in the vertical form, with assets at the top of the page, followed by liabilities, and capital at the bottom. Most are usually drawn up in the vertical format, as opposed to the more old-fashioned horizontal style.

balances with the Bank of England *plural noun* money deposited by commercial banks and building societies with the Bank of England, either to settle accounts with other banks or as a reserve

balancing items *plural noun* items in the balance of payments such as mistakes or omissions, receipts which are late or other irregular items which, together with the current balance and capital account, make it balance

bank *noun* a business which holds money for its clients, which lends money at interest, and trades generally in money. Apart from the main commercial banks this category includes some former building societies and other financial institutions. Banks are licensed by the regulatory authorities such as the Bank of England or, in the USA, the Federal Reserve. ■ *verb* to put or keep money in a bank

bank account *noun* an arrangement that a customer has with a bank, where the customer can deposit and withdraw money (NOTE: The US term is **banking account**.)

bank advance *noun* same as **bank loan**

bank bill *noun US* same as **banknote**

bank credit *noun* credit in the form of loans or overdrafts accorded by banks to their customers

bank deposits *plural noun* all money placed in banks by private or corporate customers

Bankers' Automated Clearing Services *noun* a company set up to organise the payment of direct debits, standing orders, salary cheques and other payments generated by computers. It operates for all the British clearing banks and several building societies, and forms part of APACS. Abbreviation **BACS**. Compare **Clearing House Automated Payments System**

banker's draft *noun* an order by one bank telling another bank (usually in another country) to pay money to someone

Bank for International Settlements *noun* a bank which acts as a clearing bank for the central banks of various countries, through which they settle their currency transactions and also acts on behalf of the IMF. It is based in Basel, Switzerland. Abbreviation **BIS**

banking account *noun US* same as **bank account**

banking system *noun* the system of banks in a country, including commercial banks, merchant banks and the central bank

bank loan *noun* a loan made by a bank to a customer, usually against the security of a property or asset. Also called **bank advance**

banknote *noun* a promissory note issued by a bank that is payable to the bearer on demand and is acceptable as money (NOTE: The US term is **bill**.)

Bank of England *noun* the central British bank, owned by the state, which, together with the Treasury, regulates the nation's finances. The Bank of England issues banknotes which carry the signatures of its officials. It is the lender of last resort to commercial banks and supervises banking institutions in the UK. Its Monetary Policy Committee is independent of the government, and sets interest rates. The Governor of the Bank of England is appointed by the government.

bank rate *noun* the discount rate of a central bank. Formerly, it was the rate at which the Bank of England lent to other banks (then called the Minimum Lending Rate (MLR), and now the base rate).

bankruptcy *noun* the state of being bankrupt. In the UK, bankruptcy is applied only to individual persons, but in the USA the term is also applied to corporations. In the UK, a bankrupt cannot hold public office (e.g., he or she cannot be elected an MP) and cannot be the director of a company. A bankrupt also cannot borrow money. In the USA, there are two types of bankruptcy: involuntary, where the creditors ask for a person or corporation to be made bankrupt; and voluntary, where a person or corporation applies to be made bankrupt (in the UK, this is called voluntary liquidation). (NOTE: The plural is **bankruptcies**.)

bank statement *noun* a written statement from a bank showing the balance of an account

bar chart *noun* a chart where values or quantities are shown as thick columns of the same width but different heights. Also called **bar graph, histogram**

bargaining *noun* the act of discussing a price, usually wage increases for workers

bargaining theory of wages *noun* the theory behind collective bargaining, that an agreement should be reached which is acceptable to both management and workers, and which is not detrimental to the overall profitability of the company

bar graph *noun* same as **bar chart**

barometric price leader *noun* a firm which fixes the price for a good or service in a market, which other firms then follow

barrier *noun* something which restricts commercial activity, such as laws restricting movement of capital or labour

barrier to entry *noun* something which makes it difficult for a firm to enter a market and compete with firms already in that market. Barriers to entry are mainly government legislation, the cost of starting up a new business, the current ownership of resources and patents, and the strength of companies already in the market. Barriers to entry may be created, as when companies already in a market have patents that prevent their goods from being copied, when the cost of the advertising needed to gain a market share is too high, or when an existing product commands very strong brand loyalty.

barrier to exit *noun* something which make it difficult for a firm to leave a market, such as its inability to get a good price for assets which it wants to sell. Barriers to exit may be created, for example, when a company has invested in specialist equipment which is only suited to manufacturing one product, when the costs of retraining its workforce would be very high, or when withdrawing one product would have a bad effect on the sales of other products in the range

barter *noun* a system where goods are exchanged for other goods and not sold for money. This is an inefficient system where money is readily available, as it implies that each party has to carry large stocks of what the other party wants. ■ *verb* to exchange goods by the barter system

base date *noun* the date from which something is calculated, usually a date on which something started

base period *noun US* a period against which an index is measured, usually taken as equalling 100

base rate *noun* the basic rate of interest on which the actual rate a bank charges on loans to its customers or interest on deposits is calculated. Loans are charged at a percentage above base rate and interest at a percentage below it.

base year *noun* the first year of an index, against which changes occurring in later years are measured

basis point *noun* one hundredth of a percentage point (0.01%), the basic unit used in measuring market movements or interest rates

batch production *noun* production in small batches, which is more sensitive to the individual requirements of the customer than mass production. It also allows better control over work teams.

Bayes, Thomas 18th century English clergyman who was also a mathematician. He published his original theorem in 1761.

Bayesian statistics *noun* a statistical theory which uses observations of what happened in the past alongside current observations to give an estimate of the probability of something happening in the future

Bayes' theorem, Bayes' Law *noun* the fundamental mathematical law which shows how confident someone can be in predicting something in the future based on available evidence that something happened in the past

bear *noun* STOCK EXCHANGE on the Stock Exchange, a person who sells shares, commodities or currency in the belief that the price will fall and he or she will be able to buy again more cheaply later (NOTE: The opposite is **bull**.)

bearer bond, bearer security *noun* a bond which is payable to the bearer and does not have a name written on it. This is useful if the owner wishes to avoid being identified by the income tax authorities.

bear market *noun* a period when share prices fall because shareholders are selling, since they believe the market will fall further (NOTE: The opposite is a **bull market**.)

beggar-my-neighbour policy *noun* action by a country to protect its own commercial interests which has a bad effect on other countries. Such an action might be the introduction of swingeing tariffs on imports to protect local industry.

behavioural theory of the firm *noun* a theory about how firms behave when making decisions, based on the observation that firms are composed of departments and individuals who come to decisions independently or jointly which relate to their own positions within the firm rather than the firm's position in the market. Decisions taken by sales managers may not agree with decisions taken by finance departments, and a compromise position has to be reached.

below-the-line *adjective, adverb* set against net profits after tax

below-the-line expenditure *noun* exceptional payments which are separated from a company's normal accounts because they do not arise from the company's normal activities

benefit-cost analysis *noun* same as **cost-benefit analysis**

Bentham, Jeremy (1748–1832) British economist who followed on the work of Adam Smith. He did not believe that public and private interests were identical, but that the guiding principle of existence is the happiness of the individual, and that governments must apply themselves to achieve this aim.

Bernoulli, Daniel (1700–82) Swiss mathematician who studied hydrodynamics, gases, and harmonics as well as calculating how an increase in value of a person's assets affects his or her moral expectations

Bernoulli's hypothesis *noun* the theory that risk-taking mainly involves not the consideration of possible money gain, but the possibility of losing the utility of the money being risked. It takes account of the diminishing marginal utility of the money at risk.

Bertrand, Joseph (1822–1900) French mathematician who worked mainly on the theory of probability

Bertrand competition, Bertrand duopoly *noun* a model for pricing decisions by which Firm A believes that Firm B will not reduce its prices in response to a price reduction by Firm A; in fact, Firm B does reduce prices and Firm A reduces its prices again, ensuring that price competition drives the market, even if both firms may reach a point where they do not cover costs

bezzle *noun* money which had been illegally acquired by investors who wanted to profit from the US stock market in the 1920s, but which was discovered when the stock market crashed. The term was invented by J. K. Galbraith. He saw that in boom periods, the bezzle increases, while in times of depression it decreases because everyone is more careful in auditing accounts.

bias *noun* error which occurs when carrying out random sampling by which the results are either too high or too low

bid *noun* an offer to buy something (such as a share, currency, commodity, company or a unit in a unit trust) at a certain price ■ *verb* to offer to pay a particular price for something such as a share, commodity, company or a unit in a unit trust

bid price *noun* the price at which units in a unit trust are sold back to the trust by an investor. The opposite, i.e. the price offered by the purchaser, is called the offer price; the difference between the two is the spread.

Big Bang *noun* the change in practices on the London Stock Exchange, culminating in the introduction of electronic trading on 27 October 1986. The changes included the abolition of stock jobbers and the removal of the system of fixed commissions. The Stock Exchange trading floor closed, and deals are now done by phone or computer.

Big Board *noun US* same as **New York Stock Exchange** (*informal*)

bilateral aid *noun* aid from one country (the donor) to another poorer country (the recipient). Compare **multilateral aid**

bilateralism *noun* government policy aimed at balancing trade between two countries where an imbalance exists. A government can use trade barriers or other controls to reduce an unfavourable balance of trade with another country.

bilateral monopoly *noun* a situation in which there is only one purchaser and only one supplier in a market, i.e. a monopoly seller and a monopsony purchaser. This can occur when a government is purchasing weapons or when a single trade union is negotiating with an employer.

bilateral trade *noun* trade between two countries

bill *noun* **1.** a written statement of what a person or company owes for goods or services provided **2.** *US* same as **banknote** (NOTE: The UK term is **note** *or* **banknote**.) ■ *verb* to send someone a bill for goods or services provided

bill broker *noun* a firm which buys and sells Treasury bills or bills of exchange for a fee

bill of exchange *noun* a document signed by the person authorising it, which tells another to pay money unconditionally to a named person on a certain date. It is usually used in payments in foreign currency. The person raising the bill is the drawer, the person who accepts it is the drawee. The seller can then sell the bill at a discount to raise cash. This is called a trade bill. A bill can also be accepted (i.e. guaranteed) by a bank.

birth rate *noun* the number of births per thousand of population in a given year. An increase in the birth rate will result in population growth, and so will a fall in the death rate. Currently the country with the highest birth rate is Niger, with 51 births per 1,000, and the lowest is Latvia with 7.8 births. These have to be seen in conjunction with infant mortality rates, however.

BIS *abbreviation* Bank for International Settlements

black economy *noun* the part of an economy involving goods and services which are paid for in cash, and therefore not declared for tax. Also called **hidden economy, parallel economy, shadow economy**

Black Friday *noun* a sudden collapse on a stock market. It is called after the first major collapse of the US stock market on Friday 24 September 1869).

black market *noun* the buying and selling goods or currency in a way which is not allowed by law, as when a government imposes price controls or rationing. The prices on a black market are always higher than regular prices.

Black Monday *noun* Monday 19 October 1987, when world stock markets crashed

Black Tuesday *noun* Tuesday 29 October 1929, when the US stock market crashed

Black Wednesday *noun* Wednesday 16 September 1992, when the pound sterling left the European Exchange Rate Mechanism and was devalued against other currencies. It is not always seen as black, since some people believe it was a good thing that the pound left the ERM.

Blue Book *noun* an annual publication of national statistics from various UK government departments

blue-chip investments, blue-chip shares, blue-chips *plural noun* shares of very large established companies which are generally low-risk investments

board of directors, board *noun* in the UK, a group of directors elected by the shareholders to run a company. In the USA, a group of people elected by the shareholders to draw up company policy and to appoint the president and other executive officers who are responsible for managing the company. The directors are elected by shareholders at the AGM, though they are usually chosen and nominated by the chairman or chief executive. A board will consist of a chairman (who may be non-executive), a chief executive or managing director, and a series of specialist directors in charge of various activities of the company (such as production director or sales director). The company secretary will attend board meetings, but is not a director. Apart from the executive directors, who are in fact employees of the company, there may be several non-executive directors, appointed either for their expertise and contacts, or as representatives of important shareholders such as banks. These non-executive directors are paid fees. The board of a US company may be made up of a large number of non-executive directors and only one or two executive officers; a British board has more executive directors.

bogof *noun* the practice of giving free gifts to customers, e.g. one free item for each one bought

bond *noun* a contract document promising to repay money (the principal) borrowed by a company or by the government at a certain date, and paying a fixed interest at regular intervals; such documents can be traded on the market and their prices vary according to the length of time before maturity and the interest rate carried

COMMENT: Bonds are in effect another form of long-term borrowing by a company or government. They can carry a fixed interest or a floating interest, but the yield varies according to the price at which they are bought; bond prices go up and down in the same way as share prices.

bonus issue *noun* a scrip issue or capitalisation issue, where a company transfers money from reserves to share capital and issues free extra shares to the shareholders. The value of the company remains the same, and the total market value of shareholders' shares remains the same, the market price being adjusted to account for the new shares. Also called **share split** (NOTE: The US term is **stock dividend** or **stock split**.)

book value *noun* the value of an asset as recorded in the company's balance sheet

boom *noun* a time when sales or production or business activity are increasing ■ *verb* to increase in volume or activity

BOP *abbreviation* balance of payments

Boston matrix *noun* a type of product portfolio analysis, in which products are identified as stars, question marks, cash cows or dogs. Full form **Boston Consulting Group Share/Growth Matrix**

bounded rationality *noun* the limits which certain people have when dealing with complex issues like contracts. They tend to deal with problems according to a rule of thumb, with the result that an organisation like a firm, which involves several people making decisions individually, follows the best procedure.

branch banking *noun* the situation in which a national bank operates through many local offices. This is the system that applies in the UK, while in the USA banks tend to operate a unit banking system, where each state bank has only one unit under the umbrella of the local Federal Reserve Bank.

brand *noun* a make of product, which can be recognised by a name or by a distinctive design

brand loyalty *noun* the inclination of a customer to keep on buying the same brand and not to switch to another

breakeven analysis *noun* a calculation which shows at what point a product will break even

breakeven point *noun* the point where total revenue equals total costs; this is shown in break-even charts, e.g. charting the effect of a price increase or an increase in fixed costs

break-up value *noun* the value of a company if its assets are sold separately (rather than its value as an existing business)

Bretton Woods Agreement, **Bretton Woods System** *noun* an international agreement reached in 1944, setting up the International Monetary Fund and the World Bank, and a system of fixed exchange rates between currencies. At the Bretton Woods Conference the British government put forward a different plan to set up an institution similar to an international clearing house. This was called the Keynes Plan.

British Technology Group *noun* a British government organisation formed in 1981 from the National Enterprise Board (NEB) and the National Research and Development Corporation (NRDC). It aims to protect and manage intellectual property rights and invests in new technology, both as start-up companies and joint ventures. It also licences inventions to firms for commercialisation. Abbreviation **BTG**

broad money *noun* a calculation of money supply including liquid cash and money which could be used for purchases, such as money on deposit in banks. The British measure is M4.

broker *noun* a person who acts as a middleman between a seller and a buyer

brokerage, broker's commission *noun* the payment to a broker for a deal carried out

BTG *abbreviation* British Technology Group

bubble *noun* a continued rise in the value of an asset, such as a share price, which is caused by people thinking that the price will continue to rise. It has nothing to do with the inherent value of the asset, and will collapse suddenly if speculators decide that the rise cannot continue. The most famous bubble was the South Sea Bubble in the 1720s, where speculators drove up the price of shares in companies trading in the Pacific area. A recent bubble was the rise in the value of shares in electronic and internet companies in the late 1990s. Also called **speculative bubble**

budget *noun* a plan of expected spending and income (usually for one year). In general, the term refers to the annual plan of taxes and government spending proposed by a finance minister, but is also used to apply to financial planning for companies and individuals. ■ *verb* to set aside a sum of money for expected spending and income

budgetary control *noun* the use of budgets to control the performance of a company. Actual spending or income is compared regularly with budget figures, and managers use the results to plan future actions.

budget constraint *noun* a requirement to make different levels of purchase of different goods at different prices, given that the purchaser has a fixed amount of money to spend

budget deficit *noun* **1.** the deficit in a country's planned budget, where income from taxation will not be sufficient to pay for the government's expenditure. It has to be financed by borrowing. ⬧ **structural budget deficit 2.** a deficit in personal finances where a household will borrow to finance large purchases which cannot be made out of income alone

budget line *noun* a graph showing the different quantities of different goods which could be purchased at different prices, given that the purchaser has a fixed amount of money to spend. It is used in conjunction with an indifference curve to identify to identify the goods and their quantities which a customer might want to purchase. Also called **consumption possibility curve**

budget surplus *noun* a situation in which revenue is higher than expenditure, the excess being put into savings

buffer stocks *plural noun* stocks of a commodity bought by an international body when prices are low and held for resale at a time when prices have risen, with the intention of removing sharp fluctuations in world prices of the commodity

building society *noun* a financial institution which accepts and pays interest on deposits and lends money to people who are buying property against the security of the property. Building societies mainly invest the money deposited with them as mortgages on properties, but a percentage is invested in government securities. Societies can now offer a range of banking services, such as cheque books, standing orders and overdrafts, and now operate in much the same way as banks. Indeed, many building societies have changed from mutual status, where the owners of the society are its investors and borrowers, to become publicly-owned banks. The comparable US institutions are the savings & loan associations, or thrifts. Building societies are regulated by the Building Societies Ombudsman, whose duty is to investigate complaints by members of the public against building societies. All building societies belong to the Building Societies Ombudsman Scheme.

built-in stabilisers *plural noun* same as **automatic stabilisers**

bull *noun* on the Stock Exchange, a person who believes the market will rise and therefore buys shares (or commodities or currency) to sell at a higher price later (NOTE: The opposite is a **bear**.)

bullion *noun* gold or silver bars

bull market *noun* a period when share prices rise because people are optimistic and buy shares (NOTE: The opposite is a **bear market**.)

business cycle *noun* a period during which trade expands, then slows down, then expands again. Also called **trade cycle**

business rate *noun* a tax levied on business property (NOTE: The US term is **local property tax**.)

buyer concentration *noun* the number of buyers in a market. A market can be dominated by a few buyers or by a single buyer.

buyer's market *noun* a market where shares, commodities or products are sold cheaply because there is more stock available than the buyers need. The opposite is a 'seller's market'. (NOTE: The opposite is a **seller's market**.)

by-product *noun* a secondary product made as a result of manufacturing a main product which can be sold for profit

C

cabotage *noun* restriction of the transport of goods within a country by foreign hauliers. It is seen as contrary to the principles of free trade.

call *noun* the price established during a trading session

called up capital *noun* share capital in a company which has been called up. The share capital becomes fully paid when all the authorised shares have been called up.

call money *noun* money loaned for which repayment can be demanded without notice. It is used by commercial banks, placing money on very short-term deposit with discount houses. Also called **money at call, money on call**

call option *noun* an option to buy shares at a future date and at a certain price (NOTE: The opposite is a **put option**.)

Cambridge equation *noun* an equation which shows that the stock of money multiplied by its velocity of circulation equals the average price level times the number of goods sold. This shows that a stable relationship exists between the stock of money and the national income.

Cambridge school of economics *noun* a school of thought developed at Cambridge University called classical economics, based on Keynes' theories and emphasising macroeconomics, in opposition to neoclassical economics which emphasised a microeconomic approach

canon of taxation *noun* one of a series of criteria developed by Adam Smith to judge if a tax is good. The four canons are (a) the cost of collecting the tax should be much lower than the amount collected; (b) the payers must be told how much to pay and when to pay it; (c) the time and means of payment must be convenient for the payer; (d) the tax should depend on the ability of the taxpayer to pay it.

CAP *abbreviation* Common Agricultural Policy

capacity *noun* the amount which can be produced, or amount of work that can be done, or the amount of use made of the factors of production. Full capacity means that full use is made of the factors.

capacity utilisation *noun* output shown as a percentage of capacity

capital *noun* property, assets and finished goods used in a business. It is one of the four factors of production.

capital account *noun* a country's national account showing the capital invested in a infrastructure, or a firm's account showing investment in plant and other assets

capital accumulation *noun* increase in investment in capital goods

capital adequacy, capital adequacy ratio *noun* an amount of money which a bank has to have in the form of shareholders' capital, shown as a percentage of its assets (internationally agreed at 8%). Also called **capital-to-asset ratio**

capital allowances *plural noun* allowances for the purchase of fixed assets, such as machinery, which may be deducted from a company's profits and so reduce its tax liability. Under current UK law, depreciation is not allowable for tax on profits, whereas capital allowances, based on the value of fixed assets owned by the company, are tax-allowable.

capital appreciation *noun* same as **appreciation**

capital asset pricing model *noun* a model of the stock market which can be used to estimate different returns from high and low risk investments as well as the value of a company's shares. Abbreviation **CAPM**

capital assets *plural noun* property or machinery which a company owns and uses, but which the company does not buy or sell as part of its regular trade. Capital assets are divided into tangible fixed assets, intangible fixed assets and investments. Also called **fixed assets**

capital budgeting *noun* budgeting for planned purchases of fixed assets during the next budget period

capital consumption *noun* the decrease in the value a country's or a firm's stock of capital goods held as they wear out and need to be replaced

Capital Consumption Allowance *noun* the capital depreciation of the economy during a year, deducted from GDP to give the net domestic product (NDP). Abbreviation **CCA**

capital deepening *noun* increased investment of capital in a business, without changing other factors of production. Also called **capital widening**

capital employed *noun* shareholders' funds plus long-term debts of a business. ♦ **return on capital employed**

capital equipment *noun* equipment which a factory or office uses to work or in production

capital expenditure *noun* money spent on capital assets such as property, machines and furniture. Also called **capital investment, capital outlay**

capital flight *noun* the rapid movement of capital out of a country because of lack of confidence in that country's economic future in response to political unrest, war, or other conditions. Also called **flight of capital**

capital flow *noun* the movement of investment capital from one country to another. Also called **capital movement, movement of capital**

capital formation *noun* investment in fixed assets

capital gain *noun* money made by selling fixed assets or certain other types of property (such as shares, works of art, leases, etc.) (NOTE: The opposite is **capital loss**.)

capital gains tax *noun* a tax paid on capital gain. Abbreviation **CGT**

capital gearing *noun* the debts of a firm, in the form of bank borrowings, shown as a percentage of net tangible assets. ♦ **gearing**

capital goods *plural noun* one of the factors of production, goods used to manufacture other goods (i.e. factories, machinery, trucks, tools, etc.)

capital inflow *noun* movement of capital into a country by buying shares in companies, buying whole companies or other forms of investment

capital intensity *noun* the level of being capital-intensive, shown as the ratio of capital to labour in a production process

capital-intensive *adjective* (economy or business) which uses a high amount of capital in proportion to labour

capital investment *noun* same as **capital expenditure**

capitalisation *noun* the value of a company calculated by multiplying the price of its shares on the Stock Exchange by the number of shares issued. Also called **market capitalisation**

capitalisation issue *noun* a bonus issue, free issue or scrip issue, where a company transfers money from reserves to share capital and issues free extra shares to the shareholders. The value of the company remains the same, and the total market value of shareholders' shares remains the same. The market price is adjusted to account for the new shares.

capitalised value *noun* the value of a business calculated by either of two methods: the present value of future income or the share price multiplied by the number of the shares in issue

capitalism *noun* the economic system where each person has the right to invest money, to work in competitive business and to buy and sell, with no restriction from the state

capital-labour ratio *noun* the ratio of capital to labour in a production process

capital loss *noun* a loss made when selling assets (NOTE: The opposite is **capital gain**.)

capital market *noun* a financial market dealing in bonds and other financial instruments used by companies to get funds. It is the place where companies can look for long-term investment capital.

capital movement *noun* same as **capital flow**

capital outflow *noun* the movement of capital out of a country, in the form of investments in other countries

capital outlay *noun* same as **capital expenditure**

capital/output ratio *noun* the ratio of the number of units of capital needed to produce a certain output. A high capital/output ratio means that a large amount of capital will be needed.

capital redemption reserve *noun* money credited to a company's reserves if the company has bought back its shares. The company must put the same amount as they have paid to the shareholders into this reserve in order to preserve the funds available to pay the company's creditors.

capital reserves *plural noun* the share capital of a company which comes from selling new shares or revaluing assets and not from normal trading. These reserves cannot be distributed to the shareholders, except if the company is wound up. Also called **undistributable reserves**

capital stock *noun* the total value of physical stock and fixed assets in a country or firm

capital to asset ratio, **capital/asset ratio** *noun* same as **capital adequacy**

capital transfer tax *noun* formerly, a tax on gifts or bequests of money or property

capital widening *noun* same as **capital deepening**

CAPM *abbreviation* capital asset pricing model

cardinal utility *noun* the measurement of the satisfaction which a consumer gets from a good or service, based on the assumption that such satisfaction can be accurately measured; as opposed to 'ordinal utility' where the satisfaction can only be seen to be growing in comparison with another measurement

carry-over *noun* the fact of not paying an account on settlement day, but later. Also called **contango**

cartel *noun* a group of companies which try to fix the price, or to regulate the supply of a product, because they can then profit from this situation

cash *noun* money in coins or notes. Cash in circulation is part of the money supply. ■ *verb* to convert something such as a cheque into money in coins or notes

cash cow *noun* a product which consistently generates good profits and maintains its dominant position in the market, but will not provide growth because the market is only expanding slowly

cash crop *noun* an agricultural crop grown for sale to other buyers or to other countries, rather than for domestic consumption

cash discount *noun* a discount given for payment in cash. Also called **discount for cash**

cash flow *noun* a record of the cash which comes into a company from sales (cash inflow) less the money which goes out in purchases or overhead expenditure (cash outflow) during a certain period

cash-flow accounting *noun* the practice of measuring the financial activities of a company in terms of cash receipts and payments, without recording accruals, prepayments, debtors, creditors and stocks

cashless society *noun* a society where no one uses cash, all purchases being made by credit cards, charge cards or cheques

cash limit *noun* a fixed amount of money which can be spent during a certain period

cash ratio *noun* **1.** the ratio of cash or other liquid assets to the current liabilities in a business **2.** the ratio of cash to deposits in a bank (usually a percentage laid down by the central bank). Banks are required to keep some of their liabilities in the form of cash ratio deposits.

casual unemployment *noun* short-term periods of unemployment between jobs

caveat emptor *noun* 'let the buyer beware', the principle that the buyer is responsible that goods being bought are satisfactory

CBI *abbreviation* Confederation of British Industry

CCA *abbreviation* current cost accounting

CD *abbreviation* certificate of deposit

ceiling *noun* a highest point, such as the highest interest rate or the highest amount of money which a depositor may deposit

central bank *noun* the main government-controlled bank in a country, which controls the financial affairs of the country by fixing main interest rates, issuing currency, supervising and acting as banker to the commercial banks and controlling the foreign exchange rate

central government *noun* the main government in a country, as opposed to local or provincial governments

central planning *noun* a system where the government plans all business activity, regulates supply, sets production targets and itemises work to be done. Also called **state planning**. Compare **command economy**

Central Statistical Office *noun* the British government agency charged with collecting and publishing national statistics. In 1996 it merged with the Office of Population Censuses and Surveys to form the Office for National Statistics (ONS). Abbreviation **CSO**

certificate of deposit *noun* a document from a bank showing that money has been deposited at a certain guaranteed interest rate for a certain period of time. A CD is a bearer instrument, which can be sold by the bearer. It can be sold at a discount to the value, so that the yield on CDs varies. CDs are traded on the secondary market by discount houses and CD futures are traded on LIFFE. Abbreviation **CD**

certificate of incorporation *noun* a document issued by Companies House to show that a company has been incorporated

certificate of origin *noun* a document showing where imported goods come from or were made

CET *abbreviation* common external tariff

ceteris paribus Latin expression meaning 'other things being equal', used to indicate that when considering the effect that one factor has on the economy the influence of other factors is not taken into account, all other factors being considered

CGT *abbreviation* capital gains tax

change in demand *noun* the change in the level of demand for goods or services caused by factors other than price. It is shown as a shift in the demand curve.

change in supply *noun* the change in the level of supply of goods or services caused by factors other than price. It is shown as a shift in the supply curve .

channel of distribution *noun* same as **distribution channel**

chaos theory *noun* the theory describing how, when a system is sensitive to small differences in initial values, the future behaviour of that system may become unpredictable

CHAPS *abbreviation* Clearing House Automated Payments System

Chapter 11 *noun* the section of the US Bankruptcy Reform Act 1978 which allows a corporation to be protected from demands made by its creditors for a period of time, while it is reorganised with a view to paying its debts. The officers of the corporation will negotiate with its creditors as to the best way of reorganising the business.

Chapter 13 *noun* the section of the US Bankruptcy Reform Act 1978 which allows a business to continue trading and to pay off its creditors by regular monthly payments over a period of time

Chapter 7 *noun* the section of the US Bankruptcy Reform Act 1978 which sets out the rules for the liquidation of an incorporated company

charge account *noun* an arrangement which a customer has with a store to buy goods and to pay for them at a later date, usually when the invoice is sent at the end of the month. The customer will make regular monthly payments into the account and is allowed credit of a multiple of those payments.

chartist *noun* a person who studies stock market trends and forecasts future rises or falls

cheap money *noun* money which can be borrowed at a low rate of interest

check *noun US* same as **cheque**

checking account *noun US* same as **current account** 1

checks and balances *noun* the basic principle in many constitutions that the powers of one person or group should be balanced by those of another person or group

cheque *noun* a note to a bank asking for money to be paid from your account to the account of the person whose name is written on the note (NOTE: The US spelling is **check**.)

cheque account *noun* same as **current account**

cheque card, cheque guarantee card *noun* a plastic card from a bank which guarantees payment of a cheque up to a certain amount, even if there is no money in the account

Chicago School *noun* a school of economists, based at the University of Chicago, led by Professor Milton Friedman, who believe that self-interest rules economic behaviour, that money supply determines inflation and that it is pointless for governments to hope to control the economy

child benefit *noun* money paid by the government to households with children, currently for each child under 16

Chinese walls *plural noun* imaginary barriers between departments in the same organisation, set up to avoid insider dealing or a conflict of interest (as when a merchant bank is advising on a planned takeover bid, its investment department should not know that the bid is taking place, or they would advise their clients to invest in the company being taken over)

CHIPS *abbreviation* Clearing House Interbank Payments System

CIF, c.i.f. *abbreviation* cost, insurance and freight

circular flow of income *noun* the flow of income between the producers and the households who buy their goods or services. Income moves from households to producers as the households purchase goods or services; income moves from producers to households in the form of wages or profits.

circulating capital *noun* capital in the form of cash or debtors, raw materials, finished products and work in progress required for a company to carry on its business. Also called **working capital**

city *noun* the old centre of London, where banks and large companies have their main offices; the British financial centre

City Code on Takeovers and Mergers *noun* a code of practice which regulates how takeovers should take place. It is enforced by the Takeover Panel.

City Panel on Takeovers and Mergers *noun* same as **Takeover Panel**

classical economics *noun* economic theories about the role of labour in an economy which see the market as essentially a means of distributing wealth between capitalists, landowners and labour. These theories did not see any possibility of recession or unemployment because it would be corrected by market forces. The theories are typified in the writings of Adam Smith, David Ricardo and John Stuart Mill.

classical unemployment *noun* unemployment which results from wages being too high. It can be corrected by reducing wage levels or increasing productivity.

clean float *noun* the action of floating a currency freely on the international markets, without any interference from the government

clearing bank *noun* a bank which clears cheques, one of the major High Street banks, specialising in normal banking business for ordinary customers (such as loans, cheques, overdrafts and interest-bearing deposits)

clearing house *noun* the central office where clearing banks exchange cheques, or where stock exchange or commodity exchange transactions are settled

Clearing House Automated Payments System *noun* a computerised system for clearing cheques organised by the banks. Abbreviation **CHAPS**. Compare **Bankers' Automated Clearing Services**

Clearing House Interbank Payments System *noun* computerised system for clearing cheques organised by the banks in the USA. Abbreviation **CHIPS**

cliometrics *noun* the application of econometrics to historical economics, especially the economics of the distant past

close company *noun* a privately owned company controlled by a few shareholders (in the UK, less than five) where the public may own a small number of the shares company. (NOTE: The US term is **close corporation** or **closed corporation**.)

closed economy *noun* a type of economy which does not trade internationally and is not subject to outside influences

closed shop *noun* a system where a company agrees to employ only union members in certain jobs; in the USA called a 'union shop'

closing price *noun* on the Stock Exchange, the price of a share at the end of a day's trading

Coase, Ronald (1910–) *noun* American economist who concentrated in particular on the theory of the firm, stating that firms are endogenous to the economic system. He won a Nobel prize in 1960.

Coase theorem *noun* the theory that the effects of external things (or 'externalities') can be corrected by the market, in that if property rights can be identified fairly between individuals they then can find a solution by trading between themselves

cobweb model, cobweb theorem *noun* a model of supply and demand showing fluctuations caused by time lags between the responses of producers to price changes

coefficient of correlation *noun* a measurement of correlation or relationship between two sets of data on a continuum from –1 to +1

coefficient of determination *noun* a method of measuring the accuracy of a variable by comparing it to an equation with two or more independent variables – the result can be either zero (no correlation) or one (perfect correlation). Also called **multiple correlation coefficient**

coefficient of elasticity *noun* the ratio of the change in one variable as a response to a change in another variable. ◊ **price elasticity**

coefficient of variation *noun* a measurement of the variability of data in relation to its mean. Also called **relative dispersion**

coin *noun* a piece of metal money; coins form a very small part of the total money in circulation

coincident indicator *noun* an indicator which coincides with economic activity (as opposed to a leading indicator or lagging indicator). It measures the changes in the aggregate economy.

cointegration *noun* in statistics, the calculation of the relationship between economic data measured over a long period of time

collateral security *noun* security, such as negotiable instruments, shares or goods, used to provide a guarantee for a loan

collective bargaining *noun* negotiations between employers and workers' representatives over wage increases and conditions

collinearity *noun* a problem which occurs when there is a very close relationship between a series of variables which prevents them being considered as independent. Also called **multicollinearity**

collusion *noun* a situation which occurs when companies act in secret to control a market or to influence market prices

collusive oligopoly *noun* a situation in which several very large companies dominate the market and agree among themselves to restrict prices or output

command economy *noun* a system where the government plans all business activity, regulates supply, sets production targets and itemises work to be done. Also called **planned economy, central planning**

commercial bank *noun* a bank that offers banking services to the public and to businesses, as opposed to a merchant bank. Also called **clearing bank**

commercial bill *noun* a bill of exchange issued by a company (a trade bill) or accepted by a bank (a bank bill), as opposed to a Treasury bill, which is issued by the government

commercial paper *noun* an IOU or short-term promissory note issued by a company to raise a short-term loan. Abbreviation **CP**

commission *noun* money paid to a salesperson, agent or stockbroker, usually a percentage of the sales made or the business done

commodity *noun* something sold in very large quantities, especially raw materials and food such as metals or corn. Commodities are either traded for immediate delivery (as 'actuals' or 'physicals'), or for delivery in the future (as 'futures'). Commodity markets deal either in metals (aluminium, copper, lead, nickel, silver, zinc) or in 'soft' items, such as cocoa, coffee, sugar and oil. In London, the exchanges are the London Metal Exchange and the London Commodity Exchange. Gold is traded on the London Gold Market, petroleum on the International Petroleum Exchange (IPE). In the USA, the New York Commodity Exchange (COMEX) deals in metals, the Chicago Board of Trade (CBOT) in metals, soft commodities and financial futures, and the Chicago Mercantile Exchange (CME) in livestock and livestock futures.

commodity agreement *noun* ◊ **international commodity agreement**

commodity exchange, commodity market *noun* a place where people buy and sell commodities

commodity money *noun* a commodity used as a means of exchange, as in barter, or as money on the black market

Common Agricultural Policy *noun* an agreement between members of the European Union to protect farmers by paying subsidies to fix the prices of farm produce. The European Union has set up a common system of agricultural price supports and grants. The system attempts to encourage stable market conditions for agricultural produce, to ensure a fair return for farmers and reasonable market prices for the consumer, and finally to increase yields and productivity on farms in the Union. A system of common prices for the main farm products has been established with intervention buying as the main means of market support. The first major reforms in 30 years were carried out in 1992. The objectives were to control surpluses and to reduce support costs to the taxpayer and to comply with the demands of GATT. The reforms included arable set-aside, new quotas and price reductions. Abbreviation **CAP**

common external tariff *noun* a tariff agreed by all members of the European Union customs union. Abbreviation **CET**

common law *noun* law as laid down in decisions of courts, rather than by statute. It is the general system of laws which were formerly the only laws existing in England and the USA, but which in some cases have been superseded by statute. (NOTE: You say **at common law** when referring to something happening according to the principles of common law.)

Common Market *noun* a pact between various countries to reduce trade barriers, allowing free movement of goods and people across frontiers; there are no exchange controls and business can move and set up in any country without restrictions

common stock *noun* US ordinary shares in a company giving the shareholders the right to vote at meetings and receive a dividend

Community Charge *noun* a local tax formerly levied on each adult person living in the community. ♦ **poll tax**

Companies Act *noun* GB an Act of Parliament which regulates the workings of companies, stating the legal limits within which companies may do their business. There are several of these acts on the Statute Book, the most recent dating from 1985, 1989, 1991 and 2001.

Companies House *noun* an official organisation where the records of companies must be deposited, so that they can be inspected by the public; technically speaking, called 'Companies Registration Office (CRO)'

company *noun* a group of people organised to buy, sell or provide a service for a profit

COMMENT: A company can be incorporated (with memorandum and articles of association) as a private limited company, and adds the initials 'Ltd' after its name, or as a public limited company, when its name must end in 'Plc'. Unincorporated companies are partnerships such as firms of solicitors, architects, accountants, etc., and they add the initials 'Co.' after their name.

company director *noun* a person appointed by the shareholders to help run a company

company law *noun* laws which refer to the way in which companies may work

company limited by shares *noun* same as **joint-stock company**

company reserves *plural noun* same as **revenue reserves**

comparative advantage *noun* being able to produce a good or service at a lower cost than other producers

comparative statics *noun* the analysis of an equilibrium after a determinant has been changed in comparison to the equilibrium which existed before

compensating variation *noun* the amount of extra money needed to give a customer the same utility as if the price of the good or service were to rise; the opposite, 'equivalent variation', is the extra money needed to give the customer the same utility as if the price were to fall

compensation principle *noun* principle that those who gain from an economic change should compensate those who lose; it obviously does not work if those who gain do not compensate the losers fully. Also called **Hicks-Kaldor principle**

competition *noun* the action of companies or individuals who are trying to do better than others, to win a larger share of the market, to control the use of resources, etc.

Competition Act 1998 *noun* an Act of Parliament which is designed to make business compete on equal terms and outlaws certain types of anti-competitive behaviour such as non-competing agreements or the abuse by a business of its dominant position in the market

Competition Commission *noun* a UK government body which oversees competition policy and applies the Competition Act

competition policy *noun* government policy which tries to encourage competition by keeping a check on potential monopolies and making sure that businesses act fairly in relationship to each other

competitive advantage *noun* advantage gained by one company that has lower costs than another

competitive equilibrium *noun* the state of equilibrium when markets are competitive

competitive equilibrium price *noun* the price at which the quantity supplied equals the quantity demanded

competitiveness *noun* the state of being competitive, that is, being able to compete in a market with other firms; firms are competitive because of the superior quality of their products or services, lower prices, better distribution, etc.

competitive tendering *noun* a system of choosing a supplier for goods or services, by asking companies to tender; normally the company offering the lowest price will be chosen

complementary demand *noun* demand from consumers for two goods or services which are used together. Also called **joint demand**

complementary goods, **complementary products** *plural noun* two goods which are consumed at the same time, such as frankfurters and rolls, so that the demand for one will increase if the price of the other falls. This is the opposite of substitute goods where the goods can replace each other and a rise in the price of one will increase demand for the other.

compound interest *noun* interest which is added to the capital and then earns interest itself

concentration *noun* the action of grouping a number of things together; it occurs when a market is dominated by a small number of firms (90% of the market in the hands of three firms, for example). It is a stage between perfect competition where many small firms exist but cannot influence the market and a monopoly where only one firm exists and dominates the market. Also called **market concentration**

concentration ratio *noun* a ratio showing the proportion of a market that is dominated by a few large firms. This is calculated according to information about the size distribution of firms.

concert party *noun* an arrangement where several people or companies work together in secret (usually to acquire another company through a takeover bid)

conciliation *noun* ♦ **ACAS**

Condorcet, Marquis of (1745–1794) French mathematician who wrote on the theory of calculus

Condorcet's paradox *noun* same as **paradox of voting**

Confederation of British Industry *noun* an organisation founded in 1965 representing its member firms to the government, and publishing economic forecasts and encouraging business best practice. Abbreviation **CBI**

confidence index *noun* the measurement of consumers' confidence in the economy, based on the feeling that they are better off than they were last year, or that the economy is doing better than it was last year. ◆ **feelgood factor**

confidence interval *noun* a means of quantifying a margin for error in statistical analysis; the interval gives an estimated range of values for a certain unknown parameter – the wider the interval, the more likely is an error in interpreting the parameter and more data should be collected

conglomerate *noun* a group of subsidiary companies linked together and forming a group making very different types of products

conglomerate merger *noun* the merger of two large corporations in quite different sectors of the economy

consolidated accounts *plural noun* accounts where the financial position of several different accounting entities (i.e. a holding company and its subsidiaries) are recorded together

consolidated fund *noun* in the UK, money in the Exchequer which comes from tax revenues and is used to pay for government expenditure

consolidated stock *noun* full form of **consols**

consols *plural noun GB* irredeemable government bonds. They pay an interest but do not have a maturity date.

consortium *noun* a group of companies brought together for a special purpose (NOTE: The plural is **consortia**.)

conspicuous consumption *noun* the consumption of goods for show or to get approval, rather than because they are useful

constant prices *plural noun* prices which are calculated according to the prices at a given base year

constant returns to scale *noun* situation in which a proportionate increase in all costs results in an equivalent increase in output

consumer *noun* a person or company that buys and uses goods and services

consumer behaviour *noun* the way in which consumers behave, in particular when buying goods and services

consumer confidence *noun* the confidence that consumers have in the economy. If their confidence falls it can result in a decrease in economic performance.

consumer credit *noun* credit given by shops, banks and other financial institutions to consumers so that they can buy goods. (NOTE: Lenders have to be licensed under the Consumer Credit Act, 1974. The US term is **installment credit**.)

Consumer Credit Act, 1974 *noun* an Act of Parliament which requires lenders to be licensed by the Office of Fair Trading, and requires them to state clearly the full terms of loans that they make (including the APR)

consumer durables *plural noun* items such as washing machines, refrigerators or cookers which are bought and used by the public

consumer equilibrium *noun* the point where a consumer's spending results in maximum satisfaction

consumer expenditure *noun* private spending by consumers on services, durables and non-durables; it is one of the elements that makes up 'aggregate expenditure.' ♦ **consumption expenditure**

consumerism *noun* the theory that the interests of consumers should take precedence over the interests of the producers

consumer non-durables *plural noun* goods purchased by consumers which are used up immediately and have to be replaced, such as food and drink, gas, electricity, etc.

Consumer Price Index *noun* a US index showing how prices of consumer goods have risen over a period of time. Abbreviation **CPI** (NOTE: The UK term is **retail prices index**.)

consumer protection *noun* the protecting of consumers against unfair or illegal traders

consumer sovereignty *noun* the theory that consumers are the main element in the economy because they decide whether something is bought or not and are therefore more important than the producers

consumer's surplus *noun* the difference between the higher price a consumer might be prepared to pay for a good or service and the lower price he or she actually pays; it contributes to consumer satisfaction

consumption *noun* the purchasing of goods or services to satisfy needs, in particular in the household sector

consumption expenditure *noun* the expenditure made by the household sector on durables, non-durables and services, shown as a proportion of national income

consumption function *noun* a graph which shows the relationship between households' disposable income and what they actually spend on consumer goods; as income rises, so spending increases, but at a lower rate because saving increases also

consumption possibility curve, consumption possibility line *noun* a graph showing the different quantities of different goods which could be purchased at different prices, given that the purchaser has a fixed amount of money to spend; it is used in conjunction with an 'indifference curve' to identify the goods and their quantities which a customer might want to purchase. Also called **budget line**

consumption tax *noun* a tax on spending by consumers, such as a sales tax or VAT

contango *noun* the payment of interest to a stockbroker for permission to carry payment for shares from one account day to the next. Also called **carry-over**

contestable market *noun* a theoretical market which does not involve a new entrant in higher costs than other existing producers and does not involve losses on exit; the only constraint on producers is the competition within the market

contingency reserve *noun* money set aside in case it is needed urgently

contingent liability *noun* a liability which may or may not occur, but for which provision is made in a company's accounts (as opposed to 'provisions', where money is set aside for an anticipated expenditure)

contingent protection *noun* measures to protect domestic producers, such as anti-dumping laws, which are only used when necessary

contract *noun* an agreement between two or more parties to create legal obligations between them. Some contracts are made 'under seal', i.e. they are signed and sealed by the parties; most contracts are made orally or in writing. The essential elements of a contract are: (a) that an offer made by one party should be accepted by the other; (b) consideration (i.e. payment of money); (c) the intention to create legal relations. The terms of a contract may be express or implied. A breach of contract by one party entitles the other party to sue for damages or to ask for something to be done.

contract curve *noun* a series of points along a curve in the Edgeworth box which indicate where two parties get the same utility from a commodity on the curve and less utility from a commodity away from the curve

contractionary fiscal policy *noun* government policy which aims at decreasing government spending or increasing taxes; this would have the effect of reducing demand in the economy. Also called **deflationary fiscal policy**

contractionary monetary policy *noun* government policy which aims at restricting demand by reducing money supply. Also called **deflationary monetary policy**

contract of employment *noun* a contract between management and an employee showing all the conditions of work. Also called **employment contract**

contractual liability *noun* the legal responsibility for something as stated in a contract

convergence *noun* the theory that the economic factors, especially productivity, applying in a group of countries should move closer together. It also was applied in the Maastricht Treaty to economic factors within the European Union, especially regarding interest rates, government deficits, exchange rates and inflation.

convergence criteria *plural noun* economic criteria, such as those in the Maastricht Treaty, which countries must satisfy to be able to join a monetary union

conversion *noun* the action of changing convertible loan stock into ordinary shares

conversion discount, conversion premium *noun* the difference between the price of convertible stock and the ordinary shares into which they are to be converted. If the convertible stock is cheaper, the difference is a 'conversion premium'; if the stock is dearer, the difference is a 'conversion discount'.

convertibility *noun* the ability to exchange one currency for another currency or for gold easily

convertible currency *noun* currency which can easily be exchanged for another

convertible debenture *noun* a debenture which can be converted into ordinary shares at a certain date

convexity *noun* the convex shape of a curve. The theory is that if points in a set are connected and the line between any two points is included in the set, then the set is convex. In economics, this corresponds to diminishing marginal utility. In finance it can represent a convex curve in price yield of a bond.

coordinates *plural noun* values used to locate a point on a graph or map. Y-coordinates show the vertical axis and X-coordinates the horizontal axis.

copyright *noun* an author's legal right to publish his or her own work and not to have it copied. This lasts for fifty years after the author's death under the Berne Convention, but in 1995, the European Union adopted a copyright term of 70 years. ■ *verb* to protect a work by copyright ■ *adjective* protected by copyright

corner the market *verb* to own most or all of the supply of a certain commodity and so control the price

corporate bond *noun* loan stock officially issued by a company to raise capital, usually against the security of some of its assets. The company promises to pay a certain amount of interest on a set date every year until the redemption date, when it repays the loan.

corporate governance *noun* the way a company or other organisation is run, including the powers of the board of directors, audit committees, ethics, environmental impact, treatment of workers, directors' salaries and internal control. Corporate governance reporting in the UK developed from the 1992 Cadbury Committee on the Financial Aspects of Corporate Governance. That was followed by the Greenbury report on directors' remuneration. Both were later updated by the Hampel Committee. In 1999 the Turnbull Report dealing with internal control introduced the concept that companies should adopt a system to analyse all the risks to the business, not just narrow financial ones. In the USA, corporate governance is mostly prescribed by state law, though the Securities and Exchange Commission has imposed a degree of conformity federally.

corporate sector *noun* the sector of the economy which covers privately-owned businesses that trade, which together with the financial sector and personal sector forms the private sector, as opposed to the public sector (nationalised industries and government agencies)

corporation *noun* a large limited liability company; especially a limited liability company which is incorporated in the USA. ◊ **incorporation**

COMMENT: A corporation is formed by registration with the Registrar of Companies under the Companies Act (in the case of public and private companies) or other Acts of Parliament (in the case of building societies and charities).

corporation tax *noun* a tax on profits made by companies, calculated after interest and payments to the Inland Revenue, but before dividends are paid. Abbreviation **CT**

correlation *noun* ◊ **coefficient of correlation**

correspondent bank *noun* a bank that acts as an agent for other banks, especially foreign banks who have no local office

cost *noun* the value of the inputs (i.e. the amount of money) which are used to produce a good or service ■ *verb* to have a particular monetary value

cost, insurance, and freight *noun* an estimate of a price, which includes the cost of the goods, the insurance and the transport charges. Abbreviation **CIF, c.i.f.**

cost accounting *noun* the branch of management accounting concerned with the recording of manufacturing and sales costs, budgets and the calculation of profitability

cost-benefit analysis *noun* an examination of the ratio between total social costs and total social benefits, especially in considering large-scale public building programmes. The externalities involved can be costs such as pollution and benefits such as better access to markets; if social costs are less than social benefits then the construction programme can be justified. Also called **benefit-cost analysis**

cost centre *noun* a person or group within a firm whose costs can be itemised and to which fixed costs can be allocated

cost-effectiveness, cost efficiency *noun* the most economical way of achieving a desired result, either in the public sector or the private. It is essentially using the resources available to the best advantage.

cost function *noun* the relationship between the cost of inputs from factors of production and the cost of outputs in a firm

cost inflation *noun* same as **cost-push inflation**

cost of capital *noun* the interest which has to be paid on the capital borrowed to operate a business; the more risky the business the higher the interest

cost of goods sold *noun* same as **cost of sales**

cost-of-living increase *noun* a way of measuring the cost of living which is shown as a percentage increase on the figure for the previous year;

similar to the consumer price index, but including other items such as the interest on mortgages

cost of sales *noun* all the costs of a product sold, including manufacturing costs and the staff costs of the production department, before general overheads are calculated. Also called **cost of goods sold**

cost-plus pricing *noun* a method of pricing goods or services, which is based on the total cost plus a percentage mark-up which is the profit for the producer. This can encourage producers to keep costs high, because their total profit will be higher.

cost price *noun* a selling price which is the same as the price that the seller paid for the item (either the manufacturing price or the wholesale price)

cost-push inflation *noun* inflation caused by increased wage demands and increased raw materials costs, which lead to higher prices and in turn lead to further wage demands. Also called **cost inflation**

countercyclical policy *noun* same as **demand management**

counterparty *noun* the other party in a deal

countertrade *noun* trade which does not involve payment of money, but rather barter, buy-back deals, etc.

countervailing duty *noun* a duty imposed by a country on imported goods, to increase the price to a position where they do not offer unfair competition to locally-produced goods, especially where the price of the goods imported includes a subsidy from the government in the country of origin. Also called **anti-dumping duty**

countervailing power *noun* the use of corporate power to counter the effect of another power, as when a supermarket chain uses its buying power to counter the price rises imposed by a large supplier

country risk *noun* the risk associated with lending to, or investing in, a particular country. It is the level of bad debt associated with a country, which sets its international credit rating.

coupon *noun* **1.** a piece of paper from a producer or supplier which is given as a gift and which must be exchanged for a certain product **2.** a piece of paper used in place of money

Cournot, Antoine (1801–1877) mathematician who examined the conditions for equilibrium and monopolies, taxes, and international trade

CP *abbreviation* commercial paper

CPI *abbreviation* Consumer Price Index

CPP *abbreviation* current purchasing power

CPP accounting *noun* same as **current purchasing power accounting**

crawling peg *noun* a method of controlling exchange rates, where they are fixed at a certain rate but then allowed to move up or down by small amounts repeatedly

creative accountancy, **creative accounting** *noun* the adaptation of a company's figures to present a better picture than is correct (to appear to make a company more attractive to a potential buyer, or for some other reason which may not be strictly legal)

creative destruction *noun* the theory of Joseph Schumpeter that economic growth is caused by entrepreneurs who take risks and destroy previous business practices by their innovations. He believed that this was the essential force of capitalism.

credit *noun* **1.** the period of time a customer is allowed before he or she has to pay a debt incurred for goods or services **2.** the amount entered in accounts to show an increase in assets or expenses or a decrease in liabilities, revenue or capital. In accounts, credits are entered in the right-hand column. Compare **debit** ■ *verb* to enter an amount in an account to show an increase in assets or expenses or a decrease in liabilities, revenue or capital

credit account *noun* an account which a customer has with a shop which allows him or her to buy goods and pay for them later

credit card *noun* a plastic card which allows someone to borrow money and to buy goods up to a certain limit without paying for them immediately, but only after a period of grace of about 25–30 days

credit control *noun* a limit on bank lending imposed by a government

credit creation *noun* the increase of credit lent to customers by banks who lend money deposited with them on to other banks who then lend it to their customers

credit guarantee *noun* a guarantee offered to a lender, usually by the government, that a borrower will repay a sum even without security to cover it

creditor *noun* a person or company that is owed money. A company's creditors are its liabilities.

creditor nation *noun* a country which has positive overseas assets, in the form of outward investments or loans to other countries. It has a balance of payments surplus. Compare **debtor nation**

creditors' committee *noun* in the USA, a group of creditors of a corporation being reorganised under Chapter 11, who meet officials of the corporation to discuss the progress of the reorganisation

creditors' meeting *noun* a meeting of all persons to whom an insolvent company owes money, to decide how to obtain the money owed

credit squeeze *noun* a reduction in bank lending, or in money supply and an increase in interest rates introduced by a government to reduce demand in the economy

credit union *noun* a group of people who pay in regular deposits or subscriptions which earn interest and are used to loan to other members of the group

creeping inflation *noun* the normal inflationary position in many countries, where inflation increases by small amounts each year

critical path analysis *noun* the analysis of the way a project is organised in terms of the minimum time it will take to complete, defining tasks or jobs and the time each requires, arranged in order to achieve completion on time but calculating which parts can be delayed without holding up the rest of the project and which need to be accelerated. It uses PERT (Program Evaluation and Review Techniques).

CRO *abbreviation* Companies Registration Office

cross-border capital flows *plural noun* movements of capital from one country to another

cross-border trade *noun* trade between one country and another

cross-elasticity of demand, cross-price elasticity of demand *noun* the change in the demand for a good which results from the change in price of another good, shown as a percentage, assuming that the price of the first good remains constant; if the two goods are substitutes the demand for one will rise as the price of the other increases, but if they are complements then the demand for the first will fall as the price of the second increases

cross rates *plural noun* same as **exchange cross rates**

cross-subsidisation *noun* subsidisation within a firm, where one department or product is subsidised by the profits from another. This will help the production of a good which otherwise would have made a loss, but can be a factor in increasing inefficiency.

crowding out effect *noun* the reduction of the level of personal investment because of high government spending which has the effect of increasing interest rates

CSO *abbreviation* Central Statistical Office

CTT *abbreviation* capital transfer tax

cum coupon *noun* the price of a bond including the right to receive the next interest payment

cum dividend, cum div *noun* the price of a share including the next dividend still to be paid

cumulative preference share, cumulative preferred stock *noun* a preference share which will have the dividend paid at a later date even if the company is not able to pay a dividend in the current year

currency *noun* money in coins and notes which is used in a particular country

currency appreciation *noun* an increase in the value of a currency against another currency

currency depreciation *noun* a fall in the value of a currency against another currency

currency devaluation *noun* a forced reduction in value of a currency against other currencies

currency revaluation *noun* a forced increase in the value of a currency against other currencies

currency swap *noun* an agreement to use a certain currency for payments under a contract in exchange for another currency. The two companies involved each can buy one of the currencies at a more favourable rate than the other.

currency unit *noun* a main item of currency of a country (a dollar, pound, yen, etc.)

current account *noun* **1.** a bank account which pays little or no interest, but from which the customer can withdraw money when he or she wants by writing cheques. Also called **cheque account** (NOTE: The US term is **checking account**.) **2.** an account of the balance of payments recording a country's imports and exports of goods and services and the money paid on or received from investments

current assets *plural noun* assets used by a company in its ordinary work (such as materials, finished products, monies owed by customers, or cash)

current cost accounting *noun* same as **replacement cost accounting**. Abbreviation **CCA**

current expenditure *noun* expenditure on day-to-day items for a household, firm or government

current liabilities *plural noun* debts that a company has to pay within the next accounting period. In a company's annual accounts, these would be debts that must be paid within the year and are usually payments for goods or services received.

current purchasing power accounting *noun* a method of accounting which takes inflation into account by using constant monetary units (actual amounts multiplied by a general price index). Also called **CPP accounting**

current-weighted index *noun* same as **Paasche index**

current yield *noun* dividend calculated as a percentage of the current price of a share on the stock market

customer *noun* a person or company which buys goods or services. The customer may not be the consumer or end user of the product.

Customs and Excise *noun* a UK government department which organizes the collection of taxes on imports, excise duty on alcohol, etc., and VAT

customs drawback *noun* a refund of duty paid on goods on entry into a country when they are subsequently re-exported

customs duty *noun* a tax paid on goods brought into or taken out of a country

customs tariff *noun* same as **tariff**

customs union *noun* an agreement between several countries that goods can travel between them, without paying duty, while goods from other countries have to pay special duties

cyclical fluctuation *noun* short-term changes which take place around a long-term variable

cyclically adjusted *adjective* calculated assuming that the economy is running at the normal level. A cyclically adjusted PSBR is calculated to remove the effects of cyclical fluctuations from the economy.

cyclical unemployment *noun* unemployment caused by a fall in demand during a recession

D

data mining *noun* comparing two sets of data in order to find a connection between them, as by comparing the results of two unconnected companies and basing an investment strategy on them

date of maturity *noun* same as **maturity date**

dawn raid *noun* sudden planned purchase of a large number of a company's shares at the beginning of a day's trading (up to 15% of a company's shares may be bought in this way, and the purchaser must wait for seven days before purchasing any more shares; it is assumed that a dawn raid is the first step towards a takeover of the target company)

DCE *abbreviation* domestic credit expansion

DCF *abbreviation* discounted cash flow

deadweight debt *noun* debt which is incurred to pay for current expenditure but which does not produce any asset, such as a bank loan to cover business losses

deadweight loss *noun* a reduction in consumers' surplus caused by a fall in quantities of a product produced, especially when a monopoly producer keeps production low to maintain high prices

dear money *noun* money which has to be borrowed at a high interest rate, and so restricts expenditure by companies. Also called **tight money**

death duty *noun* US taxes paid on the property left by a dead person. Also called **death tax** (NOTE: The UK term is **inheritance tax**.)

death rate *noun* number of deaths per thousand of population in a given year. An increase in the death rate will result in a fall in population, and so will a decrease in the birth rate.

death tax *noun* same as **death duty**

debenture *noun* an acknowledgement of a debt issued by a limited company. Debentures pay a fixed interest and are very long-dated. They use the company's assets as security. In the UK, debentures are always secured on the company's assets; in the USA, debenture bonds are not secured.

debit *noun* an amount entered in accounts which shows an increase in assets or expenses or a decrease in liabilities, revenue or capital. In accounts, debits are entered in the left-hand column. Compare **credit**

debit card *noun* a plastic card, similar to a credit card, which debits the holder's account immediately through an EPOS system

debt *noun* **1.** an amount of money borrowed by a company to finance its activities **2.** an amount of money owed by an individual

debt burden *noun* the cost of servicing a debt, i.e. the interest payments payable on a loan

debt for equity *noun* a method of making loans to poorer countries less onerous by converting them into shares in the companies to which the loans are made. This may be preferable to the lender since he or she may be able to share in the profits of the scheme if it works well which would not be possible in the case of a pure loan.

debt management *noun* the managing of a debt, such as that of a firm, by calculating when further borrowing is needed, when interest payments or principal repayments are due and similar matters

debtor *noun* a person who owes money. In accounts, debtors are all the money owed to an accounting entity.

debtor nation *noun* a country whose foreign debts are larger than money owed to it by other countries

debt service *noun* the payments due under a loan agreement, i.e. interest payable and repayments of capital

debt-service ratio *noun* the debts of a company shown as a percentage of its equity

decentralisation, decentralization *noun* the removal of power from a central organisation, such as a central government, and the transferring of it to local authorities

decile *noun* one of a series of nine figures below which one tenth or several tenths of the total fall

decision *noun* a piece of binding legislation of the European Union. A decision is binding in its entirety on those to whom it is addressed. A decision may be addressed to a member state, to an organisation or even to an individual person.

decision tree *noun* a model for decision-making, showing the possible outcomes of different decisions

declaration of income *noun* same as **income tax return**

decreasing returns to scale *plural noun* a situation in which further inputs are made but output does not rise proportionately

deep discounted bonds *plural noun* bonds which are issued at a very large discount to the redemption price but which produce little or no interest. They do however produce a substantial capital gain when redeemed.

default *noun* a failure to carry out the terms of a contract, especially failure to pay back a debt ■ *verb* to fail to carry out the terms of a contract, especially to pay back a debt

deferred shares, deferred stock *noun* shares which receive a dividend only after all other dividends have been paid

deficiency payment *noun* a payment made to producers when a government feels that the price at which a product is sold is not enough to give the producer a reasonable income. It is applied in particular to farmers.

deficit *noun* an amount by which spending is higher than income

deficit financing *noun* planning by a government to cover the shortfall between tax income and expenditure by borrowing money

deflate *verb* to reduce the level of economic activity as a means of fighting inflation

deflation *noun* reduction in economic activity, resulting in falls in output, wages, prices and similar effects, either caused by a fall in demand or created when a government reduces money supply or lowers interest rates (NOTE: The opposite is **inflation**.)

deflationary fiscal policy *noun* same as **contractionary fiscal policy**

deflationary gap *noun* the difference between the normal level of business activity and the lower level during a recession. Also called **output gap**

deflationary monetary policy *noun* same as **contractionary monetary policy**

deflator *noun* an amount by which a country's GNP is reduced to take inflation into account

degrees of freedom *plural noun* the number of variables in a set that are free to vary independently of each other

deindustrialisation, deindustrialization *noun* a reduction in the proportion of a country's economy represented by manufacturing, usually being replaced by service industries

demand *noun* the desire on the part of consumers to acquire a good or service, together with their ability to pay for it ■ *verb* to express a desire for something in a way that is difficult to refuse

demand curve *noun* a graph showing the quantities of a good that consumers would want to buy at different prices. The curve only takes prices into account, and not other factors such as income or consumer expectations. It is based on a demand schedule. Also called **market demand curve**

demand-deficient unemployment *noun* unemployment caused by the lack of demand in an economy

demand deposit *noun US* an amount of money in an account which can be taken out when the account holder wants it by writing a cheque

demand elasticity *noun* same as **elasticity of demand**

demand for labour *noun* the need for workers in firms. It is dependent on the level of wages paid and on the sales of the product produced. If labour costs become too high, or the product does not sell, demand for labour will fall.

demand for money *noun* the need for money by individuals and firms so that they can make purchases. Also, when the future of an economy is uncertain, holding money in liquid form is seen as a safer way of investing.

demand function *noun* a calculation of the way prices, customer expectations and substitute products are reflected in the demand for a good or service

demand inflation, **demand-led inflation** *noun* inflation caused by increased demand for goods or services. In a situation of full employment demand may exceed the potential supply and leads to increased prices and increased money supply. ♦ **cost-push inflation**

demand management *noun* a government's attempts to control demand in the economy and to reduce the fluctuations of the business cycle. Also called **countercyclical policy, stabilisation policy**

demand-pull inflation *noun* same as **demand inflation**

demand schedule *noun* a list of prices of a good and the quantities consumers would want to buy. It is used to construct a demand curve.

demerger *noun* a separation of a company into several separate parts, especially of a company which has grown by acquisition

demographic time-bomb *noun* the crisis which the developed world faces as populations become older, people live longer and birth rates fall. The most obvious consequence is that a smaller working population has to support a larger retired population, making increased pension provisions essential.

demographic transition *noun* the change from high birth and death rates seen in less developed countries to low birth and death rates seen in developed countries

demography *noun* the study of populations, and how they increase and decrease

dependency culture *noun* the culture by which people become dependent on welfare payments, and those who try to escape the poverty trap to improve their status find themselves penalised. People in work may find that they earn less or pay more tax than those who are unemployed and in receipt of welfare.

dependency ratio *noun* the proportion of a country's population who are not of working age seen as a ratio of those who are of working age. The more children under 15 or the more old people over 65 there are in a population, the greater the strain put on the actual working population who have to support them. Also called **support ratio**

dependent variable *noun* variable which is influenced by another variable (called the independent variable). For example, the price of a product may influence the demand for it.

deposit *noun* **1.** an amount of money placed in a bank for safekeeping and to earn interest **2.** an amount of money given in advance so that the thing which you want to buy will not be sold to someone else ▪ *verb* to place something with a person or institution for safekeeping

deposit account *noun* an account which pays interest, but on which notice usually has to be given to withdraw money. Also called **time account**

deposit-taking institution, depository institution *noun* an institution such as a building society, bank or friendly society which is licensed to receive money on deposit from private individuals and to pay interest on it. Also called **licensed deposit-taker**

depreciate *verb* **1.** to write down the capital value of an asset over a period of time in a company's accounts **2.** to lose value

depreciation *noun* **1.** loss of value of a currency when compared to other currencies **2.** the writing down of the capital value of an asset over a period of time in a company's accounts. Various methods of depreciating assets are used, such as the straight line method, where the asset is depreciated at a constant percentage of its cost each year, and the reducing balance method, where the asset is depreciated at a constant percentage which is applied to the cost of the asset after each of the previous years' depreciation has been deducted.

depreciation rate *noun* the rate at which an asset is depreciated each year in the accounts

depressed area *noun* a part of a country suffering from economic depression

depression *noun* a period of economic crisis with high unemployment and loss of trade

deregulation *noun* the reduction of government control over an industry, especially over private firms

derivatives, derivative instruments *plural noun* forms of traded security, such as option contracts, which are derived from ordinary bonds and shares, exchange rates or stock market indices. Derivatives traded on stock exchanges or futures exchanges include options on futures or exchange rates or interest rate. While they can be seen as a way of hedging against possible swings in exchange rates or commodity prices, they can also produce huge losses if the market goes against the trader.

derived demand *noun* demand for an input which is dependent on the demand for the output

determinant *noun* a figure calculated from the elements of a square matrix, used to verify if the figures in the matrix are correct

devaluation *noun* a reduction in the value of a currency against other currencies

developed country *noun* a country which has fully developed industrial sectors and service sectors, with a high per capita GNP

developing country, developing nation *noun* a country which is not fully industrialised

development area *noun* an area which has been given special help from a government to encourage businesses and factories to be set up there. Also called **development zone**

development economics *noun* the section of economics that deals with the economics of developing countries

development zone *noun* same as **development area**

deviation *noun* the difference between a variable and its mean value

difference equation *noun* an equation which shows the values of variables at different times, so the current value of a dependent variable is shown as a function of an earlier value

differential tariffs *plural noun* different tariffs for different classes of goods as when imports from certain countries are taxed more heavily than similar imports from other countries

diffusion of innovations *noun* the process by which innovations become accepted by firms or individual consumers, either at home or internationally

DIG *abbreviation* disability income guarantee

diminishing marginal product *noun* the way in which increased inputs tend to result in proportionately fewer outputs

diminishing marginal rate of substitution *noun* same as **marginal rate of substitution**

diminishing marginal utility *noun* the way in which a consumer's satisfaction at acquiring a good diminishes as more units of the good are purchased

direct cost *noun* a cost which can be directly related to the making of a product

direct debit *noun* a system where a customer allows a company to charge costs to his or her bank account automatically and where the amount charged can be increased or decreased with the agreement of the customer

direct investment *noun* investment in physical items, such as stock or machinery

directive *noun* a piece of legislation of the European Union which is binding, but which member states can implement as they wish. A directive is binding as to the result to be achieved, but leaves to the national authorities the choice of form and method.

direct labour *noun* the workers employed to make a good or provide a service, as opposed to indirect labour which does not actually make a good but provides backup to the direct labour force

director *noun* **1.** a person appointed by the shareholders to help run a company **2.** the person who is in charge of a project, an official institute or other organisation

COMMENT: Directors are elected by shareholders at the AGM, though they are usually chosen by the chairman or chief executive. A board will consist of a chairman (who may be non-executive), a chief executive or managing director and a series of specialist directors in charge of various activities of the company (such as a finance director, production director or sales director). The company secretary will attend board meetings, but need not be a director. Apart from the executive directors, who are in fact employees of the company, there may be several non-executive directors, appointed either for their expertise and contacts, or as representatives of important shareholders such as banks. The board of an American company may be made up of a large number of non-executive directors and only one or two executive officers. A British board has more executive directors.

direct tax *noun* a tax (such as income tax) paid directly to the government

direct taxation *noun* the use or collection of direct taxes

dirigisme *noun* a situation where the state interferes in the running of the economy (NOTE: The opposite is **laissez-faire**.)

dirty float *noun* same as **managed float**

Disability Income Guarantee *noun* payments made by the government to increase the incomes of disabled people on low incomes and bring them up to a higher level. It is a form of Income Support. Abbreviation **DIG**

discount *noun* **1.** a percentage by which a full price is reduced to a buyer by the seller; a discount for cash, or cash discount, means that you pay less if you pay in cash; a discount for quantity purchases, or bulk discount means that you pay less if you buy a large quantity **2.** the amount by which something is sold for less than its value ■ *verb* to sell something at a discount

discounted cash flow *noun* the calculation of the forecast return on capital investment by discounting future cash flows from the investment, usually at a rate equivalent to the company's minimum required rate of return. Abbreviation **DCF**

COMMENT: Discounting is necessary because it is generally accepted that money held today is worth more than money to be received in the future. The effect of discounting is to reduce future income or expenses to their 'present value'. Once discounted, future cash flows can be compared directly with the initial cost of a capital investment which is already stated in present value terms. If the present value of income is greater than the present value of costs the investment can be said to be worthwhile.

discount house *noun* a financial company which specialises in buying and selling bills at a discount, using money which has been borrowed short-term from commercial banks to finance the operation

discount market *noun* the market for borrowing and lending money, through instruments such as Treasury bills or certificates of deposit

discount rate *noun* the percentage used in a discounting calculation, such as to find the present value of future income

discount window *noun* the way in which the US Federal Reserve grants loans to a bank by giving advances on the security of Treasury bills which the bank is holding

discouraged worker *noun* a worker who has been unemployed and makes no effort to get back into work, because of age, lack of skills or depression

discrete variable *noun* a variable which can only take on certain values, such as an integer

discretionary policy *noun* a policy where it is left to the policymakers to decide what action to take or when to act

discretionary spending *noun* government spending which it is not obliged by law to make, but which it makes because it decides that this is the best action to take

discriminating monopoly *noun* a situation in which a monopoly provider sells in different markets at different prices which it calculates depending on the circumstances prevailing each market (such as higher prices in developed countries, lower prices in developing countries)

diseconomies of scale *plural noun* a situation in which increased production actually increases unit cost. After having increased production using the existing workforce and machinery, giving economies of scale, the company finds that in order to increase production further it has to employ more workers and buy more machinery, leading to an increase in unit cost.

disembodied technical progress *noun* advances in techniques which are not caused by new machinery, but by new skills acquired by workers

disequilibrium *noun* a situation which is not stable (as when a country's balance of payments is in deficit)

disguised unemployment *noun* a situation in which the official unemployment statistics hide the fact that some people are not registered as unemployed when they could be. This applies to people such as those who have taken early retirement or women who have stopped work temporarily to have families. Also called **hidden unemployment**

disincentive *noun* any factors (such as a high marginal tax rate) which makes it less attractive to work, make money or save money

disinflation *noun* a slowdown in the rate of inflation. Compare **deflation**

disintermediation *noun* the cutting out of intermediaries, as when a lender lends money direct to a borrower

disinvestment *noun* reduction of investments by selling shares

dissaving *noun* the action of a household which spends more than its income either by selling assets or by incurring debts

distribution *noun* the act of sending goods from the manufacturer to the wholesaler and then to retailers

distributional efficiency *noun* the situation in which the distribution of goods and services to consumers is carried out in the most efficient way

distribution channel *noun* a way of sending goods from a manufacturer to a retailer. Also called **channels of distribution** (NOTE: A distribution channel usually consists of a chain of intermediaries, for example wholesalers and retailers, that is designed to move goods from the point of production to the point of consumption in the most efficient way.)

disutility *noun* the measure of the dissatisfaction a consumer experiences with a good or service he or she has bought

diversification *noun* the addition of another quite different type of business to a firm's existing trade

divestment *noun* the action of closing a business or part of a business, in order to release investment funds for expansion in other areas, or simply to sell the business

dividend *noun* a part of a company's profits paid to shareholders. It is usually expressed as an amount per share (2p per share) or as a percentage of the nominal value of the share (5.2% per share).

COMMENT: The dividend is calculated as the proportion of profits a company can pay to its shareholders after tax has been paid, always keeping some of the profit back to reinvest in the company's products or activities. Large companies usually pay dividends twice a year, once after the half-year results have been declared (called the 'interim dividend') and gain when the final results are published.

dividend check *noun US* same as **dividend warrant**

dividend cover, dividend payout ratio *noun* the percentage of profits which is paid in dividends to shareholders. Also called **times covered** (NOTE: The opposite is **payout ratio**.)

dividend warrant *noun* a cheque which makes payment of a dividend (NOTE: The US term is **dividend check**.)

dividend yield *noun* a dividend expressed as a percentage of the current market price of a share

division of labour *noun* the way in which workers specialise in certain aspects of a job, no one worker doing all the job. This is particularly the case in manufacturing industries.

divorce of ownership from control *noun* same as **separation of ownership from control**

DJIA *abbreviation* Dow Jones Industrial Average

dog *noun* a product which has a low market share and a low growth rate, and so is likely to be dropped from the company's product line

dollar *noun* the unit of currency used in the USA and other countries, such as Australia, Bahamas, Barbados, Bermuda, Brunei, Canada, Fiji, Hong Kong, Jamaica, New Zealand, Singapore and Zimbabwe. Without specific mention of a country, it usually refers to the currency of the USA.

dollar area *noun* the area of the world where the US dollar is the main trading currency

Domar, Evsey (1914–1997) Russian-born American economist who wrote mainly on economic growth and government debt

Domar growth model *noun* same as **Harrod-Domar growth model**

domestic credit expansion *noun* the proportion of an increase in money supply which does not come from a surplus in the balance of payments but from domestic bank lending. Abbreviation **DCE**

dominant firm *noun* a firm which supplies a large proportion of a good or service, without however being a monopoly

dominant strategy *noun* in game theory, a strategy which gives better results than another strategy which is dominated and then discarded

donor country *noun* a country which gives aid to another poorer country (the recipient)

double A *noun* ◊ **A**

double coincidence of wants *noun* a situation which exists in barter, where each party wants something offered by the other and so the two parties can barter goods or services

double counting *noun* the counting of a cost or benefit element twice when doing analysis. This can happen when calculating the total sales in a market as the sum of all sales made by firms, without deducting the purchases firms make from other firms in the market.

double-entry bookkeeping *noun* a method of bookkeeping in which both debit and credit entries are recorded in the accounts at the same time (e.g. as a sale is credited to the sales account, the purchaser's debt is debited to the debtors account)

double option *noun* the option to buy or sell at a certain price in the future (a combination of call and put options)

double taxation *noun* taxation of the same income twice, first in the country where the income arises and then in the home country of the earner

Dow 30 *noun* same as **Dow Jones Industrial Average**

Dow Jones Average *noun* same as **Dow Jones Industrial Average**

Dow Jones Index *noun* any of several indices published by the Dow Jones Co., based on prices on the New York Stock Exchange. The main index is the Dow Jones Industrial Average. Other Dow Jones indexes are: the Dow Jones 20 Transportation Average; the Dow Jones 15 Utility Average; the Dow Jones 65 Composite Average (formed of the Industrial Average, the Transportation Average and the Utility Average taken together and averaged); and the Dow Jones Global-US Index (a capitalisation weighted index based on June 30, 1982=100). A new European-based index is the Dow Jones Euro Stoxx 50 Index, comprising fifty blue-chip companies from various European countries.

Dow Jones Industrial Average *noun* an index of share prices on the New York Stock Exchange, based on a group of thirty major corporations. Abbreviation **DJIA**. Also called **Dow Jones Average, Dow 30**

downside risk *noun* the risk that an investment will fall in value (NOTE: The opposite is **upside potential**.)

downsizing *noun* reduction in the size of something, especially reduction of the number of people employed in a company to make it more profitable

drawee *noun* a person who accepts a bill of exchange

drawer *noun* a person who raises a bill of exchange

drawing rights *plural noun* the right of a member country of the IMF to borrow money from the fund in a foreign currency. ♦ **special drawing rights**

dual economy *noun* an economy where both technically advanced and technically primitive sectors exist, as in developing countries where advanced technology is applied to extracting minerals or manufacturing while at the same time large parts of the country exist at subsistence level

duality *noun* a mathematical term by which a problem can be stated in two different, opposing ways, as when considering a market from the point of view of maximising utility or minimising costs at the same time

dummy variable *noun* a variable with the value of either 1 or 0, used to indicate that some characteristic is present or absent

dumping *noun* the act of getting rid of excess goods cheaply in an overseas market

duopoly *noun* a situation in which two persons or companies control all the market in the supply of a product. Compare **monopoly**

duopsony *noun* a situation in which there are only two buyers in a market

durable goods, durables *plural noun* goods which have a relatively long life, such as electric goods, cars or machinery

Dutch auction *noun* a type of auction where the auctioneer offers an item for sale at a high price and gradually reduces the price until someone makes a bid

dynamics *noun* the study of changes in an economy which take place over a long period of time

E

earmarking *noun* the linking of a tax to a particular service, such as earmarking road taxes for the upkeep of roads. Also called **hypothecation**

earned income *noun* the income from sources such as wages, salaries and pensions (as opposed to unearned income from investments)

earnings *plural noun* **1.** salary or wages, profits and dividends or interest received **2.** the profits of a business

earnings drift *noun* the amount by which wages and salaries rise above agreed rates, as when earnings are increased by bonus payments or overtime payments. Also called **salary drift, wage drift**

earnings per share *plural noun* the amount of money earned in profit per share (the total profits after tax and preference dividends have been paid, divided by the number of shares). Abbreviation **EPS**

earnings yield *noun* the amount of money earned in dividends per share expressed as a percentage of the current market price of the share. The last dividend paid is divided by the current market price of one share.

easy fiscal policy *noun* government policy when dealing with a recession by cutting taxes and increasing government borrowings to fund increased government expenditure

easy monetary policy *noun* same as **easy money policy**

easy money *noun* the money available on easy repayment terms

easy money policy *noun* government policy of expanding the economy by making money more easily available (lower interest rates, easy access to credit, etc.). Also called **easy monetary policy**

EBRD *abbreviation* European Bank for Reconstruction and Development

e-business *noun* **1.** the conducting of business via electronic means such as computers, modems, the Internet and email, as when shopping via the Internet or using email to buy shares. Also called **e-commerce 2.** a company that does its business using the Internet

EC *abbreviation* European Community (NOTE: now called the **European Union**)

ECB *abbreviation* European Central Bank

ECGD *abbreviation* Export Credits Guarantee Department

e-commerce *noun* the process of buying and selling goods over the Internet. Also called **electronic commerce** (NOTE: Although e-commerce was originally limited to buying and selling, it has now evolved and includes such things as customer service, marketing, and advertising.)

econometric model *noun* a model of an aspect of the economy, using a statistical approach. Such models are used in forecasting macroeconomic trends.

econometrics *noun* the study of the statistics of economics, using computers to analyse statistics and make forecasts using mathematical models

economic activity rate *noun* same as **activity rate**

Economic and Monetary Union *noun* same as **European Monetary Union**. Abbreviation **EMU**

economic cost *noun* the cost of a scarce factor of production used to produce a good or service, as opposed to another that could have been used, instead of the one adopted. Also called **opportunity cost**

economic development *noun* the expansion of the commercial and financial situation in developing countries by industrialisation

economic efficiency *noun* the reduction of the inputs needed to produce one unit of output, and so increasing the margin to the producer

economic growth *noun* the rate at which a country's national income grows, usually shown as an increase in GDP or GNP or an increase in per capita income

economic imperialism *noun* the domination of small countries by large multinational corporations or by other states which are economically more powerful

economic indicator *noun* a statistic which shows how the country's economy is going to perform in the short or long term (relating to factors such as unemployment rate or overseas trade)

economic man *noun* a theoretical individual found in economic models, who acts entirely for reasons of self-interest without any concern for others. As a consumer he always looks for the product that gives most satisfaction, as a producer for the product that gives most profit.

economic migrant *noun* a person who moves because he or she wants to find a job, or simply a better-paid job

economic model *noun* a computerised plan of an economic situation, used for forecasting economic trends. Also called **model**

economic rent *noun* the return on any factor of production which is more than what it should receive to remain in its present state of use. It is not the same as the profit, since it does not take account of other costs. Also called **quasi-rent**

economics *noun* **1.** the study of the production, distribution, selling and use of goods and services **2.** the study of financial structures to show how a product or service is costed and what returns it produces (NOTE: [all senses] takes a singular verb)

economic sanctions *plural noun* restrictions on trade with a country in order to harm its economy or to make its government change policy

economic surplus *noun* the amount remaining after the costs involved in producing a country's output (such as wages and cost of raw materials) are deducted from the value of the output produced

economic union *noun* a union between two or more countries where tariff barriers are reduced and fiscal and industrial policy are harmonised

economic value added *noun* the difference between a company's profit and the cost of its capital. A company does not have simply to make a profit from its business – it has to make enough profit to cover the cost of its capital, including equity invested by shareholders. Abbreviation **EVA**

economic welfare *noun* the welfare of an individual or group which comes from the purchase and consumption of goods and services

economies of scale *plural noun* a situation in which a product is made more profitable by manufacturing it in larger quantities so that each unit costs less to make. Compare **diseconomies of scale**

economies of scope *plural noun* factors which make it more profitable to produce a series of products, rather than a single product

economist *noun* a person who specialises in the study of economics, often one who advises policymakers

economy *noun* **1.** the practice of being careful not to waste money or materials **2.** the financial state of a country, and the way in which a country makes and uses its money

economy in transition *noun* same as **transition economy**

Edgeworth box *noun* a diagram devised by F. Y. Edgeworth, in the form of a box which plots the indifference curves of two individuals or firms relative to the consumption or production of two goods. The contract curve plotted shows the points where the utility to the two individuals or firms is equal.

EEA *abbreviation* European Economic Area

EEC *abbreviation* European Economic Community (NOTE: now called the **European Union (EU)**)

e-economy *noun* the various industries involved in buying and selling goods and services over the Internet

EEOC *abbreviation* Equal Employment Opportunity Commission

effective demand *noun* the desire on the part of consumers to acquire a good or service, together with their ability to pay for it

effective exchange rate *noun* the rate of exchange for a currency calculated against a basket of currencies

effective interest rate *noun* the real interest rate on a bond which is purchased at a discount, as opposed to the nominal interest rate

effective protection, effective rate of protection *noun* the calculation of the protection really given to local manufacturers by imposing a tariff on imported competing goods, less any tariff imposed on imported raw materials and parts used to make the goods locally

efficiency *noun* the ability to work well or to produce the right result or the right work quickly. There are various types of efficiency: productive efficiency is where goods and services are produced at the lowest cost; allocative efficiency is where resources are allocated to producing goods and services in the most efficient way; distributional efficiency is where the distribution of goods and services to consumers is carried out in the most efficient way.

efficient markets hypothesis *noun* the theory that stock markets respond to information about the assets being sold, so that if it is anticipated that a share will rise in value, investors will buy that share and so force up its market price. Abbreviation **EMH**

EFT *abbreviation* electronic funds transfer

EFTA *abbreviation* European Free Trade Association

EFTPOS *abbreviation* electronic funds transfer at a point of sale

EIB *abbreviation* European Investment Bank

eighty/twenty law, 80/20 law *noun* Pareto's law (so called because 80/20 is the normal ratio between majority and minority figures, so 20% of accounts produce 80% of turnover; 80% of GDP enriches 20% of the population, and so on)

EIS *abbreviation* Enterprise Investment Scheme

elastic *adjective* which can expand or contract easily (as in consumer demand for certain products which changes a lot as a result of only small changes in price: such products are said to be price-elastic)

elasticity *noun* the ability to change easily

elasticity of demand *noun* the percentage change in demand for an item in response to changes in its market price. It assumes that income and other variables remain constant. Also called **demand elasticity**

elasticity of substitution *noun* the quantities demanded of two goods shown as a proportion of a change in their prices

elasticity of supply *noun* the percentage change in the quantity of an item supplied divided by the percentage change in its price. This only applies in industries where the price is fixed by the market and not by the producer

elasticity of technical substitution *noun* the rate at which one factor of production can be substituted for another without changing the output

electronic business *noun* same as **e-business**

electronic commerce *noun* same as **e-commerce**

electronic funds transfer *noun* a system for transferring money from one account to another electronically (as when using a smart card). Abbreviation **EFT**

electronic funds transfer at a point of sale *noun* a system for transferring money directly from the purchaser's account to the seller's, when a sale is made using a plastic card. Abbreviation **EFTPOS**

electronic point of sale *noun* a system where sales are charged automatically to a customer's credit card and stock is controlled by the shop's computer. Abbreviation **EPOS**

eligible liabilities *plural noun* liabilities which go into the calculation of a bank's reserves

embargo *noun* a government order which stops a type of trade, such as exports to, or other commercial activity with, another country ■ *verb* to put an embargo on something

embodied technical progress *noun* advances in techniques which are dependent on new machinery, not on new skills acquired by workers

emerging market *noun* a new market, as in Southeast Asia or Eastern Europe, which is developing fast and is seen as potentially profitable to fund managers

EMH *abbreviation* efficient markets hypothesis

EMI *abbreviation* European Monetary Institute

emission credits *plural noun* theoretical reductions in emissions of CO_2 and other greenhouse gases which can be bought by a country from others who do not need them and set against its targets. They are allowed under the Kyoto treaty.

empirical testing *noun* the testing of economic theories against real data

employee *noun* a person employed by a company or firm

employee share ownership plan, employee share ownership programme, employee share scheme *noun* a scheme which allows employees to obtain shares in the company for which they work (though tax may be payable if the shares are sold to employees at a price which is lower than the current market price). Abbreviation **ESOP**

employer *noun* a person or company which has regular workers and pays them

employment *noun* regular paid work

Employment Acts *plural noun* a series of UK and US acts which regulate trade unions and the labour market and establish parameters for government policies aimed at encouraging employment

employment contract *noun* same as **contract of employment**

employment service *noun* a service offered by private employment or government agencies, such as jobcentres, which list jobs available in a certain area. The Employment Service was the name of a government agency which is now part of the Jobcentre Plus network.

EMS *abbreviation* European Monetary System

EMU *abbreviation* **1.** Economic and Monetary Union **2.** European Monetary Union

endogenous growth *noun* the theory that in the long run economic growth is governed by factors within the national system and not by factors outside it. Compare **exogenous growth**

endogenous income hypothesis *noun* the theory that wealth is a factor in consumption expenditure: as individuals become richer so their expenditure increases as a proportion of their total income

endogenous money *noun* money which is an asset to the individual or firm holding it, but which is a liability to someone else. The theory is that money has to be actually in a bank before it can be lent to someone, in other words, the financial sector reacts to production and prices in the real world. The opposite, exogenous money or outside money, is money which is put into the production system from outside and production and prices react to the financial sector. Also called **inside money**

endogenous variable *noun* a variable in an economic model which affects the model and is also affected by it. Compare **exogenous variable**

Engel, Ernst (1821–1896) German economist and statistician who studied the budgets of Belgian families to develop his law

Engel curve *noun* a curve which indicates how an individual's income is spent

Engel's law *noun* a law which states that as incomes rise so a higher proportion is spent on luxury goods and a lower proportion on necessities such as food. Alternatively, the lower the family income, the more proportionately the family spends on food. This is shown by the Engel curve.

enterprise *noun* a business, especially used in statistics and official reports

Enterprise Investment Scheme *noun* a UK scheme, started in 1994, to promote investment in unquoted companies by which qualifying gains are exempt from capital gains tax or can be written off against income tax. Abbreviation **EIS**

enterprise zone *noun* an area of the country where businesses are encouraged to develop by offering special conditions such as easy planning permission for buildings and reduction in the business rate

entrepot port *noun* a town with a large international commercial port dealing in commodities which are imported and then reexported without customs duties (the entrepot trade)

entrepreneur *noun* a person who directs a company and takes commercial risks. He or she sees market opportunities and acts on them for profit.

entrepreneurship *noun* the action of directing a company and taking commercial risks as an entrepreneur

entry *noun* an item of information entered into a ledger (NOTE: The plural is **entries**.)

entry forestalling price, **entry preventing price** *noun* a price for a good or service which is set by a firm already established in a market, and which is at a level which does not encourage new entrants to the market. The action of setting such a price is called limit pricing.

envelope curve *noun* a curve that encloses other curves

envelope theorem *noun* a theory that the mathematical relationship between variables can be shown as a curve (the envelope curve) which plots the relationship between variables and indicates the optimum course of action to take

environment *noun* the surroundings of an organism, including the physical world and other organisms. Firms and governments are vary sensitive to the environment and the impact of businesses on it. Such an impact can be regularly analysed in an environmental audit or environmental impact assessment.

environmental audit *noun* an assessment made by a company or organisation of the financial benefits and disadvantages to be derived from adopting a more environmentally sound policy

environmental impact assessment, **environmental impact analysis** *noun* the assessment of the impact that a projected expenditure will have on the environment

environmental impact statement *noun* a statement required under US law for any major federal project, evaluating the effect of the project on the environment. Abbreviation **EIS**

epos, EPOS, EPoS *abbreviation* electronic point of sale

EPS *abbreviation* earnings per share

Equal Employment Opportunity Act 1972 *noun* a US act which emphasises the right of individual workers to equal treatment in employment

Equal Employment Opportunity Commission *noun* a US government organisation set up in 1965 to eliminate discrimination in the workplace. It monitors employers' performance and enforces the Equal Employment Opportunity Act. Abbreviation **EEOC**

Equal Opportunities Commission *noun* a UK government organisation set up in 1975 which aims to prevent discrimination in the workplace, in particular discrimination on sexual grounds. Abbreviation **EOC**

equal pay *noun* the situation in which all workers get equal pay for the same jobs, or for jobs which are deemed to be equivalent, irrespective of factors such as age, sex or race

equation *noun* a set of mathematical rules applied to solve a problem

equation of international demand *noun* according to J. S. Mill, the terms of trade between two countries which are established according to the level of demand for each other's goods.

equilibrium *noun* a situation in which there is no tendency for people to change what they are doing

equilibrium level of national income *noun* the level of national income where there is no tendency to change, that is, where consumption expenditure and production coincide

equilibrium price *noun* the price at which the quantity supplied equals the quantity demanded, so that there is no excess of supply or demand

equilibrium quantity *noun* the quantity supplied at the equilibrium price

equities *plural noun* ordinary shares in companies

equity *noun* **1.** the value of an asset, such as a house, less any mortgage on it **2.** the ordinary shares in a company

COMMENT: 'Equity' (also called 'capital' or 'shareholders' equity' or 'shareholders' capital' or 'shareholders' funds') is the current net value of the company including the nominal value of the shares in issue. After several years a company would expect to increase its net worth above the value of the starting capital. 'Equity capital' on the other hand is only the nominal value of the shares in issue.

equity accounting *noun* the accounting practice of including part of the profits of an associated company in the investor company's profit and loss account and showing the balance sheet value of the investment as cost plus a share of the associate's retained profit

equity capital *noun* a company's capital which is invested by holders of ordinary shares giving them the right to unlimited returns. Note that preference shares are not equity capital, since they involve less risk and do not share in the profitability of the company – if the company is wound up none of the equity capital would be distributed to the preference shareholders. Also called **shareholders' equity**

equity gearing *noun* the ratio between a company's borrowings at interest and its ordinary share capital

equity risk premium *noun* the extra yield from an increased dividend or higher than usual profits which an investor looks to receive from more risky investments. Abbreviation **ERP**

equivalent variation *noun* the amount of extra money needed to give a customer the same utility as if the price of the good or service were to fall. The opposite, compensating variation, is the extra money needed to give the customer the same utility as if the price were to rise.

ERDF *abbreviation* European Regional Development Fund

ERM *abbreviation* exchange rate mechanism

ERP *abbreviation* equity risk premium

escalator clause *noun* a clause in a contract allowing for regular price increases because of increased costs

ESF *abbreviation* European Social Fund

ESOP *abbreviation* employee share ownership plan

estate duty *noun* formerly, a tax on property left by a dead person (NOTE: now called **inheritance tax**)

estimator *noun* a statistical formula by which estimated quantities can be calculated

EU *abbreviation* European Union

Euler, Leonhard (1707–1783) Swiss mathematician who worked in Germany and Russia. Among other things he proposed e as the base of natural logarithms.

Euler's theorem *noun* the theory that a rigid body with one fixed point will rotate around an axis. In economics it is the theory which relates distribution to marginal productivity.

euro *noun* the currency adopted as legal tender in several European countries from 1 January 1999. The countries which are joined together in the European Monetary Union and adopted the euro as their common currency in 1999 are: Austria, Belgium, Finland, France, Germany, Ireland, Italy, Luxembourg, the Netherlands, Portugal and Spain. The conversion of these currencies to the euro was fixed on 1 January 1999. Greece joined on 1 January 2001. The CFA franc and CFP franc were pegged to the euro at the same time. (NOTE: The plural is **euro** or **euros**.)

Eurobond *noun* a medium- to long-term bearer bond issued by an multinational corporation or government or public body outside its country of origin and sold to purchasers in several countries who pay in a eurocurrency (sold on the Eurobond market)

Eurobond market *noun* the market in Eurobonds

Eurocurrency *noun* the currency of a European country held by a non-resident of that country

Eurocurrency market *noun* the market in Eurocurrencies

Eurodollar *noun* a US dollar deposited in a bank outside the USA, used mainly for trade within Europe

European Bank for Reconstruction and Development *noun* a bank, based in London, which channels aid from the European Union to Eastern European countries. Abbreviation **EBRD**

European Central Bank *noun* the central bank for most of the countries in the European Union, those which have accepted European Monetary Union and have the euro as their common currency. It is based in Frankfurt. Abbreviation **ECB**

European Commission *noun* the administration of the European Union, made up of members nominated by each member state. Also called **Commission of the European Community**

European Community *noun* same as **European Economic Community**. Abbreviation **EC**

European Development Fund *noun* a fund set up by the EC to help the 71 countries linked to the community under the Lomé convention. Abbreviation **EDF**

European Economic Area *noun* an area covered by an agreement on trade between the EU and the members of EFTA. Abbreviation **EEA**

European Economic Community *noun* a grouping of European countries which later became the European Union. Abbreviation **EEC**. Also called **European Community**

European Free Trade Association *noun* a group of countries (Iceland, Liechtenstein, Norway and Switzerland) formed in 1960 to encourage freedom of trade between its members. EFTA countries are linked with the EU countries to form the EEA . Abbreviation **EFTA**

European Investment Bank *noun* an international European bank set up in 1958 to provide aid to small companies in the poorer parts of the European Union. Abbreviation **EIB**

European Monetary Co-operation Fund *noun* formerly, a fund set up by the EC to manage the exchange rates of its member states; now part of the European Central Bank

European Monetary Fund *noun* a system for managing exchange rates within the EC before 1979, when it was replaced by the European Monetary System

European Monetary Institute *noun* an organisation set up in 1994 to act as the preliminary stage before setting up the European Central Bank and introducing the euro as the common European currency. Abbreviation **EMI**

European Monetary System *noun* a system for managing exchange rates within the EC, set up in 1979 to replace the European Monetary Fund. It was itself replaced in 1999 when the single currency was introduced. Abbreviation **EMS**

European Monetary Union *noun* the process by which the majority of the member states of the EU joined together to adopt the euro as their common currency on 1st January 1999. Abbreviation **EMU**

European Recovery Programme *noun* a programme set up in 1947 by George Marshall, the US Secretary of State, to help rebuild the economies of European countries after the Second World War. Also called **Marshall Plan**

European Regional Development Fund *noun* an EU fund set up in 1975 to provide grants to underdeveloped parts of Europe. Abbreviation **ERDF**

European Social Fund *noun* an EU fund which aims to help workers find jobs or get training, and helps develop a proper business spirit. Abbreviation **ESF**

European Union *noun* a group of European countries linked together by the Treaty of Rome. The European Community was set up in 1957 and changed its name to the European Union when it adopted the single market. It has now grown to include fifteen member states. These are: Austria, Belgium, Denmark, Finland, France, Germany, Greece, Ireland, Italy, Luxembourg, the Netherlands, Portugal, Spain, Sweden and the United Kingdom. The member states of the EU are linked together by the Treaty of Rome in such a way that trade is more free, that money can be moved from one country to another freely, that people can move from one country to another more freely and that people can work more freely in other countries of the group (the four fundamental freedoms).

EVA *abbreviation* economic value added

exact interest *noun* annual interest calculated on the basis of 365 days (as opposed to ordinary interest, calculated on 360 days)

ex ante *adverb* as seen in advance, expectations of what will happen in the future have an effect on planning. Compare **ex post**

exceptional items *plural noun* items which arise from normal trading but which are unusual because of their size or nature. Such items are shown separately in a note to the company's accounts but not on the face of the profit and loss account unless they are profits or losses on the sale or termination of an operation, or costs of a fundamental reorganisation or restructuring which have a material effect on the nature and focus of the reporting entity's operations, or profits or losses on the disposal of fixed assets.

excess capacity *noun* spare capacity which is not being used. It exists when firms production does not match its expectations. Since maintaining capacity is expensive, any excess should be avoided.

excess capacity theory *noun* the theory that all firms tend to work at less than 100% capacity and make up the difference by overtime working or other means

excess demand *noun* a situation in which the demand for a good or service exceeds the supply. This usually results in increased prices.

excess profit *noun* a profit which is higher than what is thought to be normal

excess reserves *plural noun* reserves held by a US bank which are more than required by law. Compare **required reserves**

excess supply *noun* a situation in which the supply of a good or service is more than the demand

exchange *noun* **1.** the process of giving of one thing for another **2.** a market for shares, commodities, futures and similar instruments ■ *verb* to give one thing for another

exchange control *noun* the control by a government of the way in which its currency may be exchanged for foreign currencies

exchange cross rates *plural noun* rates of exchange for two currencies, shown against each other, but in terms of a third currency, often the US dollar. Also called **cross rates**

Exchange Equalisation Account *noun* a UK government account with the Bank of England in gold and foreign currencies. It is used by the government when buying or selling foreign currency to influence the sterling exchange rate. The US equivalent is the Exchange Stabilizer Fund.

exchange rate *noun* a price at which one currency is exchanged for another. Also called **rate of exchange**

exchange rate mechanism *noun* a former method of stabilising exchange rates within the European Monetary System, where currencies could only move up or down within a narrow band (usually 2.25% either way, but for certain currencies widened to 6%) without involving a realignment of all the currencies in the system. Abbreviation **ERM**

Exchange Stabilizer Fund *noun* a US government account with a Federal Reserve Bank in gold and foreign currencies. It is used by the government when buying or selling foreign currency to influence the dollar exchange rate. The UK equivalent is the Exchange Equalisation Account.

Exchequer *noun* the fund of all money received by the government of the UK from taxes and other revenues

Exchequer stocks *plural noun* same as **Treasury stocks**

excise duty *noun* a tax on certain goods consumed in a country (such as alcohol, petrol or cigarettes). The duty on goods imported into a country is called customs duty.

excludability *noun* the fact of being the exclusive property of, or being exclusively available to, a certain individual. The theory is that certain forms of knowledge should be exclusively enjoyed by someone, such as an invention by the patent holder.

exclusion *noun* the act of not including someone, as when a consumer is prevented from using a good; the good is then a private good which can be bought or sold. If a good is available to anyone, free of charge, then it is a public good.

exclusion clause *noun* a clause in an insurance policy or warranty which says which items or events are not covered

exclusion principle *noun* a principle applying to private goods, that some consumers will be excluded from purchasing them, as opposed to public goods which are available to everyone

exclusive dealing *noun* an arrangement between a producer and distributor that they will only trade with each other. Such exclusive arrangements apply to certain areas, and are felt to be to the disadvantage of the ultimate customer who has no choice of supplier, and therefore does not benefit from price competition.

ex coupon *adverb* sold without the current interest coupons. It refers to bonds.

ex dividend, ex div *adjective* not including the right to receive the next dividend. It applies to shares. Abbreviation **xd**

exit *noun* the act of leaving a market, usually because of losses incurred

exit price *noun* the price at which an investor sells an investment or at which a firm sells up and leaves a market

exogenous growth *noun* the theory that in the long run economic growth is governed by factors outside the national system and not by factors within it. Compare **endogenous growth**

exogenous money *noun* money which is put into the production system from outside, where production and prices react to the financial sector. The opposite, money which is inside the banking system is called endogenous money or inside money. Also called **outside money**

exogenous variable *noun* a variable outside an economic model which affects the model but is not affected by it. Compare **endogenous variable**

expectations *plural noun* what people think will happen. Expectations have a major influence on economic decisions in particular in times of uncertainty when there is no clear picture of future trends.

expectations-augmented Phillips curve, expectations-adjusted Phillips curve version curve where the expected rate of inflation is taken into account when measuring wage increases and demand

expectations lag *noun* the period which elapses before the expected value of a variable changes to allow for a change in a current value. In adaptive expectations it is the time which elapses between the moment of the observation of a trend by an individual and the change in his or her expectations caused by it.

expected inflation, expected rate of inflation *noun* the rate of inflation which the public expects to exist in the future. It is not possible to measure it accurately.

expected utility *noun* the satisfaction to a consumer from something where the benefits are uncertain, as in shares in risky companies or betting on a lottery

expected value *noun* the future value of a certain course of action, weighted according to the probability that the course of action will actually occur. If the possible course of action produces income of £10,000 and has a 10% chance of occurring, its expected value is 10% of £10,000 or £1,000.

expenditure *noun* the amount of money spent, by individuals, firms or the government. Totalised it forms the aggregate demand.

expenditure switching *noun* the moving of present expenditure from one purchase to another, such as from purchasing imports to purchasing home-produced goods

expenditure tax *noun* a tax on money as it is spent, as opposed to income tax which taxes income as it is received. An expenditure tax is sometimes considered a better progressive tax in that individuals with low income spend less than those with high incomes. VAT, sales tax, excise duty and customs duty are all expenditure taxes.

explicit cost *noun* the cost of paying for factors involved in buying or producing a good or service where the factors come from outside producers. The opposite, implicit cost represents payments for factors which a firm actually produces or owns itself.

exploitation *noun* the use of someone's labour cheaply, either by a firm underpaying its workers or by a developed country paying less for imports from a developing country

exponent *noun* number indicating how many times a base number is to be multiplied to produce a certain power. It is printed in small characters after the base number.

exponential *adjective* with a variable exponent which relates to the base e, the basis of a natural logarithm

export *noun* **1.** a product which is sold and transported to a foreign country. ◊ **exports 2.** the practice or business of sending goods to foreign countries to be sold ■ *verb* to sell and transport a product to a foreign country

Export Credits Guarantee Department *noun* a UK government department which insures sellers of exports sold on credit against the possibility of non-payment by the purchasers. Abbreviation **ECGD**

export incentive *noun* a way of encouraging exports, e.g. guaranteeing credit, subsidies for exported goods or special tax concessions so that exporters pay lower tax on profits from exports

export-led growth *noun* growth in a national economy which is caused by increased exports. It is less inflationary than domestic growth.

export multiplier *noun* the ratio of the increase in a country's national income to the increase in the value of exports

export promotion *noun* the promoting of the sale of exports by means such as government incentives, government-sponsored exhibitions or subsidies to exporters

exports *plural noun* goods, services or capital sold to foreign countries (NOTE: usually used in the plural, but the singular form is used before a noun)

export subsidy *noun* a government subsidy to exporters, to encourage trade. Direct export subsidies are banned under international agreements.

ex post *adverb* as seen after the event. Compare **ex ante**

exposure to risk *noun* the amount of risk which a lender or investor has. Exposure can be the amount of money lent to a customer (a bank's exposure to a foreign country) or the amount of money which an investor may lose if his investments collapse (such as his or her exposure in the Australian market).

extended fund facility *noun* a means of giving help to IMF members whose economies are suffering from balance of payments difficulties, similar to standby credit but with longer repayment terms

external balance *noun* the situation in which a country invests abroad the same amount as other countries invest in it. It implies rising foreign currency reserves and a low overseas debt.

external benefits *plural noun* ◊ **externalities**

external costs *plural noun* ◊ **externalities**

external debt *noun* money owed by foreign countries

external deficit *noun* a deficit in a country's balance of payments

external diseconomy *noun* ◊ **externalities**

external economy *noun* ◊ **externalities**

external growth *noun* the growth of a firm by buying other companies, rather than by expanding existing sales or products (NOTE: The opposite is **internal growth** or **organic growth**.)

externalities *plural noun* costs or benefits involved in a transaction which do not accrue to the individual or firm which is carrying out the transaction. External costs (or external diseconomies) might include damage to the environment from a mining industry, while external benefits (or external economies) could be the pleasure incurred in an artificial lake created by hydroelectric works.

external labour market *noun* a system in which jobs in an organisation are advertised so that people working outside the organisation can apply. This is opposed to an internal labour market where preference is given to employees already working in the organisation.

external trade *noun* same as **foreign trade** (NOTE: The opposite is **internal trade**.)

extraordinary items *plural noun* formerly, large items of income or expenditure which did not arise from normal trading and which did not occur every year. They were shown separately in the profit and loss account, after taxation.

extrapolation *noun* the extending of a trend beyond the timescale or quantities of the data on which the trend is based

extrapolative expectations *plural noun* expectations which are based on an extrapolation of existing trends, i.e. assuming that existing trends will continue at the same rate

F

face value *noun* the value written on a coin, banknote or share certificate or bill of exchange. Also called **nominal value, par value**

factor cost *noun* the value of a good or service as the price paid for it, i.e. not including tax such as VAT

factor endowment *noun* the factors of production which a country has available

factor income *noun* income which comes from selling factors of production, such as hiring out labour or renting land

factoring *noun* the business of buying debts from a firm at a discount and then getting the debtors to pay. Many businesses resort to factoring to improve their cash flow.

factor market *noun* the market for a factor of production, such as the labour market or the capital market

factor of production *noun* one of the four things needed to produce a product (land, labour, machinery and capital)

factory gate price *noun* the price of a product bought directly from the manufacturer. The factory gate price includes direct costs such as labour, raw materials and energy, and overhead costs such as interest on loans, plant maintenance and rent.

fair trade *noun* an international business system in which countries charge import duties on certain items imported from their trading partners where those imports are believed to be unfairly cheap, usually because of labour costs which are cheaper than in the importing country

Fair Trading Act 1973 *noun* an act which provided for the regulation of monopolies and competition and set up the Office of Fair Trading

Family Expenditure Survey *noun* since 1957, a regular annual official survey of household income and expenditure based on a sample of about 10,000 households. It covers incomes and expenditure, especially on regularly paid items, such as gas, electricity and telephone, together with insurance, travel costs and hire purchase costs. The results are used to provide the weighting for the RPI. Abbreviation **FES**

Fannie Mae *noun* same as **Federal National Mortgage Association** (*informal*)

fao *abbreviation* for the attention of

farm subsidies *plural noun* subsidies paid to farmers. In the European Union the Common Agricultural Policy protects farmers by paying subsidies to fix prices of farm produce; the US federal government has a comprehensive scheme to subsidise farmers growing certain crops, mainly grain and cotton – these subsidies go more to large farming businesses rather than to small farmers.

FASB *abbreviation* Financial Accounting Standards Board

FCI *abbreviation* Finance Corporation for Industry

FDI *abbreviation* foreign direct investment

FDIC *abbreviation* Federal Deposit Insurance Corporation

Fed *noun US* same as **Federal Reserve Board** (*informal*)

Federal Deposit Insurance Corporation *noun* a US Federal agency which supervises banks, guarantees investors' deposits and makes sure that financial products and services give a fair deal to the customer. Abbreviation **FDIC**

Federal funds *plural noun* deposits by commercial banks with the US Federal Reserve Banks, which can be used for short-term loans to other banks. Also called **Fed funds**

Federal Home Loan Bank Board *noun* a former US Federal agency set up in 1932 to supervise the Federal Home Loan Bank System. It regulated all savings and loan associations and was replaced in 1989 by the Federal Housing Finance Board. Abbreviation **FHLBB**

Federal Home Loan Bank System *noun* a US credit system which provided credit to institutions making home loans to individuals. Originally it was supervised by the Federal Home Loan Bank Board, and now by the Federal Housing Finance Board. Abbreviation **FHLBS**

Federal Housing Finance Board *noun* a US Federal agency set up in 1989 to regulate the Federal Home Loan Banks. Abbreviation **FHFB**

Federal National Mortgage Association *noun* a privately owned US organisation that regulates mortgages and helps offer mortgages backed by Federal funds. Abbreviation **FNMA**. Also called **Fannie Mae**

Federal Reserve *noun* a system of federal government control of the US banks, in which the Federal Reserve Board regulates money supply, prints money, fixes the discount rate and issues government bonds. The system is the central bank of the USA. It is run by the Federal Reserve Board, under a chairman and seven committee members (or governors) who are all appointed by the President. The twelve Federal Reserve Banks and their twenty-five branches act as lenders of last resort to local commercial banks. Although the board is appointed by the President, the whole system is relatively independent of the US government.

Federal Reserve Bank *noun* one of the twelve regional banks in the USA which with their twenty-five branches are owned by the state and directed by the Federal Reserve Board. Abbreviation **FRB**

Federal Reserve Board *noun* the committee which runs the central banks in the USA. Abbreviation **FRB**

Federal Trade Commission *noun* the US Federal agency established to keep business competition free and fair

Fed funds *US* same as **Federal funds** (*informal*)

feelgood factor *noun* a general feeling that everything is going well (leading to increased consumer spending)

FES *abbreviation* Family Expenditure Survey

FHFB *abbreviation* Federal Housing Finance Board

FHLBB *abbreviation* Federal Home Loan Bank Board

FHLBS *abbreviation* Federal Home Loan Bank System

fiat money *noun* coins or notes which are not worth much as paper or metal, but are said by the government to have a value and are recognised as legal tender

fiduciary issue *noun* bank notes which are not backed by gold, but which have a value printed on them and are accepted as having that value

FIFO *abbreviation* first in first out

FIMBRA *abbreviation* Financial Intermediaries, Managers and Brokers Regulatory Association

final product *noun* a manufactured product or finished service which is bought by the final user, such as an individual consumer

finance *noun* **1.** money available for investment, as a loan or for a similar use **2.** the business of managing money ■ *verb* to provide money for an investment, as a loan or for a similar use

Finance Act *noun* the annual act of the UK Parliament which gives the government the power to obtain money from taxes as proposed in the Budget

finance company, finance corporation *noun* a company, usually part of a commercial bank, which buys goods or equipment which it then hires or leases to companies or individuals. Also called **finance house**

Finance Corporation for Industry *noun* an organisation set up in 1945 to channel money from city institutions to help finance companies. It merged with the ICFC in 1973 to form Finance for Industry (FFI) and was renamed 3i (Investors in Industry) in 1983 and subsequently floated on the Stock Exchange. Abbreviation **FCI**

finance house *noun* same as **finance company**

financial accounting *noun* the recording of financial transactions in monetary terms according to accounting standards and legal requirements

Financial Accounting Standards Board *noun* the body which regulates accounting standards in the USA. Abbreviation **FASB**

financial assets *plural noun* assets in the form of liquid money or certificates which can be liquidated (such as government stocks, share certificates or fixed-interest bonds)

financial futures, financial futures contract *noun* a contract for the purchase of financial instruments such as gilt-edged stocks or Eurodollars for delivery at a date in the future

financial innovation *noun* a new idea introduced into the financial world which gradually becomes accepted, such as automatic bank transfers or swipe cards

financial institution *noun* an organisation such as a building society, pension fund or insurance company which invests large amounts of money in financial assets such as loans or other securities (as opposed to property)

financial instrument *noun* any form of investment in the stock market or in other financial markets, such as shares, government stocks, certificates of deposit, bills of exchange, etc.

Financial Intermediaries, Managers and Brokers Regulatory Association *noun* one of the self-regulatory bodies replaced by the FSA, originally set up to regulate the activities of people such as financial advisers and insurance brokers, giving financial advice or arranging financial services for small clients. Abbreviation **FIMBRA**

financial intermediary *noun* an institution which takes deposits or loans from individuals and lends money to clients. Banks, building societies and hire purchase companies are all types of financial intermediary.

financial ratios *plural noun* ratios which relate to the creditworthiness of a firm (such as current ratio, dividend cover or P/E ratio)

financial sector *noun* the part of the private sector of the economy which deals with money, including banks, building societies and pension funds

financial security *noun* a financial instrument such as shares, debentures or treasury bonds which are issued by corporations or the government and can be traded

Financial Services Act *noun* an act of the UK Parliament which regulates the offering of financial services to the general public and to private investors

Financial Services Authority *noun* a UK government agency set up to regulate all financial services, such as banks, stockbrokers, unit trusts, pension companies, professional bodies and stock exchanges, including the ombudsmen for these services. Abbreviation **FSA**

Financial Times *noun* an important British financial daily newspaper (printed on pink paper). Abbreviation **FT**

Financial Times Index, Financial Times Ordinary Index *noun* an index of 30 major industrial and commercial companies listed on the London Stock Exchange. It does not include banks, insurance companies or other financial institutions.

financial year *noun* the twelve-month period for which a company produces accounts (not necessarily the same as a calendar year)

fine-tuning *noun* the making of small adjustments to things such as interest rates, the tax bands or the money supply to improve a nation's economy

firm *noun* a business or partnership. Strictly speaking, a firm is a partnership or other trading organisation which is not a limited company. In practice, it is better to use the term for businesses such as a firm of accountants or a firm of stockbrokers, rather than for a major aircraft construction firm which is likely to be a Plc.

first in first out *noun* an accounting policy in which it is assumed that stocks in hand were purchased last, and that stocks sold during the period were purchased first. Compare **last in first out**

first-order conditions *plural noun* conditions for the value of a variable to be stationary at zero. Compare **second-order conditions**

fiscal drag *noun* the effect of inflation on a government's tax revenues. As inflation increases so do prices and wages, and tax revenues rise proportionately. Even if inflation is low, increased earnings will give the government increased revenues anyway.

fiscal federalism *noun* the sharing of revenues from tax between the central government and regional or local authorities. The revenues may be raised by either authority and switched between them, as VAT is raised by governments and passed to the EU for distribution.

fiscal illusion *noun* the introduction or existence of taxes (called stealth taxes) which are not transparent, and which the public who pays them may not know exist

fiscal neutrality *noun* a tax system which does not distort the economy. It is very difficult for a tax system to be devised which does not offer incentives to adopt one policy as opposed to another.

fiscal policy *noun* the government's policy regarding the use of tax revenues to influence the economy. An expansionary policy of tax cutting and increasing government spending could encourage employment; a deflationary policy of increasing tax and cutting government spending would reduce demand in the economy.

fiscal year *noun* a twelve-month period on which taxes are calculated (in the UK, 6 April to 5 April)

Fisher equation *noun* an equation devised by the mathematician Irving Fisher, which shows the quantity theory of money. The equation $MV = PT$ (where M = amount of money, V = velocity of circulation, P = average price level and T the transactions which take place) is always true.

fixed assets *plural noun* property which a company owns and uses, but which the company does not buy or sell as part of its regular trade, including the company's investments in shares of other companies

fixed capital *noun* capital in the form of fixed assets (i.e. buildings and machinery)

fixed costs *plural noun* costs paid to produce a product which do not increase with the amount of product made (such as rent or insurance). Also called **oncosts**

fixed exchange rate *noun* a rate of exchange of one currency against another which cannot fluctuate, and can only be changed by devaluation or revaluation

fixed factors *plural noun* factors of production which cannot be removed or changed

fixed income *noun* an income which does not change from year to year (as from an annuity)

fixed-interest securities *plural noun* securities (such as government bonds) which produce an interest which does not change

fixed investment *noun* an investment in fixed assets, such as buildings or machinery

fixed rate *noun* an interest rate which is fixed and cannot be changed during the life of the agreement

flag of convenience *noun* a flag flown by a ship whose owner is not a national of the country concerned; usually granted by countries which do not fully respect international shipping laws and often a cover for some sort of illegal practice

flat yield *noun* the interest rate shown as a percentage of the price paid for fixed-interest stock

flight to quality *noun* the tendency of investors to buy safe blue-chip securities when the economic outlook is uncertain

float *noun* an amount of cash taken from a central supply and used for running expenses ■ *verb* to start a new company by selling shares in it on the Stock Exchange

floating capital *noun* same as **working capital**

floating charge *noun* a charge linked to any or all of the company's assets of a certain type, but not to any specific item

floating debenture *noun* a debenture secured on all the company's assets which runs until the company is wound up, when the debenture becomes fixed

floating debt *noun* any short-term part of the national debt, such as Treasury bills

floating exchange rate *noun* an exchange rate for a currency which can vary according to market demand, and is not fixed by the government

floating rate *noun* same as **variable rate**

flotation *noun* the action of starting a new company by selling shares in it on the Stock Exchange

flow *noun* the movement of something shown as taking place over a period of time. Cash flow is the movement of cash in and out of a business; flow of income is the movement of income into the account of an individual or firm.

FNMA *abbreviation* Federal National Mortgage Association

FOB, f.o.b. *abbreviation* free on board

Food and Agricultural Organization *noun* an agency of the United Nations set up in 1945 whose work is concentrated on fighting hunger by increasing agricultural development, nutrition and food security. It advises governments on agricultural issues, directly aids development and helps organize food distribution in areas of famine. Abbreviation **FAO**

footloose industry *noun* an industry which is not tied to any particular area and which can be relocated anywhere to take advantage of cheaper costs (a call centre as opposed to a coal mine)

Footsie *noun* same as **FTSE 100** (*informal*)

forced saving *noun* a situation in which a government increases taxes and does not increase public expenditure. This forces individuals to spend less. Also called **involuntary saving**

forecast dividend *noun* a dividend which a company expects to pay at the end of the current year. Also called **prospective dividend**

forecasting *noun* calculation of what will probably happen in the future

foreclosure, foreclosing *noun* the act of forcing the sale of a property because the owner cannot repay money which he or she has borrowed using the property as security

foreign aid *noun* help given to a less developed country by a richer country

foreign balance *noun* that part of a country's balance of payments which is represented by foreign trade

foreign currency *noun* the currency (i.e. money) of another country. A foreign currency account is a bank account in the currency of another country (e.g. a dollar account in the UK).

foreign currency reserves *plural noun* money or other liquid assets held by a country and used to settle international debts. Gold and SDRs form part of a country's foreign currency reserves. Also called **foreign exchange reserves, international reserves**

foreign direct investment *noun* investment in a developing country by foreign companies or governments. Abbreviation **FDI**

foreign exchange *noun* **1.** foreign currencies in general **2.** the exchanging of the money of one country for that of another

foreign exchange controls *plural noun* government restrictions on changing the local currency into foreign currency

foreign exchange reserves *plural noun* same as **foreign currency reserves**

foreign investment *noun* money invested in other countries. Also called **overseas investment**

foreign purchasers *noun* expenditure during a given period by foreign consumers (i.e. exports minus imports). It is one of the elements that make up aggregate expenditure.

foreign sector *noun* one of the parts of the economy or the business organisation of a country, made up of companies or governments based outside the country

foreign trade *noun* trade with other countries. Also called **external trade, overseas trade**

foreign trade multiplier *noun* the effect of a rise in a country's domestic economy which not only increases trade in domestically produced goods but also increases imports

forex, Forex *noun* same as **foreign exchange**

forfaiting *noun* the providing of finance for exporters. Where an agent (the forfaiter) accepts a bill of exchange from an overseas customer; he or she buys the bill at a discount, and collects the payments from the customer in due course.

forwardation *noun* the difference between the spot and futures prices, as when the spot price of a commodity or currency is lower than the futures price (NOTE: The opposite is **backwardation**.)

forward contract *noun* an agreement to buy foreign currency or shares or commodities for delivery at a later date at a certain price

forward-exchange market *noun* a market for purchasing foreign currency for delivery at a later date (these are one-off deals, as opposed to futures contracts which are continuous)

forward exchange rate *noun* a rate for purchase of foreign currency at a fixed price for delivery at a later date

forward integration *noun* a situation in which a company joins with another which is at a later stage in the production or distribution line, as when a milk company acquires an ice cream company. Compare **backward integration**

forward market *noun* a market for purchasing foreign currency or oil or commodities for delivery at a later date (these are one-off deals, as opposed to futures contracts which are continuous)

forward rate *noun* same as **forward exchange rate**

fractional reserve banking *noun* a banking system in which banks maintain a certain liquid cash ratio to cover immediate demand from their clients. In most banking systems a minimum reserve ratio is required by law.

franchise *noun* a licence to trade using a brand name. Usually the franchisee pays a royalty for the use of the brand, being a percentage of sales. ■ *verb* to license others to use a brand name

franked investment income *noun* dividends plus tax credits received by a company from another company in which it owns shares. The tax credits can be set off against advance corporation tax if it makes its own dividend payments.

FRB *abbreviation* **1.** Federal Reserve Bank **2.** Federal Reserve Board

free competition *noun* the situation of being free to compete without government interference

freedom of entry *noun* a situation in which there are no barriers to prevent a new entrant entering a market. Also called **free entry**

free enterprise economy *noun* an economy where business is free from government interference

free entry *noun* same as **freedom of entry**

free good *noun* a good which is in plentiful supply and which has a negligible price. Consumers tend to overutilise such goods.

freehold property *noun* a property which the owner holds for ever and on which no rent is payable

free issue *noun* same as **scrip issue**

free market *noun* a market which has no restrictions placed on it (either by a government or by a firm)

free market economy *noun* an economic system in which the government does not interfere in business activity in any way, as opposed to a planned economy. Also called **market conomy**

free on board *adjective* a price including all the seller's costs until the goods are on the ship for transportation. Abbreviation **f.o.b.**

free port *noun* a port where there are no customs duties

free reserves *plural noun* the part of a bank's reserves which are above the statutory level and so can be used for various purposes as the bank wishes

free-rider *noun* a person who tries to benefit from a service without paying for it, as when the leaseholder of a flat on the first floor of a block of flats does not want to contribute the required share to the costs of a new roof because it does not directly concern him or her

free trade *noun* a system in which goods can go from one country to another without any restrictions

free trade area *noun* a group of countries practising free trade

free trade zone *noun* an area where there are no customs duties

freeze on wages *noun* same as **wage freeze**

freight *noun* the cost of transporting goods by air, sea or land ■ *verb* to transport goods by air, sea or land

freight forwarder *noun* a person or company that arranges shipping and customs documents for several shipments from different companies, putting them together to form one large shipment

frequency distribution *noun* a statistical representation in which a population is divided into various categories

frictional unemployment *noun* unemployment where workers leave their jobs to find something better or in a different place and then take some time to find it. It can be caused by market conditions, including the introduction of new technology or the arrival of new entrants in the market. It can include transitional unemployment. Also called **search unemployment**

Friedman, Milton (1912–) American economist, best known as a leading monetarist. A professor at the University of Chicago, he is a fierce defender of the principles of free trade.

friendly society *noun* a group of people who pay regular subscriptions which are used to help members of the group when they are ill or in financial difficulties. Friendly societies were formerly regulated by the UK Friendly Societies Commission which had the power to authorise friendly societies, both incorporated and registered, to carry on insurance business and non-insurance business. These powers are now with the FSA.

fringe benefit *noun* an extra item given by a company to workers in addition to a salary, such as company cars and private health insurance. Also called **perk, perquisite**

front door *noun* financing by the Bank of England of discount houses which run short of cash and ask the Bank to make them short-term loans, which it does at a high interest rate as lender of the last resort. This is opposed to back door financing where the Bank of England increases money supply by selling Treasury bills.

front-end charge *noun* initial loading of the management charges into the first premium paid for an insurance

FSA *abbreviation* Financial Services Authority

FT *abbreviation* Financial Times

FTC *abbreviation* Federal Trade Commission

FTSE 100 *noun* an index based on the one hundred largest companies by market value, listed on the London Stock Exchange (this is the main London index; it is also popularly called the 'Footsie')

FTSE 350 Index *noun* an index based on the market price of 350 companies listed on the London Stock Exchange. It includes the companies on the FTSE 100 Index and FTSE 250 Index.

FTSE All-Share Index *noun* an index based on the market price of about 800 companies listed on the London Stock Exchange (it includes the companies on the FT 350 Index, plus shares in financial institutions) (NOTE: also simply called the **All-Share Index**)

FTSE All-Small Index *noun* an index covering the FTSE SmallCap companies, plus about 750 fledgling companies which are too small to be included in the All-Share Index

FTSE Mid 250 Share Index *noun* an index based on the market price of the 250 companies listed on the London Stock Exchange after the top 100 companies which make up the FTSE 100 index

FTSE Small Cap Index *noun* an index which covers about 500 smaller companies which are too small to be included in the FTSE 350 Index

full capacity *noun* a situation making full use of the factors of production

full cost pricing *noun* a pricing method which involves covering the entire cost per unit, plus a margin for the producer. It is similar to cost-plus pricing.

full employment *noun* situation in which everyone in a country who can work and wants to work has a job

full-line forcing *noun* situation in which a producer forces a customer to buy the whole of a product line, and so reduces the customer's freedom of choice of supplier. This can lead to a monopoly situation.

function *noun* a mathematical formula, where a result is dependent upon several other numbers ■ *verb* to operate and fulfil a role

functional distribution of income *noun* the division of income in an economy between the various factors of production, mainly between capital and land

fundamental disequilibrium *noun* a situation in which a country has a long-term balance of payments deficit or surplus and can only remedy the situation by devaluing or revaluing its currency

fundamentals *noun* the basic realities of a stock market or of a company (such as its assets, profitability and dividends.)

fundamental uncertainty *noun* a type of uncertainty that gives rise to a particular form of modified auditors' report. It occurs when the magnitude of its potential impact is so great that, without clear disclosure of the nature and implications of the uncertainty, the view given by the financial statements would be seriously misleading.

funded debt *noun* a short-term debt which has been converted into long-term by selling long-term securities such as debentures to raise the money

funding *noun* the provision of money for spending

futures *plural noun* trading in shares, currency or commodities for delivery at a later date. They refer to fixed amounts, and are always available for sale at various dates.

futures contract *noun* a contract for the purchase of commodities for delivery at a date in the future. If an investor is bullish, he or she will buy a contract, but if the investor feels the market will go down, he or she will sell one.

COMMENT: A futures contract is a contract to purchase; if an investor is bullish, he or she will buy a contract, but if he or she feels the market will go down, he or she will sell one.

futures market *noun* a market for purchasing a continuous supply of foreign currency for delivery at later dates, as opposed to the forward exchange market which deals in one-off contracts

G

G10 *abbreviation* Group of Ten

G7 *abbreviation* Group of Seven

G8 *abbreviation* Group of Eight

GAB *abbreviation* General Arrangements to Borrow

gains from trade *plural noun* advantages which a country gets from trading with other countries: firstly the economies of scale when large amounts are produced and secondly the exchange of commodities between countries which means the certain countries can specialise in certain commodities making them cheaper

galloping inflation *noun* very rapid inflation which it is almost impossible to reduce. Also called **rapid inflation**

game theory *noun* the use of games to determine how people act in different economic or commercial situations

GATT *abbreviation* General Agreement on Tariffs and Trade

GDP *abbreviation* gross domestic product

GDP deflator *noun* the amount by which a country's GDP is reduced to take inflation into account. Also called **gross domestic product deflator**

gearing *noun* **1.** the ratio of capital borrowed by a company at a fixed rate of interest to the company's total capital. High gearing (when a company is said to be highly geared) indicates that the level of borrowings is high when compared to its ordinary share capital. A lowly-geared company has borrowings which are relatively low. High gearing has the effect of increasing a company's profitability when the company's trading is expanding. If the trading pattern slows down, then the high interest charges associated with gearing will increase the rate of slowdown. **2.** the borrowing of money at fixed interest which is then used to produce more money than the interest paid ▶ also called **leverage**

General Agreement on Tariffs and Trade *noun* an international agreement to try to reduce restrictions in trade between countries. Abbreviation **GATT**

General Arrangements to Borrow *noun* an agreement between members of the G10 group of countries, by which its members make funds available to the IMF to cover loans which it makes. Abbreviation **GAB**

general equilibrium *noun* the state when prices and quantities of commodities have been reached an equilibrium

general equilibrium analysis *noun* the study of equilibrium in various sectors of an economy which react on each other

Generalized System of Preferences *noun* a system instituted in 1968 by which developed countries agreed not to impose tariffs on imports from developing countries. It has gradually been replaced by the World Trade Organization agreements. Abbreviation **GSP**

general obligation bond *noun US* a municipal or state bond issued to finance public undertakings such as roads but repaid out of general funds. Abbreviation **GO bond**

geographical immobility *noun* the situation in which people or resources do not move easily from one location to another

geometric progression *noun* a sequence of numbers where each number is a multiplier of the previous one, such as 3, 6, 12, 24, as opposed to arithmetic progression where the sequence has a constant difference between each number

Gibrat's law of proportionate growth, Gibrat process *noun* a general rule stated by the French economist Robert Gibrat in 1931, that the growth of any firm is not connected to the size of the firm, but is random and is subject to various factors including chance. Also called **law of proportionate growth**

Giffen, Robert (1837–1910) Scottish lawyer and statistician

Giffen good *noun* a theoretical good which is inferior in quality and has no substitutes, with the result that the demand falls if the price falls and the demand rises if the price rises. It comes from observations of poor consumers in the 19th century: if the price of bread rose they spent more on it and less on other more expensive commodities. Also called **inferior good**

gift tax *noun* in the USA, a tax on gifts. It is levied on people who have given gifts: only gifts between husband and wife are exempt.

gilt-edged securities *plural noun* UK government bonds, bearing a fixed interest, which are traded on the Stock Exchange

Gini coefficient *noun* a way of measuring inequality in incomes within a society developed by Corrado Gini (1884–1965), an Italian statistician. It is the ratio between the 45° line and a Lorenz curve below the 45° line.

Ginnie Mae *abbreviation* Government National Mortgage Association (*informal*)

giro system *noun* a banking system in which money can be transferred from one account to another without writing a cheque. The money is first removed from the payer's account and then credited to the payee's account. It is opposed to a cheque payment, which is credited to the payee's account first and then claimed from the payer's account.

globalisation, globalization *noun* the tendency of more multinational corporations to develop as tariff barriers are reduced. Globalisation is due to technological developments which make global communications possible, political developments such as the fall of communism and developments in transportation which make travelling faster and more frequent. It can benefit companies by opening up new markets, giving access to new raw materials and investment opportunities and enabling them to take advantage of lower operating costs in other countries.

GNMA *abbreviation* Government National Mortgage Association

GNP *abbreviation* gross national product

GNP deflator *noun* the amount by which a country's GNP is reduced to take inflation into account. Also called **gross national product deflator**

GO bond *abbreviation* general obligation bond

gold *noun* a very valuable yellow metal. Gold is the traditional hedge against investment uncertainties. People buy gold in the form of coins or bars, because they think it will maintain its value when other investments such as government bonds, foreign currency or property may not be so safe. Gold is relatively portable, and small quantities can be taken from country to country if an emergency occurs.

golden hallo *noun* a cash inducement paid to someone to encourage him or her to change jobs and move to another company

golden handcuffs *plural noun* a contractual arrangement to make sure that a valued member of staff stays in his or her job, by which the employee is offered special financial advantages if he or she stays and heavy penalties if he or she leaves

golden handshake *noun* a large, usually tax-free, sum of money given to a director who resigns from a company before the end of his or her service contract

golden parachute, golden umbrella *noun* a special contract for a director of a company, which gives him or her advantageous financial terms if he or she has to resign when the company is taken over

golden rule *noun* the rule that governments should only borrow to fund investment, not expenditure

gold exchange standard *noun* same as **gold standard**

gold fixing *noun* the system where the world price for gold is set twice a day in US dollars on the London Gold Exchange and in Paris and Zurich

gold point *noun* the amount by which a currency which was linked to gold could vary in exchange with another currency also linked to the gold standard. It came about when differences in exchange rates made slight differences to the gold value of each currency.

gold standard *noun* the linking of the value of a currency to the value of a quantity of gold. The pound sterling was linked to the gold standard until 1931. Also called **gold exchange standard**

good *noun* an item which is made and is for sale

Goodhart's Law *noun* the law proposed by Charles Goodhart, Professor at the London School of Economics and formerly Chief Adviser to the Bank of England and a member of the Monetary Policy Committee, that when a measure becomes a target it ceases to be a measure. So if a central bank has a money supply target to aim for, then the measure of money used will soon have no meaning. It also applies to inflation targets.

goods *plural noun* physical items which can be sold, as opposed to services which do not exist physically

goodwill *noun* the good reputation of a business, which can be included in a company's intangible asset value. Purchased goodwill is defined as the difference between the cost of an acquired entity and the aggregate of the fair values of that entity's identifiable assets and liabilities.

COMMENT: Goodwill can include the trading reputation, the patents, the trade names used, the value of a 'good site', etc., and is very difficult to establish accurately. It is an intangible asset, and so is not shown as an asset in a company's accounts, unless it figures as part of the purchase price paid when acquiring another company.

governance *noun* the philosophy of how something should be ruled, whether a country or a company

government *noun* the organisation which administers a country

government bonds *plural noun* bonds or other paper issued by a government on a regular basis as a method of borrowing money for government expenditure

government debt *noun* money owed by a government, municipality or local authority. It may also include the debts of nationalised industries.

government expenditure *noun* spending by a government, municipality or local authority. It covers things such as spending on health, education and social services, and is funded by tax revenue. It is one of the elements that make up aggregate expenditure. Also called **government spending**

Government National Mortgage Association *noun* a US federal organisation which provides backing for mortgages. Abbreviation **GNMA**

government sector *noun* same as **public sector**

government spending *noun* same as **government expenditure**

graduated taxation *noun* same as **progressive taxation**

Granger causality *noun* tests devised by Professor Clive Granger, a British-born US econometrician, to determine if one variable is an indicator over a period of time. It is assumed that the relationship between variables remains stable.

grant *noun* a quantity of money or assets given to a business by a central government, a local government or a government agency ■ *verb* to give a grant to a person or business

grant-in-aid *noun* an amount of money given by the central government to local government to help fund a specific project

graph *noun* a diagram which represents statistical information along two axes

gravity model *noun* a model showing how a customer's buying decisions are governed by the distance that has to be travelled between his or her base and the market

Great Depression *noun* the world economic crisis of 1929–33

greenhouse gases *plural noun* gases (carbon dioxide, methane, CFCs and nitrogen oxides) which are produced by burning fossil fuels and which rise into the atmosphere, forming a barrier which prevents heat loss

Green Paper *noun* a report from the UK government on proposals for a new law to be discussed in Parliament. Compare **White Paper**

green pound *noun* the value of the pound sterling as used in calculating agricultural prices and subsidies in the EU

green revolution *noun* the development of new forms of cereal plants such as wheat and rice and the use of more powerful fertilisers, which give much higher yields and increase the food production especially in tropical countries

Gresham, Sir Thomas (1518–1579) English financier and entrepreneur, who founded the Royal Exchange in London as a business centre

Gresham's law *noun* the law that bad money will drive out good. Where two forms of money with the same denomination exist in the same market, the form with the higher metal value will be driven out of circulation when people hoard it and use the lower-rated form to spend (as when paper money and coins of the same denomination exist in the same market).

grey market *noun* an unofficial market run by dealers, where new issues of shares are bought and sold before they officially become available for trading on the Stock Exchange (even before the share allocations are known)

gross domestic fixed capital formation *noun* gross investment in fixed assets

gross domestic product *noun* the annual value of goods sold and services paid for inside a country. Abbreviation **GDP**

gross domestic product deflator *noun* same as **GDP deflator**

gross income *noun* income before tax has been deducted

gross investment *noun* total investment in an economy during a certain period

gross margin *noun* the percentage difference between the unit manufacturing cost and the received price

gross national product *noun* the annual value of goods and services in a country including income from other countries. Abbreviation **GNP**

gross national product deflator *noun* same as **GNP deflator**

gross profit *noun* profit calculated as sales income less the cost of sales

gross trading profit *noun* the profit of a company before allowing for depreciation and before deducting debt interest. It is the profit on the company's trading activities.

Group of Eight *noun* the G7 expanded to include Russia. Abbreviation **G8**

Group of Seven *noun* the central group of major industrial nations (Canada, France, Germany, Italy, Japan, the UK and the USA) who meet regularly to discussed problems of international trade and finance. Abbreviation **G7**

Group of Ten *noun* the major world economic powers working within the framework of the IMF: Belgium, Canada, France, Germany, Italy, Japan, Netherlands, Sweden, the UK and the USA. There are in fact now eleven members, since Switzerland has joined the original ten. Abbreviation **G10**. Also called **Paris Club**

growth *noun* the rate at which a country's national income grows over a period of time, usually shown as an increase in GDP or GNP or an increase in per capita income

growth company *noun* a company whose share price is expected to rise in value

growth rate *noun* the speed at which something grows

growth theory *noun* any of several theories developed since the 19th century and related to economic growth related to factors such as increases in population or progress in technology

GSP *abbreviation* Generalized System of Preferences

guarantee *noun* a legal document which promises that a machine will work properly or that an item is of good quality ■ *verb* to provide a legal document which promises that a machine will work properly or that an item is of good quality

guaranteed wage *noun* a wage which a company promises will not fall below a certain figure

H

hammer *verb* to remove a business from the Stock Exchange because it has failed

hard currency *noun* currency of a country which has a strong economy and which can be changed into other currencies easily. Also called **scarce currency** (NOTE: The opposite is **soft currency**.)

hard landing *noun* a change in economic strategy to counteract inflation which has serious results for the population (such as high unemployment orrising interest rates)

harmonisation *noun* standardisation, making things the same in several countries. In the EU plans to harmonise tax regimes are controversial.

Harrod, Sir Roy (1900–1978) British economist who saw economic growth as a continually changing situation involving both multipliers and accelerators

Harrod-Domar growth model *noun* a theoretical growth model which examines the problems of growth in an economy when a fixed capital/output ratio is seen together with a fixed propensity to save. There are three elements: warranted growth, which firms believe will occur without any extra investment; natural growth, which comes from a growth in the labour force; and actual growth, which is the final actual result. Compare **Solow economic growth model**. Also called **Domar growth model**

headline inflation rate *noun* the UK inflation figure which includes items such as mortgage interest and local taxes, which are not included in the inflation figures for other countries. Compare **underlying inflation rate**

Heckscher, Eli (1879–1952) Swedish economic historian who saw mercantilism as the basis for developing the political and economic values of developing nations

Heckscher-Ohlin model *noun* a model of a country's international trade, which shows that a country will export goods which make use of the factors of production it has in abundance and import goods which use factors of production which are scarce

hedge *noun* a protection against a possible loss (by taking an action which is the opposite of an action taken earlier), as by buying investments at a fixed price for delivery later ■ *verb* to take measures as a protection against a possible loss

Herfindahl index *noun* an index developed by the US economist Orris Herfindahl (1918–72), used to calculate the dominance of a market by a small number of firms. The index is a simple way of calculating market concerntration, by calculating the market share of various firms, then squaring it and summing the squares. It gives the number of firms in the market and the relative size of each. It was subsequently further refined to form the Herfindahl-Hirschmann index.

heteroscedasticity *noun* a state in which data has different variances, as opposed to homoscedasticity where data is constant

Hicks, Sir John (1904–1989) British economist who worked on marginal productivity and imperfect competition

Hicks-Kaldor principle *noun* same as **compensation principle**

hidden economy *noun* same as **black economy**

hidden reserves *plural noun* reserves which are not easy to identify in the company's balance sheet. Reserves which are illegally kept hidden are called secret reserves.

hidden unemployment *noun* same as **disguised unemployment**

high gearing *noun* ◊ **gearing**

high leverage *noun* ◊ **gearing**

high-powered money *noun* same as **monetary base**

hire *noun* the act of paying money to use a piece of equipment or a mode of transport such as a car or boat for a period of time. Such an agreement involves two parties: the hirer and the owner. The equipment remains the property of the owner while the hirer is using it. Under a hire-purchase agreement, the equipment remains the property of the owner until the hirer has complied with the terms of the agreement (i.e. until he or she has paid all monies due). ■ *verb* to pay the owner for the use of something for a period or time

hire purchase *noun* a system of buying something on credit by paying a sum regularly each month, which includes part debt repayment and part interest. Abbreviation **HP** (NOTE: The US term is **installment credit**, **installment plan** or **installment sale**.)

COMMENT: An agreement to hire a piece of equipment, etc., involves two parties: the hirer and the owner. The equipment remains the property of the owner while the hirer is using it. Under a hire-purchase agreement, the equipment remains the property of the owner until the hirer has complied with the terms of the agreement (i.e. until he has paid all monies due).

histogram *noun* same as **bar chart**

historical cost *noun* the actual cost of purchasing something which was bought some time ago

historical cost accounting *noun* the preparation of accounts on the basis of historical cost, with assets valued at their original cost of purchase (as opposed to their current or replacement cost), without adjustment for inflation or other price variations. Compare **replacement cost accounting**

historical cost depreciation *noun* depreciation based on the original cost of the asset

hoarding *noun* the buying of large quantities of money or food to keep in case of need

hog cycles *plural noun* cycles during which there is overproduction and underproduction of a good, because of the time lags involved in the production process. The name comes from the production of pigs, where high demand one year will lead to excess supply the following year.

holding company *noun* a company which has a controlling interest in one or more other companies (NOTE: The US term is **proprietary company**.)

homogeneous products *plural noun* identical products sold in the same market by different producers

homoscedasticity *noun* a state in which data has the same variances, as opposed to heteroscedasticity where variances are different

horizontal equity *noun* the theory that individuals in similar situations should be treated in the same way, such as regarding tax

horizontal integration *noun* the joining of similar companies or taking over of a company in the same line of business

hostile takeover bid *noun* a takeover where the board of the company do not recommend it to the shareholders and try to fight it

Hotelling, Harold (1895–1973) US economist who specialised in welfare economics

Hotelling's law *noun* a law proposed by Hotelling that competing suppliers in a market tend to make their goods and services as similar as possible

Hotelling's rule *noun* a rule proposed by Hotelling that the present value of a natural resource must be the same whenever the resource is exploited, because the developer of the resource has to choose between the increasing value of the resource if left unexploited and its current value if extracted and sold

hot money *noun* money which is moved from country to country or from investment to investment to get the best interest rates

household *noun* one person or several people living together in one flat or house, considered as an economic unit. Households are consumers of products and at the same are themselves factors of production.

housing benefit *noun* a UK benefit paid to low-income households to help pay rent. It does not cover mortgage interest payments.

HP *abbreviation* hire purchase

human capital *noun* the sum of knowledge and skills in individual people which forms the basis of knowhow and can be increased by training

human resources *plural noun* the workforce considered as a factor of production. Abbreviation **HR**. Also called **personnel**

hyperbola *noun* a geometric form produced when a cone is cut by a plane. Mathematically it is the path traced by a point moving from a fixed focus where the ratio of the distance from the focus and a straight line is a constant.

hyperinflation *noun* inflation which is at such a high percentage rate that it is almost impossible to reduce

hypothecation *noun* **1.** the use of property such as securities as collateral for a loan without transferring legal ownership to the lender (as opposed to a mortgage, where the lender holds the title to the property) **2.** same as **earmarking**

hypothesis *noun* a prediction based on theory, but one which can nevertheless be tested in practice (NOTE: The plural is **hypotheses**.)

hypothesis testing *noun* the testing of the value of a hypothesis, either resulting in its validation or not

hysteresis *noun* the way in which equilibrium is dependent on changes which take place as a situation, such as an economy, changes

I

IBRD *abbreviation* International Bank for Reconstruction and Development

ICC *abbreviation* Interstate Commerce Commission

ICFC *abbreviation* Industrial and Commercial Finance Corporation

IDA *abbreviation* International Development Association

IDC *abbreviation* industrial development certificate

identification problem *noun* the difficulty in identifying variables when changes are actually taking place

identity *noun* the fact that two things are the same; usually indicated by the equals sign (=), but to be more precise in equations the three-line symbol ≡ is used

idle money *noun* money which is not being used to produce interest, which is not invested in business. Also called **inactive money**

IFC *abbreviation* International Finance Corporation

IHT *abbreviation* inheritance tax

illiquidity *noun* (of an asset) not being easy to change into cash

ILO *abbreviation* International Labour Organization

IMF *abbreviation* International Monetary Fund

immiserising growth *noun* theoretical economic growth which actually reduces the welfare of the individuals in a country. This could happen in theory when a less developed country expands the growth of a single commodity by reducing the price so that income actually falls.

impact effect *noun* the immediate effect of an economic event, such as an increase in government spending

imperfect competition *noun* a situation in which there are only a few sellers whose products are similar but not substitutes. The producers do not have a large enough share of the market to be important enough to influence the market. The situation is not quite a monopoly. Also called **monopolistic competition**

imperfect market *noun* a monopolistic market where the conditions of a perfect market do not apply; that is, there are many different products which are therefore are not produced at the lowest cost possible, so that each firm raises its costs so as to differentiate its products and in so doing makes abnormal profits

imperialism *noun* the act of controlling other countries as if they were part of an empire. Although imperialism is used to refer to states which have or had colonies (such as Britain, France, Belgium and the Netherlands) it is now widely used to refer to states which exert strong influence over other states. This influence can be political, military or commercial. ♦ **economic imperialism**

implementation lag *noun* the time which passes between the moment when a policy is decided and when it is actually implemented

implicit contract *noun* an agreement which is considered to be a contract, because the parties intended it to be a contract or because the law considers it to be a contract

implicit cost *noun* the cost of paying for factors involved in buying or producing a good or service where the factors are actually produced or owned by the firm itself. Explicit cost is the payment for factors which are bought from outside producers.

implicit function *noun* a function where there are no dependent variables (i.e. it relates in the same way to two variables)

import *noun* a product which is bought and brought in from a foreign country. ◊ **imports** ■ *verb* to bring goods from abroad into a country for sale

import deposit *noun* a deposit which has to be placed with a central bank by an importer before he can import goods and pay for them

import duty *noun* a tax on goods imported into a country

import levy *noun* a tax on imports, especially in the EU a tax on imports of farm produce from outside the EU

import licence *noun* a government licence or permit which allows goods to be imported

import penetration *noun* the proportion of a domestic market which is supplied by imported goods

import permit *noun* same as **import licence**

import quota *noun* a fixed quantity of a particular type of goods which the government allows to be imported

imports *plural noun* goods, services or capital bought and brought in from foreign countries (NOTE: usually used in the plural, but the singular is used before a noun)

import substitution *noun* the replacement of imported goods by goods made locally, as a method of industrialising less developed countries

import surcharge *noun* an extra duty charged on imported goods, to try to prevent them from being imported and to encourage local manufacture

import tariffs *plural noun* taxes on imports

impossibility theorem *noun* the theory that it is impossible to devise a voting system which gives a reliable list of preferences for a group of individual voters

imputation system *noun* a system of taxation of dividends, in which the company pays advance corporation tax on the dividends it pays to its shareholders, and the shareholders pay no tax on the dividends received, assuming that they pay tax at the standard rate (the ACT is shown as a tax credit which is imputed to the shareholder). The imputation system is used in the UK, Ireland, Australia and other countries.

imputed cost, imputed income *noun* the value which is given to the cost of using an asset which is not actually used, such as the value of the income from the rent of a house which an owner occupies personally and does not rent out

IMRO *abbreviation* Investment Management Regulatory Organisation

inactive money *noun* same as **idle money**

incentive pay scheme *noun* a plan to encourage better work by paying higher commission or bonuses

incidence of taxation *noun* the way in which the burden of direct and indirect taxes is distributed. The burden of income tax falls on the individual taxpayer, but the burden of indirect taxes such as VAT may fall on the consumer or the producer.

income *noun* the money which an organisation receives as gifts or from investments

income consumption curve *noun* a curve that shows the relationship between income and demand. Normally as income rises, so demand rises also, but it can happen, as in the case of low value goods, that when income rises demand falls as purchasers switch to higher-priced products.

income distribution *noun* the way in which income is distributed between various individuals or firms who receive it

income effect *noun* the effect of a change of income on the amount of a good or service consumed. If the consumer's income rises because the price of a product falls, the demand for the product may increase if the product is superior.

income elasticity of demand *noun* a proportional increase in demand in response to an increase in income

income gearing *noun* the ratio of the interest a company pays on its borrowings shown as a percentage of its pretax profits (before the interest is paid)

income method *noun* a way of calculating domestic product by totalising net income, as opposed to the output method, which totalises the value of net outputs

income per head, income per capita *noun* same as **per capita income**

income redistribution *noun* the moving of income from wealthy individuals to poorer people by means such as taxation and government benefits

incomes policy *noun* the government's ideas on how incomes should be controlled

income statement *noun US* same as **profit and loss account**

income support *noun* a class of payment made by the government to increase the incomes of individuals on low incomes and bring them up to a higher level. It is a means-tested benefit and was formerly called income per head Supplementary Benefit. In the case of people over the age of 60 it is also known as Minimum Income Guarantee (MIG) and in the case of disabled people it is also known as Disability Income Guarantee (DIG). Abbreviation **IS**

income tax *noun* tax on an individual's income (both earned and unearned)

income tax return *noun* a statement declaring income to the tax office. Also called **declaration of income**

income-tax schedule *noun* one of six types of income as classified for tax in the UK. These are Schedules A, B, C, D, E and F.

income velocity of circulation *noun* in the quantity theory of money, the proportion of the money value of national income to the stock of money in circulation

incomplete contract *noun* a contract which does not cover all the possibilities which might exist when the work in the contract is carried out

incorporation *noun* the act of forming a corporation, or of giving a company or other body the legal form of a corporation. A corporation (a body which is legally separate from its members) is formed in one of three ways: 1. registration under the Companies Act (the normal method for commercial companies); 2. granting of a royal charter; 3. by a special Act of Parliament. A company is incorporated by drawing up a memorandum and articles of association, which are lodged with Companies House. In the UK, a company is either a private limited company (they print Ltd after their name) or a public limited company (they print Plc after their name). A company must be a Plc to obtain a Stock Exchange listing. In the USA, there is no distinction between private and public companies, and all are called corporations (they put Inc. after their name).

increasing returns to scale *plural noun* increases in productivity that follow from increasing inputs

independent variable *noun* a variable that influences another variable (called the dependent variable). For example, the price of a product may influence the demand for it.

indexation *noun* the linking of a payment or value to an index

index-linked *adjective* which rises automatically by the percentage increase in the cost of living

index number *noun* a number which shows the percentage rise of something over a period of time, usually one year

index number problem *noun* a problem which occurs when trying to compare two sets of values which are each aggregated into a single figure: if the base figure against which the current figure is compared changes to take account of new circumstances, then the comparison will not be correct

indicative planning *noun* a method of controlling a country's economy by producing forecasts for various sectors of the economy which will encourage consumers and producers to think that the economy will perform better, and so they spend and invest more

indifference curve *noun* a graph used with the 'budget line' to show the different quantities of goods which give the customer the same amount of satisfaction

indifference map *noun* a graph containing several indifference curves, showing the individual's comparative satisfaction with two products

indirect costs *plural noun* same as **overhead costs**

indirect labour *noun* workers who do not actually make a good but who provide backup to the direct labour force. Examples would be accounts department or sales department in a firm.

indirect labour costs *plural noun* the costs of paying workers which cannot be allocated to a cost centre (such as workers who are not directly involved in making a product)

indirect tax *noun* a tax (such as sales tax) which is not deducted from income directly, but is paid to someone who then pays it to the government. VAT is an indirect tax.

indirect taxation *noun* the use or collection of indirect taxes

indirect utility function *noun* a function showing the quantity of goods consumed as a utility of the consumer. Utility is an increasing function of non-work income and a decreasing function of prices of goods.

Individual Savings Account *noun* a scheme by which individuals can invest by putting a limited amount of money each year into a tax-free account. ISAs replaced PEPs and TESSAs and money from maturing TESSAs can be reinvested in ISAs. Abbreviation **ISA**

indivisibility *noun* the minimum level at which any factor of production can operate. If a firm adds a machine which outputs 2000 items when it actually needs a machine which outputs only 500, then such a machine is cannot be split, and so is underproductive; only by increasing output to 2000 units can the machine become effective.

induced consumption *noun* a change in consumption which is due to changes in income

induced investment *noun* a change in investment which is due to changes in income or output

industrial action *noun* a strike or go-slow

Industrial and Commercial Finance Corporation *noun* an organisation set up to finance small start-up companies. It merged with FCI in 1973 to form Finance for Industry (FFI) and was renamed 3i (Investors in Industry) in 1983 and subsequently floated on the Stock Exchange. Abbreviation **ICFC**

industrial bank *noun* a finance house which lends to business customers

industrial democracy *noun* a situation in which the workforce has a say in the running of a business. Workers are consulted through works councils or through trade union representatives.

industrial development certificate *noun* formerly, a certificate given to firms to allow them to establish plants in certain areas. Abbreviation **IDC**

industrial dispute *noun* an argument between management and workers, usually about conditions of work or terms of employment

industrial economics *noun* economics as applied to the organising of businesses, in particular concerning pricing

industrial espionage *noun* the activity of trying to find out the secrets of a competitor's work or products, usually by illegal means

industrialisation, industrialization *noun* the changing of the economy of a less developed country from one based on agriculture to one based on industry

industrial policy *noun* a government's policy relating to industry

industrial production *noun* production by manufacturing industries, as opposed to service industries or agriculture

industrial relations *plural noun* relations between management and workers, usually through trade union representatives

industrial sector *noun* the sector of the economy dealing with industry which produces goods. Also called **secondary sector**

industry *noun* all factories, companies or processes involved in the manufacturing of products

inefficiency *noun* failure to use resources in the best possible way

inelastic *adjective* not responsive to change

inequality *noun* the situation of not being equal, in particular in reference to the distribution of income among the population

infant industry *noun* a new industry which cannot in its early years compete with others. It is used as a reason for imposing tariffs on imported goods so as to support the local industry.

inferior good *noun* same as **Giffen good**

inflation *noun* a situation in which prices rise to keep up with increased production costs, with the result that the purchasing power of money falls Inflation affects businesses, in that as their costs rise, so their profits may fall and it is necessary to take this into account when pricing products

COMMENT: The inflation rate in the UK is calculated on a series of figures, including prices of consumer items; petrol, gas and electricity; interest rates, etc. This gives the 'underlying' inflation rate which can be compared to that of other countries. The calculation can also include mortgage interest and local taxes which give the 'headline' inflation figure; this is higher than in other countries because of these extra items. Inflation affects businesses, in that as their costs rise, so their profits may fall and it is necessary to take this into account when pricing products.

inflation accounting *noun* an accounting system in which inflation is taken into account when calculating the value of assets and the preparation of accounts

inflationary gap *noun* a situation in which demand exceeds the level of output possible with full employment and so forces a rise in prices. Demand has to be reduced by deflationary measures to correct the situation.

inflationary spiral *noun* a situation in which price rises encourage higher wage demands which in turn make prices rise. Also called **price-wage spiral**

inflation rate *noun* the percentage increase in prices over a twelve-month period. The inflation rate in the UK is calculated on a series of figures, including prices of consumer items, petrol, gas and electricity and interest rates. This gives the underlying inflation rate which can be compared to that of other countries. The calculation can also include mortgage interest and local taxes which give the headline inflation figure; this is higher than in other countries because of these extra items. Also called **rate of inflation**

inflation target *noun* the inflation rate which the government aims to reach at some date in the future. The Bank of England's Monetary Policy Committee has a target of 2.5% inflation.

inflation tax *noun* a type of taxation which a government operates by altering the money supply. If the supply of money increases then the value of existing money falls, so creating a type of tax on existing holders of money. Also called **seigniorage**

informal sector, **informal economy** *noun* the sector of the economy which represents self-employed artisans, often paid in cash, and generally not listed in official figures

information *noun* what someone knows about something. Knowledge of secondhand cars is invaluable to a buyer; knowledge about the market, a firm's plans or a product's sales can be valuable to rivals. Market research is a form of information gathering.

information agreement *noun* an agreement between firms to share their information about the market with each other. This allows their trade association to distribute the information to all its members, though this may be considered a restrictive practice.

infrastructure *noun* the roads, rail network, sewers, hospitals, schools and other basic utilities which are owned by a government and provided for public use. Also called **social overhead capital**

inheritance tax *noun* a tax on wealth or property above a certain amount, inherited after the death of someone. Abbreviation **IHT** (NOTE: The US term is **death duty**.)

Inland Revenue *noun* the UK government department which deals with taxes (such as income tax, corporation tax, capital gains tax and inheritance tax), but not duties such as Value Added Tax. Duties are collected by the Customs and Excise. (NOTE: The US term is the **Internal Revenue Service** or **IRS**.)

innovation *noun* the act of developing something new, such as new form of product or service, which allows a firm to maintain a market position in advance of its rivals. It is the application of an invention to the commercial world.

input *noun* a resource applied to production, one of the four factors of production (land, labour, machinery and capital)

input-output analysis *noun* the study of economics seen as the relationship between inputs and outputs in the economy

inside money *noun* same as **endogenous money**

insider buying, insider dealing *noun* illegal buying or selling of shares by staff of a company or other persons who have secret information about the company's plans

insiders and outsiders *plural noun* people who are employed and people who are not employed; the insider-outsider theory says that collective bargaining by unions on behalf of their members (who are insiders) is partly responsible for keeping unemployment higher than it would otherwise be

insider trading *noun* same as **insider buying**

insolvency *noun* the situation of not being able to pay debts when they are due. A company is insolvent when its liabilities are higher than its assets: if this happens it must cease trading. Note that insolvency is a general term, but is usually applied to companies; individuals or partners are usually described as bankrupt once they have been declared so by a court.

Insolvency Act *noun* a UK act which sets out how insolvent companies are treated. An insolvent company may enter into a scheme of arrangement with its creditors; it may be put into receivership and its assets sold, or it can be wound up and its assets liquidated.

installment credit, installment plan, installment sales, installment buying *noun US* same as **hire purchase**

instalment *noun* a part of a payment which is paid regularly until the total amount is paid (NOTE: The US spelling is **installment**.)

institutional economics *noun* the branch of economics which deals with institutions, such as social and political structures, and their importance in the development of a country's economy

institutional investor *noun* a financial institution which invests money in securities

insurance *noun* an agreement that in return for regular small payments, a company will pay compensation for loss, damage, injury or death

insurance company *noun* a company whose business is to receive payments and pay compensation for loss or damage

intangible assets, **intangibles** *plural noun* assets which have a value, but which cannot be seen (such as goodwill, copyrights, a patent or a trademark)

integer *noun* a mathematical term to describe a whole number. It may be positive, negative or zero.

integration *noun* the process of bringing several businesses together under a central control, by mergers of takeovers

COMMENT: In a case of horizontal integration, a large supermarket might take over another smaller supermarket chain; on the other hand, if a supermarket takes over a food packaging company the integration would be vertical.

intellectual property *noun* ownership of something (such as a copyright, patent or design) which is intangible

intensity *noun* ◊ **capital intensity**

inter-bank market *noun* the market where banks lend to or borrow from each other

interest *noun* a part of the ownership of something, such as money invested in a company giving a financial share in it

interest cover *noun* the ratio of a company's earnings during a period to the interest payable on borrowings during that period

interest equalization tax *noun* a former US tax imposed to try to stop US citizens from investing abroad, in particular in Europe or Japan

interest payment *noun* a payment made to cover the interest on a loan. A firm's interest payments are deducted from the trading profit before calculating the gross profit.

interest rate *noun* the percentage charge for borrowing money. Also called **rate of interest**

interest rate swap *noun* an agreement between two companies to exchange borrowings. A company with fixed-interest borrowings might swap them for the variable interest borrowings of another company. Also called **plain vanilla swap**

interim dividend *noun* a dividend paid during an accounting period, usually at the end of a half-year

interim report, **interim statement** *noun* a report given at the end of a half-year

interlocking directorates *plural noun* a situation in which the same people are directors on the boards of different companies. Any individual can act as a director of several companies, and often it is to the advantage of the companies that they share directors and can therefore receive informal advice based on accurate information about each other's position.

intermediary *noun* a person who tries to help people or groups to reach an agreement, or who acts on behalf of one in dealings with the other

COMMENT: Banks, building societies and hire purchase companies are all types of financial intermediaries.

intermediate good, **intermediate product** *noun* same as **producer good**

intermediate technology *noun* technology which is between the advanced electronic technology of industrialised countries and the primitive technology in developing countries

intermediation *noun* an arrangement of finance or insurance by an intermediary

internal balance *noun* a situation in which a national economy enjoys full employment and stable prices, leading to a stable rate of inflation

internal growth *noun* expansion of a company which is based on profits from its existing trading. Also called **organic growth** (NOTE: The opposite is **external growth**.)

internalisation, **internalization** *noun* the action of combining different activities within a firm in order to maximise profit and reduce costs (as in vertical and horizontal integration)

internal labour market *noun* a system in which jobs in an organisation are advertised to employees already working in the organisation. This is opposed to an external labour market where jobs are advertised so that people working outside the organisation are encouraged to apply. Abbreviation **ILM**

Internal Market *noun* the EU considered as one single market, with no tariff barriers between its member states. Also called **single European market**

internal rate of return *noun* the discount rate at which the cost of an investment and its future cash inflows are exactly equal. Abbreviation **IRR**

International Bank for Reconstruction and Development *noun* a part of the World Bank group founded in 1945 which aims to reduce poverty in poorer and less developed countries by promoting development through loans and advisory services. Abbreviation **IBRD**

international commodity agreement *noun* an agreement between producer countries (and some consumer countries) to stabilise the price of an international commodity, such as coffee or cocoa, by fixing an international price and buying buffer stocks if necessary to maintain this price

international competitiveness *noun* the situation of being competitive in international trade

international debt *noun* the amount of money owed by individuals, firms or governments to others who are not resident in their own country, including debts to international agencies such as the World Bank

International Development Association *noun* a part of the World Bank group set up in 1960 to provide aid to less developed countries which have a per capita GNP below a certain level and are not able to raise loans on normal market terms. Abbreviation **IDA**

International Finance Corporation *noun* a part of the World Bank group established in 1956 which makes loans to private companies and supports private sector projects. Abbreviation **IFC**

International Labour Office *noun* an agency of the United Nations, based in Geneva, which specialises in issues concerned with work and employment and tries to improve working conditions and workers' pay in member countries. Abbreviation **ILO**

international liquidity *noun* liquid assets used as a means of international trade, such as reserve currencies like the US dollar. Also called **international money**

International Monetary Fund *noun* (part of the United Nations) a type of bank which helps member states in financial difficulties, gives financial advice to members and encourages world trade. Abbreviation **IMF**

international monetary system *noun* the system by which international trade is paid for, allowing exchange rates for different currencies and sufficient international currency reserves to allow payments to take place

international money *noun* money accepted when making foreign currency transactions. The commonest is the US dollar.

international payments *plural noun* payments made between individuals, firms or governments to accounts outside the countries in which they reside

international reserves *plural noun* same as **foreign currency reserves**

International Standard Industrial Classification *noun* a method of classifying economic activity introduced by the United Nations with the aim of making international comparisons more meaningful. Abbreviation **ISIC**

international trade *noun* trade in goods and services between different countries

International Trade Organization *noun* a projected body to organise international trade. It was superseded by GATT and then WTO. Abbreviation **ITO**

Internet *noun* the international electronic network which provides file and data transfer, together with electronic mail functions for millions of users round the world. Anyone can use the Internet.

Interstate Commerce Commission *noun* a US Federal agency which regulates business activity involving two or more of the states in the USA. Abbreviation **ICC**

intertemporal substitution *noun* the reallocation of goods and services to different times, so that if some service is more expensive at a certain time, consumers may purchase it at a different time to obtain a better price

intervention *noun* an act to make a change in a system, such as an attempt by a government to influence the exchange rate, by buying or selling foreign currency

intervention mechanism *noun* the means used by central banks in maintaining exchange rate parities (such as buying or selling of foreign currency)

in the bank *noun* a situation in which banks withdraw their money at call from discount houses which then need to borrow money from the Bank of England, the lender of last resort

intraindustry trade *noun* international trade in similar products, but usually of different quality or different brands or at different times of the year

introduction *noun* an act of bringing an established company to the Stock Exchange (i.e. getting permission for the shares to be traded on the Stock Exchange). It is used when a company is formed by a demerger from an existing larger company, and no new shares are being offered for sale.

invention *noun* **1.** a new product or process **2.** the creation of new products or processes which are then developed for commercial use through innovation

inventory *noun* (*especially US*) stock or goods in a warehouse or shop (NOTE: The UK term is **stock**.)

inventory control *noun* US same as **stock control**

inventory investment *noun* the investment in stocks of goods, usually for sale at a later date

inverse elasticity rule *noun* same as **Ramsey pricing**

investment *noun* the placing of money so that it will increase in value and produce an income (either in an asset, such as a building, or by purchasing shares, placing money on deposit, etc.)

investment appraisal *noun* the analysis of the future profitability of capital purchases as an aid to good management

investment bank *noun* US a bank which deals with the underwriting of new issues, and advises corporations on their financial affairs (NOTE: The UK term is **issuing house**.)

investment company *noun* same as **investment trust**

investment expenditure *noun* expenditure during a given period by businesses; it is one of the elements that make up aggregate expenditure

investment incentives *plural noun* financial incentives from the government to encourage companies to invest

investment income *noun* income (such as interest and dividends) from investments, not from salary, wages or profits of a business. Also called **unearned income**

Investment Management Regulatory Organisation *noun* a self-regulatory organisation which formerly regulated managers of investment funds, such as pension funds. Since 2001 it has been part of the FSA. Abbreviation **IMRO**

investment trust *noun* a company whose shares can be bought on the Stock Exchange and whose business is to make money by buying and selling stocks and shares. Also called **investment company**

Investors in Industry *noun* a finance group formed in 1983 as a new name for Finance for Industry (FFI) and subsequently floated on the Stock Exchange. It provides finance to smaller companies and especially to those in hi-tech areas. It is usually called Three i. Abbreviation **3i**

invisible *adjective* not recorded or reflected in economic statistics

invisible balance *noun* the balance of trade in invisible exports, that is the excess in value of invisible exports over invisible imports

invisible earnings *plural noun* foreign currency earned by a country by providing services, receiving interests or dividends, but not selling goods

invisible hand *noun* according to Adam Smith, the force of the market which drives the economy

invisibles *plural noun* invisible imports and exports

involuntary saving *noun* same as **forced saving**

involuntary unemployment *noun* unemployment which is not wanted by the persons involved, but is caused by a fall in the number of jobs available

inward investment *noun* investment from outside a country, as when a foreign company decides to set up a new factory there

iron law of wages *noun* a law current in the 18th and 19th centuries which states that wages are paid out of anticipated sales, and are governed by the amount of savings invested. The supply of labour determines the wages paid, and if the labour supply increases, then wages tend to fall to subsistence level.

IRR *abbreviation* internal rate of return

irredeemable security, **irredeemable bond** *noun* a government bond which has no date of maturity and which therefore provides interest but can never be redeemed at full value. In the UK, the War Loan is irredeemable.

irrevocable letter of credit *noun* a letter of credit which cannot be cancelled or changed, except if agreed between the two parties involved

IRS *abbreviation US* Internal Revenue Service

IS *abbreviation* income support

ISA *abbreviation* Individual Savings Account

ISIC *abbreviation* International Standard Industrial Classification

IS-LM model *noun* a theoretical model with two curves showing the investment and saving (IS) and interest rates and national income (LM) parts of economy at the same time

isocost curve *noun* a graph showing the amounts of different input factors that can be purchased for the same amount of money

iso-product curve, isoquant curve *noun* a curve showing the amounts of different input factors that produce the same amount of output

issued capital *noun* the amount of capital which is formed of money paid for shares issued to shareholders

issuing house *noun* a bank which organises the selling of shares in new companies (NOTE: The US term is **investment bank**.)

J

J curve *noun* a line on a graph shaped like a letter J, with an initial short fall, followed by a longer rise (used to describe the effect of a falling exchange rate on a country's balance of trade)

JIT *abbreviation* just-in-time

job *noun* a position providing regular paid work

jobber *noun US* a wholesaler

job centre *noun* a government office which lists jobs which are vacant in a certain area

jobseeker's allowance *noun* an amount of money paid by the government to people who are out of work and actively looking for jobs. Abbreviation **JSA**

joint costs *plural noun* costs which are allocated to two products

joint demand *noun* same as **complementary demand**

joint float *noun* a situation in which several currencies maintain a fixed exchange rate to each other and move together against other currencies

joint product *noun* one of several products made at the same time from the same raw materials, each product being equally important

joint profit maximisation *noun* a situation in which two firms making similar goods agree to price their goods so that they both make equally good profits

joint-stock company *noun* a company which issues shares to those who have contributed capital to it. If it is a private company, its shares are not listed on the stock exchange and it is called Limited or Ltd in its name; if it is a public company whose shares are listed on the Stock Exchange, then it is called a Public Limited Company or Plc. Also called **company limited by shares**

joint supply *noun* a situation in which two goods are produced together, and cannot be separated, so that the demand for one is always linked to the output of the other

joint venture *noun* a single business undertaking entered into by two or more businesses or partners

JSA *abbreviation* jobseeker's allowance

Juglar, Clément (1819–1905) French doctor and statistician, who was one of the first economists to develop the economic theory of business cycles and identified the 7–11 year cycle that has been associated with his name

Juglar cycle *noun* a business cycle about ten years in length

junk bond *noun* a high-interest bond raised as a debenture on the security of a company which is the subject of a takeover bid. The security has a very low credit rating, and the bond has a very low rating also.

just-in-time *noun* a system in which goods are made or purchased just before they are needed, so as to avoid carrying high levels of stock. Abbreviation **JIT**

K

Kaldor, Nicholas (1908–1986) Hungarian-born economist, based at Cambridge University, who worked principally on development theory. ♦ **Hicks-Kaldor principle**

Kennedy round *noun* the sixth round of negotiations on international tariffs under the auspices of GATT, held in 1963–67. It aimed to increase trade between the USA and the EEC, and also set up the Anti-Dumping Agreement which made rules for the export of low-priced goods. ♦ **Tokyo round, Uruguay round**

Keynes, John Maynard (1883–1946) British economist who elaborated theories concerning ways of counteracting the depression of the 1930s. He criticised the Versailles Treaty ending the First World War for the unfairness of the terms imposed on Germany. He published his *Treatise on Money* in 1930 and his *General Theory of Employment, Interest and Money* in 1935.

Keynesian economics *noun* the belief that full-employment is not possible unless governments intervene to achieve it by adjusting the level of demand. This should be done either during a depression by reflationary policies such as increasing government expenditure and reducing taxation, or during a boom by deflationary policies such as cutting government expenditure and increasing taxation.

Keynesian unemployment *noun* unemployment due to lack of demand for goods and services, as opposed to unemployment due to excessively high wages

Keynes Plan *noun* a plan put forward by the UK government at the Bretton Woods Conference to set up an institution similar to an international clearing house. It was the work of J.M. Keynes. It did not get the agreement of the USA, and the International Monetary Fund and the World Bank were set up instead.

key rate *noun* an interest rate which gives the basic rate on which other rates are calculated (the former bank base rate in the UK, or the Federal Reserve's discount rate in the USA)

kinked demand curve *noun* a demand curve which shows that firms believe that if they raise their prices, competing firms will not raise theirs, while if they cut their prices, the competition will cut theirs also

know-how *noun* the knowledge about how something works or how something is made

Kondratieff cycles *plural noun* long business cycles of around 56 years, suggested by the Russian economist N. D. Kondratieff. He identified cycles from 1780 to the 1840s, then from the 1840s to the 1890s, and then again from the 1890s to 1914. He divided the development of a national economy into four stages: firstly inflationary growth, with low interest rates, rising prices and rising corporate profits; second, stagflation, where prices continue to rise as do interest rates, and the stock market falls while debt also rises; third, deflationary growth, with falling prices and interest rates and rising stock markets and profits; finally depression, with falling prices but increasing commodity prices, stable interest rates and falling stock markets and profits.

Kyoto treaty *noun* an international treaty signed in 1997, by which governments agreed to reduce their emissions of greenhouse gases to lower than their 1990 levels by 2010. The main point of the treaty was that signatories would reduce their emissions of CO_2 and other greenhouse gases by 2010; but in order to achieve this, the main industrialised countries can buy emission reductions (called emission credits) from other countries, instead of reducing their own emissions themselves. This allows the USA, for example, to acquire emission credits for reductions in emissions in Ukraine, where, because of the collapse of the economy, emissions are already lower than stipulated in the treaty. Another scheme allows the richer countries to get credit for emission reductions in schemes which they finance in poorer countries.

L

labour *noun* one of the factors of production, the ability of human beings to do productive work and the number of human beings available to do the work (NOTE: The US spelling is **labor**.)

labour force *noun* all workers in employment and unemployed workers who are actively seeking employment. Also called **working population**

labour force participation rate *noun* same as **activity rate**

labour force survey *noun* a survey of the labour market conducted by the Office for National Statistics. It aims to give a set of national and regional statistics for employment and unemployment which can be compared with those of other EU countries. It contains details of things such as lifestyles, education, ethnic origins, income, mobility and housing. Abbreviation **LFS**

labour hoarding *noun* the practice of keeping more workers on the payroll than are necessary for the current output

labour-intensive industry *noun* an industry which needs large numbers of workers or where labour costs are high in relation to turnover

labour market *noun* the number of workers who are available for work

labour supply *noun* the amount of labour available in a market, either the total active population or the number of workers with certain qualifications

labour supply curve *noun* same as **backward-bending supply curve**

labour theory of value *noun* the theory that the value of goods and services is dependent on the value of the labour which produced them, without considering the value of the raw materials used or the cost of capital. This was the theory propounded by Adam Smith and Ricardo, as well as Karl Marx.

labour turnover *noun* the movement of labour into and out of businesses, as old workers leave and new workers arrive. There are several factors involved, including retirement of older workers, mobility of workers who move from area to area as new jobs are created, and sacking of workers by management for various reasons. In general there is a higher turnover of workers in boom conditions than in recession. Also called **turnover of labour**

Laffer, Arthur (1941–) US economist, a member of the Economic Policy Advisory Board

Laffer curve *noun* a chart showing that cuts in tax rates increase output in the economy, or alternatively, that increases in tax rates initially produce more revenue and then less as the economy slows down

LAFTA *abbreviation* Latin American Free Trade Association

lagged relationship *noun* a relationship between two or more variables under different time scales

lagging indicator *noun* an indicator (such as the gross national product) which shows a change in economic trends later than other indicators (NOTE: The opposite is **leading indicator**.)

Lagrange multiplier *noun* an equation developed by the French mathematician Lagrange, by which a function can be minimised without solving external constraints

laissez-faire economy *noun* an economy where the government does not interfere because it believes it is right to let the economy run itself. It is the opposite of dirigisme.

land *noun* an area of earth, which can have plants or buildings on its surface and minerals under the surface. Land is a tangible fixed asset and one of the factors of production.

Laspeyres, Ernst (1834–1913) German economist and statistician

Laspeyres index, **Laspeyres price index** *noun* an index of which the weighted average is based on figures for a base year

last-in, first-out *noun* an accounting method in which stock is valued at the price of the latest purchases. Abbreviation **LIFO**

last in first out *noun* an accounting method where stock is valued at the price of the earliest purchases. It is assumed that the most recently purchased stock is sold first.

Latin American Free Trade Association *noun* a group of Latin American countries, formed in 1960 and eventually covering the whole area, with the aim of setting up a free trade area in Latin America. By 1980 it had ceased to exist. Abbreviation **LAFTA**

LAUTRO *abbreviation* Life Assurance and Unit Trust Regulatory Organization

law of demand *noun* ◊ demand curve

law of diminishing marginal utility *noun* a general rule that each unit consumed adds less satisfaction to the consumer than the previous one, i.e. the marginal utility of any good or service diminishes as each new unit of it is consumed

law of diminishing returns *noun* a general rule that as more factors of production (land, labour and capital) are added to the existing factors, so the amount they produce is proportionately smaller

law of large numbers *noun* a general rule that the behaviour of large groups is easier to predict than that of individuals because groups behave in a more uniform fashion

law of one price *noun* a general rule that where the same good is sold in different markets its price will be the same. If the prices do vary then arbitrageurs will intervene and correct the price differential.

law of proportionate growth, law of proportionate effect *noun* same as **Gibrat's law of proportionate growth**

law of supply and demand *noun* a general rule that the amount of a product which is available and the needs of possible customers are brought into equality by market forces

LBO *abbreviation* leveraged buyout

L/C *abbreviation* letter of credit

LDCs *abbreviation* least developed countries

LDT *abbreviation* licensed deposit taker

leading indicator *noun* an indicator (such as manufacturing order books) which shows a change in economic trends earlier than other indicators (NOTE: The opposite is **lagging indicator**.)

leads and lags *plural noun* the acts of moving forward or delaying settlement of transactions to take advantage of possible changes in the exchange rate

lead underwriter *noun* an underwriting firm which organises the underwriting of a share issue (NOTE: The US term is **managing underwriter**.)

learning by doing *noun* a situation in which workers learn new skills from their work, and so increase productivity

learning curve *noun* the gradual process of learning new skills. A steep learning curve implies having to learn new skills fast.

lease *noun* a written contract for letting or renting a building or a piece of land or a piece of equipment for a period against payment of a fee ■ *verb* to let or rent a building or a piece of land or a piece of equipment for a period against payment of a fee

lease-back *noun* an arrangement where property is sold and then taken back on a lease

leasehold *noun* **1.** the holding of property on a lease from a freeholder (the ground landlord) **2.** a property held on a lease from a freeholder ■ *adjective* on a lease from a freeholder

least developed countries *plural noun* the 49 poorest countries as defined by the United Nations. They are countries which have very low per capita GDP and low human assets and are perceived as economically vulnerable. Abbreviation **LDCs**

legal tender *noun* coins or notes which can be legally used to pay a debt. Small denominations cannot be used to pay large debts.

lemon problem *noun* same as **adverse selection**

lender of last resort *noun* a central bank which lends money to commercial banks when they are short of funds. In the UK, this is the Bank of England, and in the USA it is the Federal Reserve Banks.

Leontief paradox *noun* a paradox noted in 1954 by the Russian-born US economist Wassily Leontief, that the USA, in spite of being the world's richest country, had exports which were more labour-intensive than its imports. The paradox was later resolved by showing that in a country which produces more than two goods the high ratio of capital to labour does not imply that its exports are more labour-intensive than its imports.

Lerner, Abba (1903–1982) US economist who based his theory of how a country's balance of trade could affect its exchange rate after the devaluation of its currency on the principles of Alfred Marshall. ◊ **Marshall-Lerner condition**

less developed countries *plural noun* same as **least developed countries**. Abbreviation **LDCs** (*dated*)

level of significance *noun* in hypothesis testing, the probability that a hypothesis will be rejected when it should have been accepted

leverage *noun* same as **gearing**

leveraged buyout, leveraged takeover *noun* a buyout of all the shares in a company by borrowing money against the security of the assets of the company to be bought. Abbreviation **LBO**

LFS *abbreviation* labour force survey

liabilities *plural noun* debts of an individual or a business, including dividends owed to shareholders

liability *noun* **1.** the fact of being legally responsible for damage or loss **2.** responsibility for a payment, such as the repayment of a loan

LIBOR *abbreviation* London Interbank Offered Rate

licensed deposit taker, licensed institution *noun* same as **deposit-taking institution**. Abbreviation **LDT**

life assurance *noun* same as **assurance**

life-cycle hypothesis *noun* a hypothesis (proposed by Franco Modigliani) that current disposable income is not the sole factor in consumption, but that future anticipated earnings are also involved. Consumers spend or borrow more or less as a proportion of their incomes according to the point they are at in their personal life cycles. This may have an effect on savings rates as individuals live longer and tend to save more and spend less.

life insurance *noun* same as **assurance**

lifestyle audit *noun* a study of a person's living standards to see if it is consistent with their reported income

LIFO *abbreviation* last in first out.

limit *noun* the point at which something ends or at which someone can go no further. Limit up and limit down show the upper or lower limits to share price movements which are regulated by some stock exchanges. ■ *verb* to introduce a limit to something

limit down *verb* ◊ **limit**

limited company *noun* a company in which a shareholder is responsible for the company's debts only to the face value of the shares he or she owns, or to the amount unpaid (if any) on those shares. Also called **limited liability company**. Abbreviation **Ltd**

limited liability *noun* a situation in which someone's liability for debt is limited by law

limited liability company *noun* same as **limited company**

limited partnership *noun* a registered business in which the liability of the partners is limited to the amount of capital they have each provided to the business and where the partners may not take part in the running of the business

limit pricing *noun* a policy adopted by firms already in a market to reduce their prices so as to make it unprofitable for other firms to try to enter the market. The price established is called an entry forestalling price.

limit up *verb* ◊ **limit**

linear programming *noun* a method of mathematically breaking down a problem so that it can be solved by a computer

liquid assets *plural noun* cash, or bills which can easily be changed into cash

liquidation *noun* **1.** the sale of assets for cash **2.** the closing of a company and selling of its assets

liquidity *noun* **1.** a situation of having cash **2.** assets which can be changed into cash

liquidity preference *noun* a situation in which people prefer to hold money in cash rather than spend it or invest it

liquidity ratio *noun* the ratio of liquid assets (i.e. current assets less stocks, but including debtors) to current liabilities, giving an indication of a company's solvency. Also called **acid test ratio, quick ratio**

liquidity trap *noun* a situation in which a government is incapable of reducing real interest rates. This will happen if the interest rates are reduced to zero and people feel that holding money in cash is better than investing it. According to Keynes the only solution is for a government to increase spending.

listed company *noun* a company whose shares can be bought or sold on the Stock Exchange

listed securities *plural noun* shares which can be bought or sold on the Stock Exchange. These shares appear on the official Stock Exchange list.

Lloyd's, Lloyd's of London *noun* the London international insurance market. Lloyd's is an old-established insurance market. The underwriters who form Lloyd's are divided into syndicates, each made up of active underwriters who arrange the business and non-working underwriters (called names) who stand surety for any insurance claims which may arise.

LM curve *noun* one of the curves in the IS-LM diagram which indicated interest rates combined with national income to give equilibrium in the money markets

loan *noun* an amount of money which has been lent ■ *verb* to lend something

loanable funds *plural noun* funds which are available for lending. The theory of loanable funds is that interest rates are determined by the supply of money available for lending. The market for loanable funds is the general money market .

loan capital *noun* the part of a company's capital which is a loan from an outside source and has to be repaid at a later date

loan stock *noun* stock issued by a company at a fixed rate of interest, as a means of raising a loan

lobbying *noun* the activity of asking someone (such as an MP or local official) to do something on your behalf

local content *noun* the proportion of inputs which come from the country itself, as opposed to those imported

local content rule *noun* a rule concerning the content of manufactured goods which must contain a certain proportion of material which is locally produced and not imported. In free-trade areas goods which are exempt from tariffs must contain a certain percentage of material from member countries of the area. Also called **rule of origin**

lock-out *noun* an industrial dispute in which the management will not let the workers into the factory until they have agreed to the management's conditions

locomotive principle *noun* the idea that growth in the world economy is driven by an important country or new industry, which is the locomotive which pulls other economies along

logarithm *noun* the power by which a base number has to be raised to give a certain number

log-linear function *noun* a function where the logarithm of a variable is linear

log-normal distribution *noun* a distribution where the logarithms of variables are normal

log-rolling *noun* action by members of parliament or elected local councillors to help each other's interests, even though this may not be in the general interest of the country or local area

Lomé Convention *noun* an agreement drawn up in 1975 by which African, Caribbean and Pacific states have open EU markets for their manufactured goods and most of their agricultural produce. They also receive EU aid in return. The agreement replaced the earlier Yaoundé convention.

London Interbank Offered Rate *noun* the rate at which banks borrow money from other banks (in sterling or Eurodollars) on the London Interbank market. Abbreviation **LIBOR**

long-dated securities *plural noun* bonds or bills of exchange which mature in fifteen years' time

long position *noun* a situation in which dealers or speculators hold stocks which they do not intend to sell immediately. Compare **short position**

long rate *noun* the rate of interest on long-dated securities. Compare **short rate**

long run *noun* the period of time which in theory is long enough for everything to be varied, in particular the factors of production. Compare **short run**

long-run average cost *noun* the total costs divided by the number of units produced over a long period

long-run cost-curve *noun* a curve showing the relationship between the cost of producing something and the actual output, over a long period. In this case all inputs can be adjusted.

long-run marginal cost *noun* the additional cost of adding a unit to the production quantity shown over a long period where all inputs are variable

long-term capital *noun* funds employed in a business over a long period, such as debentures

long-term interest rate *noun* the interest rate on long-dated securities, i.e. those with fifteen years to maturity

long-term unemployment *noun* unemployment for a period of longer than one year, which is more difficult to correct than short-term unemployment. People who have been unemployed for long periods tend to find it harder to get employment than those who have been unemployed for short periods.

Lorenz, Max (1880–1962) US economist who initially studied the tariffs on the US railroads and become the chief statistician of the Interstate Commerce Commission

Lorenz curve *noun* a curve developed by the economist Max Lorenz which shows the inequality of incomes, plotting cumulative income against the cumulative variable of the population which is being examined

loss *noun* **1.** the situation of having less money than before or of not making a profit **2.** an amount of money lost

low gearing *noun* ◊ **gearing**

Ltd *noun* same as **limited company**

Lucas, Robert (1937–) US macroeconomist, winner of the Nobel prize in 1995, who specialises in the theory of business and in particular rational expectations

Lucas critique *noun* the suggestion that economists should not believe that economic relationships will continue even if economic circumstances change. Economic models based on existing policies will not predict correctly what will happen if the policies are changed.

Luddites *plural noun* people who resist technological change. The term comes from the name for workers who destroyed new equipment in the 19th century.

lump of labour *noun* the theory that there is only a certain amount of employment available, so that if technological advances mean that fewer people are needed to produce a product, then unemployment will rise, or that if hours of work are reduced, employment will rise. This is not necessarily the case, as the new technologies may create new demand, which in turn creates new employment opportunities, while reducing hours of work may reduce the value of the work actually done.

lump-sum tax *noun* a tax paid as one single amount which does not vary. Such a tax has no effect on consumers' choice patterns.

luxury product *noun* a product whose consumption varies with disposable income. The wealthy spend more of their income on luxury products than people with lower incomes.

luxury tax *noun* an extra tax levied on luxury products

M

M0 *noun* the narrowest UK measure of money supply, including coins and notes in circulation plus the balances of commercial banks with the Bank of England

M1 *noun* a measure of money supply which includes all coins and notes in circulation, plus personal money in current accounts (i.e. accounts against which cheques can be written), plus traveller's cheques, and in the USA, money in NOW accounts

M2 *noun* a measure of money supply which includes M1 and personal money in deposit accounts (in the USA, only deposits of less than $100,000 are included)

M3 *noun* a British measure of sterling money supply which includes coins and notes, personal money in current and deposit accounts and government deposits and certificates of deposit

£M3 *noun* a UK measure of sterling money supply, including coins and notes, personal money in current and deposit accounts and government deposits

M4 *noun* a calculation of broad money supply including M3 plus money on deposit in banks and Treasury bills

M5 *noun* a money supply figure formed of M4 plus building society accounts and accounts with national savings

Maastricht Treaty *noun* a treaty signed in 1992 which sets out the principles for a European Union and the convergence criteria for states wishing to join the EMU. Apart from the monetary union, the treaty also emphasised the importance of coordinating foreign and defence policy and legal systems throughout the European Union, including citizenship of the Union for citizens of member states.

Macmillan Committee *noun* the Advisory Committee on Finance and Industry (1929–31), a committee set up by the UK government after the crash of 1929 to examine the state of the British economy. J. M. Keynes was a prominent member of it.

macroeconomics *noun* the study of the macroeconomy. Compare **microeconomics** (NOTE: takes a singular verb)

macroeconomy *noun* the economy of a whole area or a whole country

mainstream corporation tax *noun* the total tax paid by a company on its profits (before 1999 less any Advance Corporation Tax, which a company had already paid when distributing profits to its shareholders in the form of dividends). Abbreviation **MCT**

majority good *noun* a good which is manufactured in large quantities to meet a required demand. Compare **minority good**

majority interest *noun* a group of more than half of all the shares in a company

majority shareholder *noun* a person who owns more than half the shares in a company

managed currency *noun* a currency where the central bank intervenes in the foreign exchange markets to influence the exchange rate

managed float *noun* the floating of a currency in which the government intervenes to regulate the exchange rate. Also called **dirty float**

managed trade *noun* international trade which is organised by governments as opposed to normal market-based trade between companies

management *noun* the directing or running of a business

management accountancy, management accounting *noun* the providing of information to managers, which helps them to plan, to control their businesses and to take decisions which will make them run their businesses more efficiently

management accounts *plural noun* financial information prepared for a managers so that they can make decisions (including monthly or quarterly financial statements, often in great detail, with analysis of actual performance against the budget)

management buyin *noun* the purchase of a company by a group of outside directors. Abbreviation **MBI**

management buyout *noun* the takeover of a company by a group of employees, usually senior managers and directors. Abbreviation **MBO**

management by objectives *noun* a way of managing a business by setting work targets for the managers and testing to see if they are achieved correctly and on time

managerial theories of the firm *plural noun* theories that a firm's success depends on the capabilities and motivation of its managers. It is in the interest of the managers to run the firm profitably and make money for themselves. In most cases the shareholders are happy to let the managers do this since it increases dividends and the firm's market value.

managing underwriter *noun US* ◊ **underwriter**

manpower planning *noun* planning to anticipate manpower requirements and trying to meet them as closely as possible

manufacturer's recommended price *noun* same as **recommended retail price**

margin *noun* the difference between the money received when selling a product and the money paid for it

marginal *adjective* very small, with respect to a change to a variable which can have an effect on each unit or product sold

marginal analysis *noun* the analysis of the effect of adding one extra unit to a variable

marginal benefit *noun* an increase in benefit which follows from producing one unit more of a good

marginal cost *noun* the additional cost of making a single extra unit above the number already planned

marginal cost pricing *noun* the pricing of a good at the marginal cost of production

marginal efficiency of capital *noun* the highest rate at which a product will break even. The rate decreases as investment increases because investors will always invest in the most profitable projects first. Abbreviation **MEC**

marginal physical product *noun* the quantity of output produced by each unit of variable input

marginal pricing *noun* the basing of the selling price of a product on the variable costs of its production plus a margin, but excluding fixed costs

marginal product *noun* the quantity of a product (either physical or in revenue) which comes from a unit of increased input

marginal productivity of capital *noun* the value of extra production of a unit of increased capital

marginal propensity to consume *noun* the proportion of the last unit of income which is spent. It is the amount that consumption changes in response to a change in disposable income. Abbreviation **MPC**

marginal propensity to import *noun* the proportion of the last unit of GDP which is spent on imports. Abbreviation **MPI**

marginal propensity to save *noun* the proportion of last unit of income which is saved. It is the amount that savings change in response to a change in disposable income. Abbreviation **MPS**

marginal propensity to tax *noun* the proportion of each extra unit of income which is taken by the government in tax. Abbreviation **MPT**

marginal rate of substitution *noun* the extra amount of one product needed to compensate a consumer for a decrease in the amount of another product. Abbreviation **MPS**. Also called **diminishing marginal rate of substitution**

marginal rate of tax, **marginal rate of taxation** *noun* the percentage of tax which a taxpayer pays on every extra pound or dollar he or she earns, and which is therefore paid at a higher rate. Also called **marginal tax rate**

marginal rate of technical substitution *noun* the extra amount of one input which has to be added to compensate for an amount of another input which decreases, in order to keep up the same production levels

marginal rate of transformation *noun* the rate at which production of one product can take the place of the production of another product by switching inputs

marginal revenue *noun* the income from selling a single extra unit more than the existing number of sales, i.e. in addition to the existing total revenue

marginal revenue product *noun* the increase in revenue resulting from the use of one more unit of a factor of production. Abbreviation **MRP**

marginal tax rate *noun* same as **marginal rate of tax**

marginal utility *noun* the consumer's satisfaction at acquiring one more unit of a good. It diminishes as more units of the good are purchased.

marginal utility of money, marginal utility of wealth *noun* the consumer's satisfaction at having one more unit of money available to spend

margin of error *noun* the number of mistakes which are accepted in a document or calculation. The percentage error which must be accepted when making forecasts.

margin of safety *noun* the quantity of units produced (or sales of these units) which are above the breakeven point

margin requirement *noun* the amount of money which one party to a deal is required to deposit to secure the deal

market *noun* **1.** a place where a product might be sold **2.** the group of people who might buy a product ■ *verb* to sell a product in or to a market

marketable securities *plural noun* stocks, shares, certificates of deposit and other financial instruments which can be bought or sold on a stock market

market capitalisation *noun* same as **capitalisation**

market clearing *noun* a situation in which the demand for a good or service is exactly the same as the quantity available, so that nothing is left; producers can set the prices of their products in such a way as to clear all the stock

market concentration *noun* same as **concentration**

market cycle *noun* the period during which a market expands, then slows down and then expands again

market demand curve *noun* same as **demand curve**

market economist *noun* a person who specializes in the study of financial structures and the return on investments in the Stock Market

market economy *noun* same as **free market economy**

market entry *noun* the entry of a new supplier into a market, usually because existing suppliers are making large profits. The new entrant may start up from cold, or more likely will buy an existing supplier and increase investment to gain market share. Entry to markets is subject to barriers to entry.

market failure *noun* the failure of a market to provide goods or services adequately, as when it is dominated by a monopoly. Market failure can be corrected by government action.

market forces *plural noun* influences on sales which bring about a change in prices

marketing *noun* **1.** the process of identifying needs and satisfying these needs with suitable goods or services, through product design, distribution and promotion, either as a business or as a non-profit-making organisation **2.** the techniques used in selling a product, such as packaging and advertising

marketing mix *noun* the combination of all the elements that make up marketing such as price, distribution and advertising

marketing research *noun* all research carried out in the interests of successful marketing, including market research, media research and product research

market interest rates *plural noun* interest rates on money deposits which are governed by the supply of and demand for money in the market

marketmaker *noun* a person who buys or sells shares on the Stock Market and offers to do so in a certain list of securities. A marketmaker operates a book, listing the securities he or she is willing to buy or sell, and makes money by charging a commission on each transaction.

market mechanism *noun* same as **price mechanism**

market power *noun* the power of a supplier to take advantage of a weak consumer, as when the market is dominated by a monopoly

market price *noun* **1.** the price at which a product can be sold **2.** the price at which a share stands on a stock market

market segmentation *noun* the dividing of the market or consumers into certain categories according to their buying habits

market sentiment *noun* a general feeling among investors or financial analysts on a stock market (either optimistic or pessimistic) which can be influenced by external factors, and which will affect the prices of the shares themselves

market share *noun* the percentage of a total market which the sales of a company cover. Also called **share of the market**

market structure *noun* the way in which a market is organised, including the concentration of suppliers or consumers, the ease of entry or barriers to entry and the competitiveness of players in the market

market value added *noun* the difference between a company's market value and the amount of its invested capital. MVA reveals how well a company has performed over the long term in using its resources to create value. Abbreviation **MVA**

mark-up *noun* an increase in price

Marshall, Alfred (1842–1924) British economist who was the first professor at Cambridge University to emphasise the importance of economics

Marshall Aid *noun* money given to European countries after the Second World War under the European Recovery Programme (Marshall Plan)

Marshall-Lerner condition *noun* a condition under which a change in a country's exchange rate leads to a change in its balance of payments. In particular a devaluation will only be successful if volumes of trade are elastic to price changes. The idea was developed by Abba Lerner on the basis of propositions by Alfred Marshall.

Marshall Plan *noun* same as **European Recovery Programme**

Marxian economics, Marxist economics *noun* an economic theory based on the writings of Karl Marx, which explains that it is the law of value which underlies all commodity production. The value of commodities is determined by the value of the labour contained in them and is expressed in money terms as commodities are exchanged. This is the law which regulates the capitalist system by competition as it affects supply and demand. Marxist economists predict the collapse of the capitalist system because competition will drive down prices to unprofitable levels resulting in lower wages and industrial discontent.

mass production *noun* the manufacturing of large quantities of goods

matrix *noun* the arrangement of data in horizontal and vertical columns (NOTE: The plural is **matrices**.)

maturity date *noun* the date when a government stock, an assurance policy or a debenture will become due for payment. Also called **date of maturity**

maximin strategy *noun* a strategy to be adopted in game theory, where the player follows the policy which gives the best result of all the bad results possible, i.e. the maximum of the minimum (NOTE: The opposite is **minimax strategy**.)

maximum *noun* the largest possible number or price or quantity (NOTE: The plural is **maxima** or **maximums**.) ■ *adjective* which is the largest possible number or price or quantity

maximum-likelihood estimation *noun* the calculation of parameter values which fit the observed data best

MBI *abbreviation* management buyin

MBO *abbreviation* management buyout

MCT *abbreviation* mainstream corporation tax

mean *adjective* calculated by adding several figures together and dividing by the number of figures added ■ *noun* an average figure, calculated by adding several figures together and dividing by the number of figures added

means test *noun* an inquiry into how much money someone earns to see if he or she is eligible for state benefits

means-test *verb* to subject someone to a means test

means-tested benefit *noun* a state benefit which is available only to people whose income falls below a certain level

MEC *abbreviation* marginal efficiency of capital

median *noun* a point in the middle of a list of numbers or values

Median Voter Theorem *noun* the theory that in politics voters in the centre are more likely to be represented in a Parliament than those with extreme views

medium of exchange *noun* something, such as money, which is used to make purchases of goods or services easier. If there is no medium of exchange, then the parties have to use barter.

Medium Term Financial Strategy *noun* a policy adopted by the UK government in the 1980s to use money supply and the Public Sector Borrowing Requirement as means of controlling the economy and reducing inflation. The aim was to reduce M3 by 1 per cent per annum. Abbreviation **MTFS**

member *noun* same as **shareholder** (*formal*)

member bank *noun* a bank which is part of the US Federal Reserve System

memorandum and articles of association, memorandum of association *noun* the legal documents setting up a limited company and giving details of its name, aims, authorised share capital, conduct of meetings, appointment of directors and registered office

menu costs *plural noun* the costs of price rises which involves activities such as printing new catalogues and price labels, reprogramming computers and retraining staff. The menu costs of inflation are the increase in inflation due to the cost of informing people about price rises.

mercantilism *noun* a policy in the 17th and 18th centuries of encouraging export trade and discouraging imports in order to increase the country's wealth. the policy is still continued in some countries today and leads to protectionism.

merchant bank *noun* a bank which arranges loans to companies, deals in international finance, buys and sells shares, and launches new companies on the Stock Exchange, but does not provide normal banking services to the general public

Mercosur *noun* a treaty signed in 1994 between Argentina, Brazil, Paraguay and Uruguay, setting up a free trade zone between the countries with the elimination of customs tariffs. The four countries have a unified policy regarding trade with other countries, and coordinate their own internal macroeconomic policies.

merger *noun* the joining together of two or more companies, usually as the result of an agreed takeover bid

merger accounting *noun* the method of preparing group accounts in which the business combination meets the strict criteria necessary for such accounting. Merger accounting seeks to treat the combining entities as if they had always been combined. The carrying values of their assets and liabilities do not need to be adjusted to fair value on consolidation. The results and cash flows of all the combining entities are brought into the group accounts from the beginning of the financial year in which the combination occurred. The corresponding figures are restated.

merit good *noun* same as **public good**

m.e.s. *abbreviation* minimum efficient scale

mezzanine debt *noun* further debt acquired by a company after the start-up finance has been provided. It is less risky than start-up finance, since the company has usually already started trading. This type of debt is aimed at consolidating the company's trading position before it is floated on a stock exchange.

MFA *abbreviation* Multi-Fibre Arrangement

MFN *abbreviation* most favoured nation

M-form *noun* same as **multidivisional form**

microeconomics *noun* the study of microeconomies. Compare **macroeconomics** (NOTE: takes a singular verb)

microeconomy *noun* the economy of a group of people or single companies

middle management *noun* the department managers of a company who carry out the policy set by the directors and organise the work of a group of workers

MIG *abbreviation* Minimum Income Guarantee

MIGA *abbreviation* Multilateral Investment Guarantee Agency

migration *noun* the movement of people from one area to another, or from one country to another. Compare **economic migrant**

Mill, John Stuart (1806–1873) English philosopher and economist. He was educated entirely by his father, James Mill, who subjected him to a rigid system of intellectual discipline. He followed the utilitarian ideas of Jeremy Bentham whose work he read when he was still a teenager. He wrote many articles and books on politics, social economy and philosophy. He is remembered for his advocacy of women's suffrage and the rights of the labouring poor.

Miller, Merton (1923–2000) US economist who developed the Modigliani-Miller theorem

minimax strategy *noun* a strategy to be adopted in game theory, where the player follows the policy which gives him the least bad result of all the bad results possible, i.e. the minimum of the maximum (NOTE: The opposite is **maximin strategy**.)

minimum *noun* the smallest possible quantity or price or number (NOTE: The plural is **minima** or **minimums**.) ■ *adjective* which is the smallest possible quantity or price or number

minimum balance *noun* the smallest amount of money which must be kept in an account to qualify for the services provided

minimum efficient scale *noun* a point on a firm's cost curve at which economies of scale no longer occur, i.e. when the long-run average cost stops falling. Abbreviation **m.e.s.**

Minimum Income Guarantee *noun* payments made by the government to increase the incomes of people over 60 on low incomes and bring them up to a higher level. It is a form of income support. Abbreviation **MIG**

minimum lending rate *noun* formerly, the rate at which the Bank of England used to lend to other banks (NOTE: now called the **base rate**)

minimum wage *noun* the lowest hourly wage which a company can legally pay its workers

Ministry of Finance *noun* ◊ **Treasury**

minority good *noun* a good which sells in small quantities, and where an increase in price will have little effect on the quantity sold

minority interest *noun* a group of shares which are less than one half of the shares in a company

minority shareholder *noun* a person who owns a group of shares but less than half the shares in a company

mint *noun* a factory where coins are made ■ *verb* to make coins

mismatch *noun* a situation in which the skills of the unemployed do not match the requirements of the jobs available

mission statement *noun* a statement which gives the aims of an organisation

mixed economy *noun* an economic system which contains both nationalised industries and private enterprise

mixed strategy *noun* the policy of using various strategies in a market, so as to make it impossible for competitors to forecast which strategy will be used

MLR *abbreviation* minimum lending rate

MMC *abbreviation* Monopolies and Mergers Commission

MNC *abbreviation* multinational corporation

mobility of capital *noun* the ability to move capital from one country to another without restriction. This is one of the four freedoms of the European Union. If capital is invested in plant and other fixed assets it stops being mobile.

mobility of labour *noun* the ability of workers to move from one area to another to find jobs. When it involves moving from one country to another without restriction this is one of the four freedoms of the European Union.

MOD *abbreviation* modulus

mode *noun* the way of doing something. A mode of payment is the way in which payment is made (such as cash or cheque).

model *noun* same as **economic model**

Modigliani, Franco (1918–) Italian-born US economist who (with Merton Miller) formulated the Modigliani-Miller theorem. He also proposed the life-cycle hypothesis that consumers aim for a level income during their life, by saving when they are earning and spending when they are retired. He was awarded the Nobel Prize for Economics in 1985.

Modigliani-Miller theorem, Modigliani-Miller proposition *noun* a proposition that in a perfect market there is no relationship between the capital structure of a firm (i.e. where it gets its capital from) and its real performance

modulus *noun* the remainder after the division of one number by another. Abbreviation **MOD**

monetarism *noun* the theory that the amount of money in the economy affects the level of prices, so that inflation can be controlled by regulating money supply

monetary base *noun* money which is under the direct control of the central bank, i.e. all currency in circulation, plus all bank deposits with the central bank. It approximates to the UK M0 level of money supply. Also called **high-powered money**

monetary policy *noun* the government's policy relating to the money supply, bank interest rates and borrowing. If a government wants to stimulate the economy it will adopt reflationary measures such as increasing spending and reducing taxation; if it wants to cool down the economy in a boom, it will adopt deflationary measures and reduce government spending and increase taxation.

Monetary Policy Committee *noun* a committee of the Bank of England, chaired by the governor of the Bank, which has responsibility for setting interest rates independently of the UK government. The aim is to set rates with a view to keeping inflation at a certain level, and avoiding deflation. Abbreviation **MPC**

monetary system *noun* the system of controls used by a country to regulate its money supply

monetary targets *noun* figures such as the money supply and PSBR which are given as targets by the government when setting out its budget for the forthcoming year

monetary unit *noun* the standard currency in a country (such as the dollar or yen) or within a group of countries (such as the euro)

monetise, monetize *verb* to convert assets into money

money *noun* coins and notes used for buying and selling. In some contexts it includes funds in deposit and current accounts.

money at call *noun* same as **call money**

money illusion *noun* the illusion that people do not realise that inflation cuts the spending power of their incomes, or that they mistake paper profits (as in the rise in house values) for real money gains

money laundering *noun* the passing of money from illegal activities, such as drug trafficking, through apparently legitimate businesses to allow it to be used further without being detected

money market *noun* the market for buying and selling short-term loans or financial instruments such as Treasury bills and CDs, which can be easily converted to cash

money multiplier *noun* the ratio of the change in lending by banks to their monetary base

money on call *noun* same as **call money**

money supply *noun* the amount of money which exists in a country. Money supply is believed by some to be at the centre of control of a country's economy. If money supply is tight (i.e. the government restricts the issue of new notes, reduces the possibility of lending and imposes similar restrictions) the amount of money available in the economy is reduced and thus may reduce spending. Money supply is calculated in various ways.

money terms *plural noun* prices or incomes shown in real terms, adjusted for inflation

money wages *plural noun* wages expressed in real terms, adjusted for inflation

Monopolies and Mergers Commission *noun* a UK government organisation which examines takeover bids at the request of the Office of Fair Trading, to see if a successful bid would result in a monopoly and so harm the consumer by reducing competition. Abbreviation **MMC**

monopolistic competition *noun* same as **imperfect competition**

monopoly *noun* a situation in which one person or company controls all the market in the supply of a product

monopoly policy *noun* government policy aimed to regulate monopolies

monopoly power *noun* the power which a monopoly has to influence a market, by means such as setting the pricing structure or barring new entrants

monopoly profit *noun* the larger than normal profit which a monopoly enjoys because of lack of competition

monopsony *noun* a situation in which there is only one buyer of a good or service and many suppliers, so that the buyer can obviously control the prices he or she pays

Monte Carlo method *noun* a statistical analysis technique for calculating an unknown quantity which has an exact value by using an extended series of random trials

Moody's Investors Service *noun* a US rating organisation which gives a rating showing the reliability of a debtor organisation (its ratings run from AAA to C). It also issues ratings on municipal bonds, running from MIG-1 (the highest rating) to MIG-4.

moral hazard *noun* the possibility that a party to a contract will do something to his or her own benefit which will harm other parties, and so obtain benefits promised under the contract. An example would be that a property owner might want to burn down the property to get the insurance money.

moratorium *noun* a temporary stop to repayments of interest or capital of money owed (NOTE: The plural is **moratoria** or **moratoriums**.)

mortgage *noun* a legal agreement where someone lends money to another person so that he or she can buy a property, the property being the security ■ *verb* to give a legal right to property to a person or organisation in exchange for a loan

most favoured nation *noun* a country which has the best trade terms. Abbreviation **MFN**

most-favoured-nation clause *noun* an agreement between two countries that each will offer the other the best possible terms in commercial contracts

movement of capital *noun* same as **capital flow**

moving average *noun* an average of share prices on a stock market, where the calculation is made over a period which moves forward regularly. The commonest are 100-day or 200-day averages, or 40-week moving averages. The average is calculated as the average figure for the whole period, and moves forward one day or week at a time. These averages are often used by chartists.

MPC *abbreviation* Monetary Policy Committee

MPM *abbreviation* marginal propensity to import

MPS *abbreviation* marginal propensity to save

MPT *abbreviation* marginal propensity to tax

MRP *abbreviation* manufacturer's recommended price

MRS *abbreviation* marginal rate of substitution

MTFS *abbreviation* Medium-Term Financial Strategy

multicollinearity *noun* same as **collinearity**

multidivisional form *noun* a method of organising a large commercial enterprise where the whole organisation is ultimately controlled by central management but most decisions are left to autonomous divisions. Also called **M-form**

Multi-Fibre Arrangement *noun* a protectionist agreement signed in 1974 to regulate the exports of fibres and cloths from less developed countries to developed countries, so as to protect employment in the importing countries. It goes against the WTO rules. Abbreviation **MFA**

multilateral aid *noun* aid from richer countries to poorer countries which is channelled through international agencies such as the World Bank

Multilateral Investment Guarantee Agency *noun* an agency of the World Bank which guarantees investment in developing countries. Abbreviation **MIGA**

multilateralism *noun* a policy of expanding international trade between many countries, rather than restricting it to bilateral deals between just two countries

multinational, **multinational company,** **multinational corporation** *noun* a company which has branches or subsidiary companies in several countries. Also called **transnational**

multiplant *adjective* based in several plants. A large firm may have several plants in the same country, and international firms may operate from plants in different countries.

multiple correlation coefficient same as **coefficient of determination**

multiple regression *noun* analysis which allows the prediction of the value of a variable from several predictor variables

multiplier *noun* **1.** a number which multiplies another **2.** a factor which tends to multiply something, as when the effect of new inputs such as investment is to produce a proportionately higher increase in national income

multiplier-accelerator **model** *noun* same as **accelerator-multiplier model**

multiplier effect *noun* a situation in which a small initial change in investment or spending produces a proportionately larger change in national income

multiproduct firm *noun* a firm which makes more than one type of product according to the Standard Industrial Classification system

mutual company *noun* same as **mutual insurance company**

mutual fund *noun* a US organisation which takes money from small investors and invests it in stocks and shares for them, the investment being in the form of units in the fund (NOTE: The UK term is **unit trust**.)

mutual insurance company *noun* an insurance company which belongs to its policy holders or a savings bank which belongs to its depositors (who may receive dividends from it). Also called **mutual company**

mutual status *noun* a situation in which the owners of a building society are its investors and borrowers

MVA *abbreviation* market value added

N

NAFTA *abbreviation* North American Free Trade Agreement

NAIRU *abbreviation* non-accelerating inflation rate of unemployment

name *noun* a person who provides security for insurance arranged by a Lloyd's of London syndicate. The underwriters who form Lloyd's are divided into syndicates, each made up of active underwriters who arrange the business and names who stand surety for any insurance claims which may arise. Because of large losses by some syndicates in the early 1990s, some names were made bankrupt.

NASDAQ *noun* a system which provides quotations via computer for the US over-the-counter market, and also for some large corporations listed on the NYSE. Full form **National Association of Securities Dealers Automated Quotations system** (NOTE: The UK term is **SEAQ**.)

Nash, John (1928–) US economist who was awarded the Nobel Prize for Economics in 1994

Nash equilibrium *noun* in game theory, a situation in which two parties are following different strategies (one maximin and the other minimax), the result being that neither party can improve his or her position because of the strategy adopted by the other party

National Association of Securities Dealers Automated Quotations system *noun* full form of **NASDAQ**

national bank *noun* a US bank which is chartered by the Federal government and is part of the Federal Reserve System as opposed to a state bank

National Bureau of Economic Research *noun* a private US organisation which provides economic analysis. Abbreviation **NBER**

National Debt *noun* the money borrowed by a government which has not been repaid

National Economic Development Council *noun* a UK government group which existed from 1962 to 1992 for the discussion of economic problems between government, trade unions and employers. Abbreviation **NEDC**

National Enterprise Board *noun* a UK government organisation set up in 1975 to help industrial development and invest public money in profitable manufacturing companies. In 1981 it merged with the National

Research and Development Corporation to form the British Technology Group. Abbreviation **NEB**

national expenditure *noun* the total expenditure in a national economy, i.e. both output and income

national income *noun* the value of income from the sales of goods and services in a country

national income accounts *plural noun* national accounts showing the value of goods and services produced and sold both domestically and exported over a period of one year. They cover both GDP and GNP, together with other income from investments abroad.

National Institute of Economic and Social Research *noun* an independent UK research organisation which provides reports on economic matters for businesses and government. It provides statistics and research into such areas as employment, productivity and household spending, and even provides advice on the teaching of mathematics. Abbreviation **NIESR**

National Insurance *noun* the UK state insurance system, organised by the government, which pays for such things as medical care, hospitals and unemployment benefits. Abbreviation **NI**

National Insurance contribution *noun* a proportion of income paid each month by an employee and the employee's company to the National Insurance. Abbreviation **NIC**

National Insurance Fund *noun* a fund, managed by the Inland Revenue, which holds the contributions to National Insurance and pays out benefits and pensions

nationalisation, nationalization *noun* the taking over of private industry by the state

nationalised industry *noun* an industry which was privately owned, but is now owned by the state

national product *noun* the money value of all goods and services produced in a country (this is the gross national product). When investment on capital goods and depreciation are deducted this gives the net national product.

National Research and Development Corporation *noun* a UK government organisation set up in 1948 to commercialise government-funded research. In 1981 it merged with the National Enterprise Board to form the British Technology Group. Abbreviation **NRDC**

National Savings & Investments *noun* part of the Exchequer, a savings scheme for small investors including savings certificates and premium bonds. Abbreviation **NS&I**

National Savings certificates *plural noun* certificates showing that someone has invested in National Savings & Investments. The NS&I issues certificates both with fixed interest rates and index-linked.

natural growth rate *noun* the growth rate which comes from an increase in the labour force and will keep unemployment at a constant level. Also called **natural rate of economic growth**. ⸰ Harrod-Domar growth model

natural logarithm *noun* a logarithm to the base e, where e is approximately 2.718

natural monopoly *noun* a situation in which economies of scale can only be achieved under a monopoly rather than under a situation of perfect competition. This was applied to some of the nationalised industries such as electricity.

natural rate of economic growth *noun* same as **natural growth rate**

natural rate of unemployment *noun* the level of unemployment which can be reached when the labour market is in equilibrium, i.e. when everyone who wants a job has one

natural resource *noun* a part of the environment considered as a factor of production and able to be used commercially (such as coal)

natural resources *plural noun* a part of the environment considered as a factor of production and able to be used commercially (such as coal)

natural wastage *noun* loss of workers because they resign or retire, not through redundancy or dismissals

NAV *abbreviation* net asset value

NBER *abbreviation* National Bureau of Economic Research

NBV *abbreviation* net book value

NDP *abbreviation* net domestic product

near money *noun* assets which can easily be converted to cash. Also called **quasi money**

NEB *abbreviation* National Enterprise Board

necessary condition *noun* a condition which must exist to guarantee a result. Compare **sufficient condition**

necessity *noun* a thing which is vitally important, without which nothing can be done or a person cannot survive (NOTE: The plural is **necessities**.)

NEDC *abbreviation* National Economic Development Council

'Neddy' *noun* same as **National Economic Development Council** (*informal*)

negative carry *noun* a deal where the cost of finance is more than the return on the capital used

negative equity *noun* a situation in which a house bought with a mortgage becomes less valuable than the money borrowed to buy it (because of falling house prices)

negative income tax *noun* a system of giving poorer families tax credits, so that instead of paying income tax they actually earn it

negative-sum game *noun* in game theory, a game where the players end up with a total sum which is less than when they started. Compare **positive-sum game, zero-sum game**

negative yield curve *noun* a situation in which the yield on a long-term investment is less than that on a short-term investment

negotiable order of withdrawal account *noun US* same as **NOW account**

neoclassical economics *noun* the school of economics which followed classical economics in the latter part of the 19th century. It studied in particular to principles of allocation of resources (i.e. the factors of production), as opposed to the distribution of wealth proposed by the classical economists.

neoclassical synthesis *noun* an economic theory developed in the 1950s which was a synthesis of neoclassical economics and Keynes' macroeconomic models. ◆ **new neoclassical synthesis**

net assets *plural noun* all the assets of a company after taking away what the company owes

net asset value *noun* the total value of an accounting entity after deducting the money owed by it. It is the value of shareholders' capital plus reserves and any money retained from profits. Abbreviation **NAV**. Also called **net worth**

net asset value per share *noun* the value of a company calculated by dividing the shareholders' funds by the number of shares issued

net book value *noun* the value of an asset in a company's books, i.e. its original purchase price less any depreciation. Abbreviation **NBV**

net cash flow *noun* the difference between the money coming in and the money going out of a firm, where more money is coming in and less money going out

net current assets *plural noun* the current assets of a company (cash and stocks) less any liabilities, which a company needs to be able to continue trading. Also called **net working capital**

net domestic product *noun* the value of all products and services produced in a country less the value of the capital used to produce them. It can be calculated by deducting the Capital Consumption Allowance (CCA) (the capital depreciation of the economy during a year) from GDP. Abbreviation **NDP**

net earnings *noun* same as **net income**

net exports *noun* a figure showing total exports less total imports

net income *noun* the total earnings of a business after tax and other deductions. Also called **net earnings**

net investment *noun* an increase in the total capital invested. It is calculated as gross capital invested less a figure for capital consumption, which can only be an estimate.

net national product *noun* a figure showing the gross national product less investment on capital goods and depreciation. Abbreviation **NNP**

net present value *noun* the value of future cash inflows less future cash outflows discounted at a certain discount rate, usually the company's cost of capital. Abbreviation **NPV**

net profit *noun* the result where income from sales is more than all expenditure. Also called **profit after tax**

net property income from abroad *noun* income received from other countries in the form of dividends, rents, etc., plus profits from companies working abroad, less rents and dividends paid to non-national companies working in this country

net tangible assets *plural noun* a company's tangible assets (i.e. not including intangibles such as goodwill and intellectual properties) less its current liabilities (i.e. not including liabilities due in the next financial year). Abbreviation **NTA**

network externality *noun* the increasing economies of working via the telephone or Internet as more people use the system

net working capital *noun* same as **net current assets**

net worth *noun* same as **net asset value**

net yield *noun* the profit from investments after deduction of tax

neutrality of money *noun* a situation in which the level of money supply only affects the level of prices in an economy. Compare **superneutrality of money**

new classical economics *noun* a school of economics which believes that the economy works in a basically rational fashion, and that unemployment is caused by state intervention in the system. It is a form of laissez-faire.

New Deal *noun* a UK government initiative to help the unemployed find jobs. It covers both young people and older people, those with disabilitiess and single parents, and offers incentives to employers to employed people who are currently unemployed.

new economy *noun* the part of a country's economy which comes from new technologies, such as broadband telephones or genetically modified foods

New International Economic Order *noun* a series of resolutions passed by the General Assembly of the United Nations in 1974, which were critical of the way in which the western developed countries interacted with and exploited the developing world and demanded affirmative action to correct inequalities of treatment. Abbreviation **NIEO**

new issue *noun* the issue of new shares to raise finance for a company

new issue market *noun* same as **primary market**

newly industrialised country *noun* a country which has recently increased its industrialisation, and which is a growing power in the world economy. Abbreviation **NIC**

new neoclassical synthesis *noun* an economic theory developed in the 1990s which applies rational expectations to the neoclassical synthesis and includes the monetarist theories of Milton Friedman

new protectionism *noun* new forms of protectionism such as preventing takeovers by foreign companies, developed to restrict international competition (in spite of the efforts of the WTO)

New York Stock Exchange *noun* the main US stock exchange, situated on Wall Street in New York. Abbreviation **NYSE**. Also called **Big Board**

NIC *abbreviation* **1.** National Insurance contributions **2.** newly industrialised country

NIEO *abbreviation* New International Economic Order

NIESR *abbreviation* National Institute of Economic and Social Research

Nikkei index, Nikkei Average *noun* the index of prices on the Tokyo Stock Exchange, based on about 200 leading shares

NNP *abbreviation* net national product

nominal interest rate *noun* the interest rate expressed as a percentage of the face value of a bond, not on its market value

nominal rate of protection, nominal protection *noun* an addition to the price of an imported good caused by import tariffs. This allows home-produced goods to support a higher price if necessary.

nominal value *noun* same as **face value**

nominal wages *plural noun* wages earned after tax and other deductions have been made, as opposed to real wages which are wages shown as a ratio of a price index

nominal yield *noun* the dividend on a share expressed as a percentage of its face value

nominee holding *noun* shares held in an account by someone who is nominated, especially someone who is appointed to deal with financial matters on the owner's behalf. Most shares are now held in nominee accounts, especially where computerised share dealing takes place. The disadvantage for the shareholder is that he or she does not see the company reports, and will not be eligible for any shareholder perks. Shares can also be purchased and held in nominee accounts so that the identity of the owner of the shares cannot be discovered.

non-accelerating inflation rate of unemployment *noun* the rate of employment when inflation remains stable (calculated at 4.5% in the USA). If unemployment falls below a certain rate, then inflation will start to rise, but if inflation falls, then unemployment will start to rise. Abbreviation **NAIRU**

non-durable goods, non-durables *plural noun* goods which are used up soon after they have been bought (such as food or newspapers)

non-excludability *noun* **1.** a situation of not being the exclusive property or being exclusively available to a certain individual **2.** the theory that no one should be excluded from enjoying something, such as an invention. The most recent cases involve the patenting of DNA.

non-executive director *noun* a director who attends board meetings and gives advice, but does not work full-time for the company, and is paid a fee for his or her advice. Non-executive directors keep an eye on the way the company is run, and in particular make sure that the executive directors are doing their work properly. They may also intervene in disputes between directors, or between shareholders and directors. Also called **outside director**

non-linear function *noun* a function which is not linear, i.e. it does not form a straight line

non-marketed economic activities *plural noun* activities which are not sold through a market and so not declared as part of the national income, such as unpaid charity work or the provision of services free to pensioners

non-performing debt, non-performing loan *noun* a loan where the borrower is not likely to pay any interest nor to repay the principal (as in the case of loans to Third World countries by western banks)

non-price competition *noun* the attempt to compete in a market through other means than price, such as quality of product and promotion

non-profit-making organisation, non-profit organisation *noun* an organisation (such as a charity) which is not allowed by law to make a profit (NOTE: The US term is **non-profit corporation**.)

non-renewable resources *plural noun* natural resources (such as coal or oil) which cannot be replaced if they are consumed

non-tariff barriers *noun* barriers to international trade other than tariffs. They include over-complicated documentation; verification of goods for health and safety reasons and blocked deposits payable by importers to obtain foreign currency. Abbreviation **NTBs**

non-voting shares *plural noun* shares which do not allow the shareholder to vote at meetings. Usually these are A shares.

norm *noun* the usual quantity, the usual rate at which something functions

normal distribution *noun* a graph of distribution which is symmetrical around a mean. It is shaped like a bell.

normal good *noun* a good for which demand increases as incomes increase

normal profit *noun* a level of profit which allows the producer to continue trading

normative economics *noun* the study of how an economy should be run, making sure that the economy is run efficiently and in a way which does not harm producers or consumers, as opposed to the study of how an economy works in practice (positive economics)

North American Free Trade Agreement *noun* an agreement between the USA, Canada and Mexico, signed in 1994, which aims to remove tariff barriers between the three countries and the reduction of non-tariff barriers, together with the free movement of capital, workers, and services. Abbreviation **NAFTA**

NOW account *noun* in the USA, an interest-bearing checking account (current account) in which a minimum of $500 has to be kept at all times. Also called **negotiable order of withdrawal account**

NPV *abbreviation* net present value

NRDC *abbreviation* National Research and Development Corporation

NS&I *abbreviation* National Savings & Investments

NTA *abbreviation* net tangible assets

NTBs *abbreviation* non-tariff barriers

null hypothesis *noun* the hypothesis that something has no effect, as that there is no relationship between income and savings. Comparing this hypothesis with data, calculations can be made to see what exactly the relationship is.

numéraire *noun* a thing used as a standard of value. It can be a good, such as a type of metal used to value other metals, or a currency such as the US dollar when used as an international trading currency.

NYSE *abbreviation* New York Stock Exchange

O

objective function *noun* a function which relates to a variable which has been chosen to optimise it

obsolescence *noun* the process of going out of date because of advances in design or technology, and therefore becoming less useful and valuable

occupational immobility *noun* the situation in which labour does not move easily from one job to another, either because workers are specifically trained for a single job, or because there are barriers to mobility

occupational pension scheme *noun* a pension scheme where the worker gets a pension from the company he or she has worked for. Also called **company pension scheme**

OECD *abbreviation* Organisation for Economic Co-operation and Development

off-balance-sheet finance *noun* financing by leasing equipment under an operating lease instead of buying it, so that it does not appear in the balance sheet as an asset

offer curve *noun* a graph showing the trade which a country can do at various price levels, or where two individuals have the same satisfaction from a good. Compare **Edgeworth box**

Office for National Statistics *noun* the UK government agency charged with collecting and publishing national statistics. It was formed in 1996 from the merger of the Central Statistical Office and the Office of Population Censuses and Surveys. Abbreviation **ONS**

Office of Fair Trading *noun* a UK government department which protects consumers against unfair or illegal business. It also decides if a takeover bid is in the interests of the ordinary customers of the two companies concerned, and may refer such a bid to the Monopolies and Mergers Commission for investigation. Abbreviation **OFT**

Office of Management and Budget *noun* the US government department which prepares the budget for the President. Abbreviation **OMB**

official financing *noun* the part of the balance of payments which is due to government actions, such as reducing reserves or repaying borrowings

Official List *noun* a daily publication by the London Stock Exchange of the highest and lowest prices recorded for each share during the trading session

official receiver *noun* an official who is appointed by the courts to run a company which is in financial difficulties, to pay off its debts as far as possible and to close it down

off-the-job training *noun* training given to workers away from their place of work (such as at a college or school)

OFT *abbreviation* Office of Fair Trading

Ohlin, Bertil (1899–1979) Swedish economist who specialised in the study of international trade. ♦ **Heckscher-Ohlin model**

Okun's law *noun* a general rule calculated by the US economist Arthur Okun, that a 1% increase in unemployment produces a corresponding loss in output of around 3%

oligopoly *noun* a situation in which only a few sellers control the market

oligopsony *noun* a situation in which only a few large buyers control the market

OLS *abbreviation* ordinary least squares

OMB *abbreviation* Office of Management and Budget

ombudsman *noun* an official who investigates complaints by the public against government departments or other large organisations. There are several ombudsmen: the main one, the Parliamentary Commissioner, is a civil servant who investigates complaints against government departments. The Banking Ombudsman and the Building Societies Ombudsman are independent officials who investigate complaints by the public against banks or building societies. The Pensions Ombudsman and Personal Investment Authority Ombudsman investigate complaints about personal pensions and employers' pension schemes, and personal investments such as unit trusts. (NOTE: The plural is **ombudsmen**.)

oncosts *plural noun* same as **fixed costs**

ONS *abbreviation* Office for National Statistics

on-the-job training *noun* training given to workers at their place of work

OPEC *abbreviation* Organization of Petroleum Exporting Countries

open economy *noun* an economy which is open for commercial transactions with the rest of the world

open-ended credit *noun* same as **revolving loans**

opening price *noun* the price at the start of the day's trading on the Stock Exchange

open-market operations *plural noun* the sale or purchase of government stock by ordinary investors on the financial markets. If they purchase government stock then money is transferred from the private sector to the government, so reducing money supply; governments use such sales as a means of influencing money supply.

operating costs, operating expenses *plural noun* the costs of production, selling and administration incurred during normal trading. Also called **operating expenses, running costs**

operating earnings *plural noun* same as **operating income**

operating expenses *plural noun* same as **operating costs**

operating income, operating profit *noun* the profit made by a company in its usual business (usually calculated after tax has been paid). Also called **operating earnings**

opportunism *noun* trying to use the terms of a contract to your own advantage

opportunity cost *noun* the cost of a scarce factor of production used to produce a good or service, as opposed to another which could have been used instead of the one adopted. Also called **economic cost**

optimal-growth theory *noun* the analysis of economic growth and its effect on social welfare. The best position is one where the rate of saving equals the rate of profit.

optimisation, optimising *noun* the choice of something which gives the best results, as shown by the Phillips curve which shows that as unemployment rises so inflation decreases

optimum *adjective* which is the best result coming from a certain series of circumstances

optimum tariff *noun* a tariff which serves to increase the wealth of the nation which imposes it

option *noun* on the Stock Exchange, the action of giving someone the right to buy or sell something such as a security, a financial instrument or a commodity at a certain price on a certain date

order-driven system, order-driven market *noun* a price system on a stock exchange in which prices vary according to the level of orders (as opposed to a quote-driven system which concentrates on high turnover shares)

ordinal utility *noun* the measurement of the satisfaction which a consumer gets from a good or service, seen in comparison with another measurement. It is opposed to cardinal utility which assumes that the satisfaction can be accurately measured on its own.

ordinary least squares *noun* the simplest calculation in regression analysis where a single independent variable is plotted against a single dependent variable and the squares of the deviations are at a minimum. Abbreviation **OLS**

ordinary shares *plural noun* shares in a company which have no special bonuses or restrictions (NOTE: The US term is **common stock**.)

ordinate *noun* the vertical value on a graph (the horizontal value is the x-value or abscissa). Also called **y-value**

organic growth *noun* same as **internal growth**

organisational slack *noun* resources used in an organisation which are more than necessary for the work involved. Such resources, like excess staff, build up over a period of time, but can be cut back easily when necessary without losing too much production capacity.

organisation theory *noun* the study of the structure and function of decision-making in organisations

organised labour *noun* workers who are members of trade unions which represent them and defend their interests

Organisation for Economic Co-operation and Development *noun* an organisation of 29 industrialised countries, aimed at encouraging international trade, wealth and employment in member countries. Abbreviation **OECD**

Organization of Petroleum Exporting Countries *noun* a group of major countries who are producers and exporters of oil. Abbreviation **OPEC**

origin *noun* a zero point on a graph

outlier *noun* a statistic which is very different from other data gathered, and which may needed to be disregarded

output *noun* the amount which a company or a person or a machine produces

output budgeting *noun* a type of budgeting which is classified according to outputs as opposed to inputs, i.e. goods and services produced rather than the costs of raw materials or labour involved in producing the goods or services

output gap *noun* same as **deflationary gap**

output method *noun* a way of calculating domestic product by totalising the value of net outputs, as opposed to the income method, which totalises the value of net income

output per hour, output per man-hour, output per hour worked *noun* the amount produced in one hour

outside director *noun* same as **non-executive director**

outside money *noun* same as **exogenous money**

outsourcing *noun* the practice of obtaining services from specialist bureaux or other companies, rather than employing full-time members of staff to provide them

over-capacity working *noun* a situation of working above normal capacity. This can happen at peak periods and can be achieved by means such as overtime working or adding more shifts.

overdraft *noun* GB an amount of money which a company or person can withdraw from a bank account with the bank's permission, and which is more than there is in the account (NOTE: The US term is **overdraft protection**.)

overfunding *noun* a situation in which the government borrows more money than it needs for expenditure, by selling too much government stock

overhead costs, overhead expenses *plural noun* the costs of the day-to-day running of a business or of part of a business (i.e. any cost, other than the cost of the goods offered for sale). Also called **indirect costs**

overheating *noun* a rise in industrial activity in an economy, leading to a rise in inflation. The economy is then said to be overheated.

overmanning *noun* the situation of having more workers than are needed to do a company's work

overseas bank *noun* a UK bank which mainly trades overseas

overseas investment *noun* same as **foreign investment**

overseas trade *noun* same as **foreign trade**

overshooting *noun* an adjustment in answer to a change in a country's economic condition which is greater than it need be, as when an exchange rate changes excessively after an external shock such as a change in oil prices

over-subscription *noun* a situation in which more shares in a new issue are subscribed for than are available

over-the-counter market *noun* a market in shares which are not listed on the Stock Exchange

overtime *noun* hours worked more than the normal working time. Such work is normally paid at a higher rate.

overtrading *noun* a situation in which a company increases sales and production too much and too quickly, so that it runs short of cash

over-valued currency *noun* a currency with an exchange rate which is too high to maintain the economy at its present level

ownership *noun* the act of owning something

own-label brand *noun* products specially packed for a store with the store's name on them

P

Paasche index *noun* a weighted index of prices developed by the German economist Hermann Paasche (1851–1925) in which the weights are given according to the latest data available. Also called **current-weighted index**

Pac-Man defence *noun* one of the ways in which a company can defend itself against a takeover bid, by bidding to take over the prospective purchaser

paid-up capital, paid-up share capital *noun* the amount of money paid for the issued capital shares. It does not include called up capital which has not yet been paid for.

P&L account *noun* same as **profit and loss account**

panel data *plural noun* data collected from a sample group repeatedly over a long period. It is more accurate than data taken from new sample groups each time.

paper gain *noun* same as **paper profit**

paper loss *noun* a loss made when an asset has fallen in value but has not been sold

paper profit *noun* a profit made when an asset has increased in value but has not been sold. Also called **paper gain, unrealised profit**

parabola *noun* a graph shaped like a U

paradox of thrift *noun* a situation, which occurs especially in a depressed economy, in which the more people save, the more the economy is depressed. Savings are only good if the result is invested in new product, and in a depression people may tend to save more than industry can invest.

paradox of value *noun* the fact that items which are rare and worth more in money terms are less useful than items which are plentiful and have a low money value (caviare and water, say). This shows that the price of something is determined by its scarcity rather than its usefulness.

paradox of voting *noun* the paradox that in a system of simple majority voting where individuals can choose between various alternatives, no single choice can come out as a preference. Also called **Condorcet's paradox**

parallel loan *noun* same as **back-to-back loan**

parallel money markets *plural noun* money markets where institutions such as banks, or organisations such as local authorities can lend or borrow money without having to go through the main money markets. Securities traded on the parallel markets include certificates of deposit and local authority bonds.

parameter *noun* a fixed limit

Pareto, Vilfredo (1848–1923) Italian economist who developed the theory of elites. He also showed that value is dependent on ordinal utility and not on cardinal utility as had been thought previously. He noted that income is distributed in the same way in all countries, no matter what tax regime is applied.

Pareto effect *noun* same as **Pareto's law**

Pareto optimality *noun* an situation in which the welfare of the community is at its maximum, and it is therefore impossible to increase the welfare of one individual without making another worse off. Also called **Pareto optimum**

Pareto-optimal redistribution *noun* the redistribution of wealth from one person to another which increases the satisfaction of both, as in the case of donations to charity

Pareto optimum *noun* same as **Pareto optimality**

Pareto's law *noun* the theory that incomes are distributed in the same way in all countries, whatever tax regime is in force; Pareto saw that a small percentage of a total is responsible for a large proportion of value or resources. Also called **Pareto effect, eighty/twenty law**

COMMENT: Also called the 80/20 law, because 80/20 is the normal ratio between majority and minority figures: so 20% of accounts produce 80% of turnover; 80% of GDP enriches 20% of the population, etc.

Paris Club *noun* the Group of Ten (so called because its first meeting was in Paris)

Parkinson's law *noun* a law, based on wide experience, that in business as in government the amount of work increases to fill the time available for it

partial adjustment *noun* a gradual adjustment by which only part of a discrepancy is adjusted during any one period, as when adjusting excessive labour costs through natural wastage rather than making workers redundant

partial derivative *noun* a derivative of a function which depends on more than one variable, when all the variables are fixed except for the particular variable which is being dealt with

partial equilibrium analysis, **partial equilibrium** *noun* the analysis of part of an economy without considering the effects that a change in this part may have on other parts which in turn may affect the sector being examined

participation rate *noun* the proportion of a group that is active in some way

partnership *noun* an unregistered business where two or more people (but not more than twenty) share the risks and profits according to a partnership agreement

partnership agreement *noun* a document which sets up a partnership, states what it is called, what the capital is, how much is contributed by each partner, the rights of each partner, profit-sharing ratios and the way the partnership may be dissolved in due course. Also called **articles of partnership**

part-time work, **part-time employment** *noun* work for part of a working day

par value *noun* same as **face value**

passive selling *noun* the practice of selling to a customer without any personal contact, as by advertising, as opposed to personal selling

patent *noun* an official document showing that a person has the exclusive right to make and sell an invention ■ *verb* to obtain a patent for an invention

paternalism *noun* a style of management in which the employer is overprotective towards the employees

pattern bargaining *noun* bargaining between unions and an employer in which the unions try to base their negotiations on past collective agreements made with employers

pay as you earn *noun* the main UK tax system, in which income tax is deducted from a salary before it is paid to the worker. Abbreviation **PAYE** (NOTE: The US term is **pay-as-you-go**.)

payback period *noun* **1.** the time taken for the total interest on an investment to equal the amount of the initial investment **2.** the period of time over which a loan is to be repaid

PAYE *abbreviation* pay as you earn

pay freeze *noun* a period when wages are not allowed to be increased

pay-off matrix *noun* a chart showing the different results for a player in a game which come from taking different decisions to those of the other player

payout ratio *noun* the dividend paid to shareholders shown as a percentage of the profits (NOTE: The opposite is **dividend cover**.)

payroll *noun* the list of people employed and paid by a company

payroll tax *noun* a tax on the people employed by a company

peace dividend *noun* money which becomes available for general government expenditure as defence spending is reduced following the ending of a war

peak *noun* a highest point, such as the highest point in a trading cycle or the highest point of customer demand for a service ■ *verb* to reach the highest point

peak-load pricing *noun* a method of pricing which charges more for a good or service supplied at peak times, and less for something supplied during off-peak periods. This applies to the supply of telephone services or electricity.

pendulum arbitration, pendular arbitration *noun* a method of arbitration in which each side makes a proposal, and the arbitrator chooses one of them, which then becomes binding on both parties

penetration pricing *noun* the giving of a product a low price to achieve market penetration

pension *noun* an amount of money paid regularly to someone who no longer works, paid either by the state or by a private company

pension fund *noun* a fund which receives contributions from employers and employees and which provides pensions for retired members of staff

PEP *abbreviation* personal equity plan

P/E ratio, PER *abbreviation* price/earnings ratio

per capita income *noun* the total national income divided by the number of population. It can be calculated more accurately by giving more weight to adults. Also called **income per capita, income per head**

per capita real GDP *noun* GDP calculated per adult member of the population. It is lower than per capita income when the country's income includes important revenue from investments abroad.

percentile, percentage point *noun* one of a series of ninety-nine figures below which a certain percentage of the total falls

perfect competition *noun* a hypothetical model of a market where all products of a particular type are identical, where there is complete information about market conditions available to buyers and sellers and complete freedom for sellers to enter or to leave the market. Also called **atomistic competition**

perfect market *noun* a hypothetical market where there is perfect competition

performance-related pay, performance pay *noun* pay which is linked to the employee's performance of their duties. Abbreviation **PRP**

peril point *noun* a term used by the Tariff Commission in the USA to indicate the point when lowering tariffs further would harm the domestic economy

perk *noun* same as **fringe benefit**

permanent income *noun* a person's estimate of his or her income over a considerable period of time in the future

permanent-income hypothesis *noun* the theory (proposed by Milton Friedman) that an individual's spending is not based on real disposable income, but on his or her estimates of whether the current income is likely to continue into the future. People base their consumption on what they consider their normal income, and try to maintain a fairly constant standard of living even though their incomes may vary considerably from month to month or from year to year. As a result, increases and decreases in income which people see as temporary have little effect on their consumption spending. According to this theory, consumption depends on what people expect to earn over a considerable period of time; they save during periods of high income and stop saving during periods of low income. This theory took the place of the relative-income hypothesis.

perpetuity *noun* same as **annuity**

perquisite *noun* same as **fringe benefit**

personal disposable income *noun* the income which an individual person has left to spend after deducting tax

personal distribution of income *noun* an analysis showing how income is divided among the population. If the population is divided into ten deciles, it can be shown what proportion of the total income is taken by each decile.

personal equity plan *noun* a government-backed scheme to encourage share-ownership and investment in industry. Individual taxpayers can each invest a certain amount of money in shares each year, and not pay tax on either the income or the capital gains, provided that the shares are held for a certain period of time. PEPs were replaced by ISAs in April 1999, but existing schemes will continue. There are several types of equity PEP: the single-company Pep, where only shares in one company are allowed, and the general Pep, where shares in several companies can be held or other types of investment can be made. Abbreviation **PEP**

personal income *noun* the income received by an individual person before tax is paid

Personal Investment Authority *noun* a self-regulatory body which regulates people such as financial advisers and insurance brokers who give financial advice or arrange financial services for clients. The PIA is now part of the FSA. Abbreviation **PIA**

personal loan *noun* a loan to a person for household or other personal use, not for business use

personal pension plan *noun* a pension plan which applies to one worker only, usually a self-employed person, not to a group. It is not connected to that person's employment or employer. Abbreviation **PPP**

personal sector *noun* one of the parts of the economy or the business organisation of a country, made up of individuals and their income and expenditure (as opposed to the corporate or public sectors)

personal selling *noun* selling to a customer by personal contact, either face to face or by telephone, as opposed to 'passive selling' by advertising

PERT *abbreviation* programme evaluation and review technique

PESC *abbreviation* Public Expenditure Survey Committee

petroleum revenue tax *noun* a UK tax on revenues from companies extracting oil from the North Sea. Abbreviation **PRT**

Phillips curve *noun* a graph showing the relationship between wage increases and unemployment plotted by the British economist A.W. Phillips (1914–1975). The theory is that low unemployment leads to higher wages, so that attempts by governments to reduce unemployment can result in higher inflation. ◆ **expectations-augmented Phillips curve**

physiocrats *plural noun* a group of French economists in the 18th century who believed that agriculture was the sole source of wealth. They favoured a laissez-faire system and were opposed to the mercantilists.

pi *noun* a Greek letter used in mathematics to indicated the quantity 3.14159. The Ancient Greeks calculated that the circumference of a circle was $2\pi r i$ (where ri is the radius) and that the area of a circle is $\pi r i^2$ but they were not able calculate an exact value for π. They knew it was slightly less than $31/7$. In fact, π does not have a finite value, being 3.14159… with a series of figures continuing to infinity.

PIA *abbreviation* Personal Investment Authority

piecework *noun* work for which workers are paid for the products produced or the piece of work done and not at an hourly rate. Usually there is a basic guaranteed minimum payment, but this is increased as the number of units produced increases.

pie chart, pie diagram *noun* a diagram in which information is shown as a circle cut up into sections of different sizes

Pigou, Arthur (1877–1959) a Cambridge economist who opposed the theories of Keynes. He believed that employment can be stimulated by the rise in value of money balances caused by a decline in prices.

Pigou effect *noun* a situation in which as real wealth increases so people spend more and this leads to a rise in employment. Also called **real balance effect**

placing *noun* the finding of a single buyer or a group of institutional buyers for a large number of shares in a new company or a company which is going public

placing a line of shares *noun* the finding of a purchaser for a block of shares which was overhanging the market

plain vanilla swap *noun* an interest rate swap in which a company with fixed-interest borrowings swaps them for the variable-rate interest borrowings of another company

planned economy *noun* same as **command economy**

Planning Programming Budgeting System *noun* a system of budgeting which is based on details of objectives, inputs used and outputs achieved. Abbreviation **PPBS**

Plc, PLC, plc *abbreviation* public limited company

plentitude *noun* the theory that in the new economy the more there is of something, the more value it has; so the more customers an internet shop has and the more products it sells, then the more money it will make. This is the opposite of old theories that value comes from scarcity and that things which are plentiful have little value.

ploughing back *noun* the investing of profits in the business (and not paying them out as dividends to the shareholders) by using them to buy new equipment or create new products

point *noun* a method of showing the change in an index by using the units in which the index is calculated, as opposed to a percentage system. If a stock exchange index moves from 3092 to 3062 it has lost 30 points or just under 1 per cent. If an index is calculated as a percentage, and moves from 3.5% to 4.5% then it is said to have gain one percentage point.

point elasticity *noun* the rate of change in response to a factor which has changed, measured at a certain point

point of inflexion, point of inflection *noun* the point on a graph where the values changes from plus to minus or vice versa

poison pill *noun* an action taken by a company to make itself less attractive to a potential takeover bid. In some cases, the officers of a company will vote themselves extremely high redundancy payments if a takeover is successful; or a company will borrow large amounts of money and give it away to the shareholders as dividends, so that the company has an unacceptably high level of borrowing.

policy instrument *noun* a government policy which is used to change the course of the economy, such as fiscal policy which affects tax, monetary policy which affects money supply, prices and incomes policy which tries influence the way producers, consumers and labour work

political economy *noun* the former name for what is now called economics

poll tax *noun* a tax which is levied equally on each person in a population

polluter-pays principle *noun* the principle that if pollution occurs, the person or company responsible should be required to pay for the consequences of the pollution and for avoiding it in future. Abbreviation **PPP**

pollution *noun* the presence of abnormally high concentrations of harmful substances in the environment, often put there by people

polynomial *noun* a mathematical expression involving the sum of terms where one or more variables are raised to a power and multiplied by a coefficient

population *noun* the number of people who live in a country or in a town

population trap *noun* a situation in which a country's economy cannot grow because its population is rising so fast that general poverty increases. The only solution is to reduce the increase in population by birth control.

portable pension, portable pension plan *noun* pension rights which a worker can take with him or her from one company to another on changing jobs

portfolio *noun* a group of loans, mortgages and investments all belonging to the same individual or company

portfolio theory *noun* the theoretical basis for managing a portfolio of investments (a mix of safe stocks and more risky ones giving a balanced income)

positional goods *plural noun* goods which are scarce and therefore valuable. They are literally irreplaceable, like works of art or beautiful views.

positive carry *noun* a deal where the cost of the finance is less than the return

positive economics *noun* the study of how an economy works in practice, as opposed to the theoretical study of how it should run in theory (normative economics)

positive-sum game *noun* in game theory, a game where the players all end up with more than they started, the total sum adding up to more than 100%. Compare **negative-sum game, zero-sum game**

positive time preference *noun* same as **time preference**

potential gross national product *noun* the total output which a country could achieve if it used all available factors of production

potential output *noun* the output which could be achieved using existing factors of production

pound *noun* the currency unit used in the UK, and in many other countries including Cyprus, Egypt, Lebanon, Malta and Syria

pound sterling *noun* ◊ **sterling**

poverty *noun* the situation in which an individual is not able to afford an adequate standard of living, i.e. not able to buy clothing, food or shelter. The level may vary from country to country.

poverty line *noun* the level of income below which an individual is not able to pay for his subsistence. It may vary from place to place.

poverty trap *noun* a situation in which an individual receiving means-tested benefits would not gain by having a better job (as he or she would lose the benefits)

PPBS *abbreviation* Planning Programming Budgeting System

PPP *abbreviation* **1.** personal pension plan **2.** polluter-pays principle **3.** purchasing-power parity

precautionary motive *noun* the motive for people or firms to hold money in case of emergencies, as opposed to the transactions motive where they hold money to use for some definite transaction in the future or the speculative motive where they hold money in the form of investments because they hope to make a capital gain

precautionary unemployment *noun* a form of unemployment which takes place when an unemployed person refuses a job offer because he or she thinks that a better offer will turn up in the near future. Also called **wait unemployment**

predatory pricing *noun* the policy of reducing prices as low as possible to try to get market share from weaker competitors

preferences *plural noun* the consumer's choice of goods or services to be bought or action to be carried out

preference shares *plural noun* shares (often with no voting rights) which receive their dividend before all other shares and which are repaid first (at face value) if the company is liquidated (NOTE: The US term is **preferred stock**.)

premium *noun* **1.** an amount paid to take out an insurance policy **2.** an amount above face value at which something such as a security sells

premium bond *noun* a UK government bond, part of the National Savings scheme, which pays no interest, but gives the owner the chance to win a monthly prize

premium offer *noun* a free gift offered to attract more customers, either attached to the product bought or given by a retailer on proof of purchase of a minimum quantity of goods

present value *noun* the value of something in the future, shown in current terms. If interest is running at 5% per annum, the sum of £100 will be worth £105 in one year's time; alternatively, £105 next year has a present value of £100.

pretax profit *noun* profit before tax has been calculated and deducted. Also called **profit before tax, profit on ordinary activities before tax**

price *noun* an amount of money which has to be paid to buy something ■ *verb* to ask an amount of money for something for sale

price ceiling *noun* the highest price which can be reached

price competition *noun* the attempt to compete in a market through lower prices

price controls *plural noun* legal measures to stop prices rising too fast

price-cutting war *noun* same as **price war**

price discrimination *noun* the action of selling the same good to different customers at different prices

price/earnings ratio *noun* the ratio between the market price of a share and the earnings per share calculated by dividing the market price by the earnings per share. The P/E ratio is an indication of the way investors think a company will perform in the future, as a high market price suggests that investors expect earnings to grow and this gives a high P/E figure; a low P/E figure implies that investors feel that earnings are not likely to rise. Also called **PE ratio**. Abbreviation **PER** (NOTE: The US term is **price/earnings multiple**.)

price effect *noun* the result of a change in price on a person's buying habits

price elasticity *noun* a situation where a change in price has the effect of causing a big change in demand

price-elasticity of demand *noun* a situation in which a change in price has the effect of causing a bigger change in demand

price-elasticity of supply *noun* a situation in which a change in price has the effect of causing a bigger change in quantities supplied. Also called **supply elasticity**

price fixing *noun* illegal agreements between companies to charge the same price for competing products

price index *noun* an index showing the increase (or more rarely, decrease) in prices of a range of goods and services over a certain period

price-inelastic demand *noun* demand which does change as much as the price of the good or service has changed

price leader *noun* a firm that uses its dominant position in a market to establish a price which other firms have to follow

price leadership *noun* the situation in which the producers model their prices on those of one leading producer

price level *noun* same as **average price level**

price mechanism *noun* a system in which decisions about production quantities and selling prices are determined by buyers and sellers in a market. Also called **market mechanism, price system**

prices and incomes policy *noun* a government policy which attempts to control prices and incomes, usually by statutory means such as by limiting price rises or wage rises to a certain percentage

price support *noun* government intervention to try to keep the price of farm produce at a certain level, so that producers can make a reasonable living

price system *noun* same as **price mechanism**

price taker *noun* a small trader on a market, whose actions will have no effect on the market as a whole and who trades at prices determined by the market

price theory *noun* the part of economics which deals with prices at a microeconomic level, in particular the theories of demand and supply

price-wage spiral *noun* same as **inflationary spiral**

price war *noun* a competition between companies to get a larger market share by cutting prices. Also called **price-cutting war**

primary market *noun* **1.** a market where companies can raise finance by issuing new shares, or by a flotation **2.** the market where new securities or bonds are issued (if the securities or bonds are resold, it is on the secondary market) ▶ also called **new issue market**

primary products *plural noun* products (such as wood, milk or fish) which are basic raw materials (as opposed to secondary products which have been processed from them)

primary sector *noun* the part of industry dealing with basic raw materials (such as coal, wood, or farm produce)

prime *noun* same as **prime rate**

prime cost *noun* a cost involved in producing a product, excluding overheads. Prime costs include direct material costs, direct labour costs and direct expenses. Because such costs can be avoided if output is reduced, they are also called avoidable costs.

prime rate *noun* the best rate of interest at which a US bank lends to its customers. This is not the same as the UK bank base rate, which is only a notional rate, as all bank loans in the UK are at a certain percentage point above the base rate. Also called **prime**

principal *noun* 1. a person or company that is represented by an agent 2. the initial amount of money invested or borrowed (NOTE: Do not confuse with **principle**.) ■ *adjective* greatest in number or importance

principal-agent problem, principal-agent theory *noun* the theory of the relationship between a principal and an agent, and the problems which can arise from this situation. The main problem occurs because the principal is unable to monitor what the agent does and the agent tends to act in his or her own interest, rather than that of the principal.

prisoners' dilemma *noun* in game theory, a situation which shows the advantages of parties making a binding agreement before taking a certain action: supposing that various prisoners are interrogated separately and each knows that if no one confesses then each will get off free then, if one confesses, he or she will receive a lesser sentence than the others who do not confess; the result is that all prisoners will confess because they hope to get lesser sentences. However if they all had agreed in advance that no one would confess, then they would all get off free. The conclusion is that if each party acts individually according to his or her own opinions, then the result is that all parties do worse than if they had acted in concert.

private costs *plural noun* costs which are incurred by individuals or firms which are paid for by the individual or firm

private enterprise *noun* businesses which are owned by private shareholders, not by the state

private good *noun* a good which must be paid for, and of which the supply is reduced as it is consumed; if a good is available to anyone, free of charge, then it is a 'public good'

private sector *noun* one of the parts of the economy of a country, which itself is made up of the corporate sector (firms owned by private shareholders), the personal sector (individuals and their income and expenditure), and the financial sector (banks and other institutions dealing in money)

private sector investment *noun* investment by private sector companies

private time preference rate, **private time preference** *noun* a higher discount rate applied by an individual to an investment project, because individuals tend to discount projects at a higher rate than society as a whole. Compare **social time preference rate**

privatisation, **privatization** *noun* the selling of a nationalised industry to private owners

probability *noun* the likelihood that something will happen, expressed mathematically. Most people calculate probability on the basis of past experience.

probability distribution *noun* the distribution of probability shown as a graph

problem children *plural noun* products which are not very profitable, and have a low market share and a high growth rate. Also called **question marks, wild cats**

procurement *noun* the activity of buying something

producer *noun* a person or company which supplies or sells goods or services. Also called **supplier**

producer good *noun* a good which is not used by the general public but which is used in the production of other goods. Many goods can be either consumer goods or producer goods, depending on their use: a saw sold to an individual to use in his house is a consumer good, but if it sold to a carpenter to use in the building trade then it is a producer good. Also called **intermediate good**

producer's surplus *noun* the amount by which the actual price of a product is more than the minimum which the producer would accept for it

product *noun* a manufactured item or a service for sale

product development *noun* improvement of an existing product line to meet the needs of the market

product differentiation *noun* the process of ensuring that a product has some unique features that distinguish it from competing ones

product innovation *noun* the production of a totally new product, rather than a new production process

production *noun* the making or manufacturing of goods for sale

production function *noun* a graph showing the relationship between the inputs (i.e. factors of production) and the resulting output of the firm

production possibility boundary, **production possibility frontier**, **production possibility curve** *noun* a graph showing the maximum production level of an economy, or the maximum production of a good or service, given the resources currently available to the producer. Also called **transformation curve**

production rate *noun* same as **rate of production**

productive efficiency *noun* a situation in which the most production is achieved from the resources available to the producer

productivity *noun* the rate of output per worker or per machine in a factory

productivity bargaining *noun* a type of wage bargaining which involves extra pay for extra productivity on the part of the worker

product life cycle *noun* stages in the life of a product in terms of sales and profitability, from its launch to its decline

product mix *noun* a group of quite different products made by the same company

product proliferation *noun* the introduction of a large number of products into a market by existing producers to prevent new entrants coming into the market

professional body *noun* an organisation which trains, validates and organises examinations for its members

profit *noun* money gained from a sale which is more than the money spent

profitability *noun* the amount of profit made, shown as a percentage of costs or sales revenue

profit after tax *noun* same as **net profit**

profit and loss account *noun* the accounts for a company with expenditure and income over a period of time, almost always one calendar year, balanced to show a final profit or loss. The balance sheet shows the state of a company's finances at a certain date. The profit and loss account shows the movements which have taken place since the end of the previous accounting period, i.e. since the last balance sheet. A profit and loss account can be drawn up either in the horizontal or in the vertical format; most are usually drawn up in the vertical format, as opposed to the more old-fashioned horizontal style, but both styles are allowed by the Companies Act. Also called **P&L account** (NOTE: The US term is **profit and loss statement** or **income statement**.)

profit before tax *noun* same as **pretax profit**

profit centre *noun* a person or department considered separately for the purposes of calculating a profit

profit margin *noun* the percentage difference between sales income and the cost of sales

profit maximisation *noun* a business strategy or policy based on achieving as high a profit as possible

profit motive *noun* the incentive to both firms and individuals to make as much profit as possible

profit on ordinary activities before tax *noun* same as **pretax profit**

profit-related pay *noun* pay which is related to the amount of profit a company makes. It can be tax free under a scheme agreed with the Inland Revenue.

profit-taking *noun* the selling of investments to realise the profit, rather than keeping them

programme evaluation and review technique *noun* a way of planning and controlling a large project, concentrating on scheduling and completion on time. Abbreviation **PERT**

progressive taxation *noun* a tax system in which the percentage of tax paid rises as the income rises. Also called **graduated taxation**. Compare **regressive taxation**

progress payment *noun* one of a series of payments made as each stage of a contract is completed

promissory note *noun* a document stating that someone promises to pay an amount of money on a certain date

propensity to consume *noun* the ratio between consumers' needs and their expenditure on goods

propensity to import *noun* the ratio between changes in the national income and changes in expenditure on imports

propensity to save *noun* the tendency of consumers to save instead of spending on consumer goods

propensity to tax *noun* the ratio between national income and the tax which is taken from it by a government

property *noun* land and buildings

property income from abroad *noun* income received from other countries in the form of dividends and rents, plus profits from companies working abroad

property rights *plural noun* the rights that an owner has over his or her property. These may be restricted under law.

proportional taxation *noun* a tax system in which the tax collected is in constant proportion to the income being taxed, i.e. as income rises so tax rises proportionately

pro rata *adjective, adverb* at a rate which varies according to the size or importance of something

protection *noun* the imposing of tariffs to protect domestic producers from competition from imports

protectionism *noun* a situation of protecting producers in the home country against foreign competitors by banning or taxing imports or by imposing import quotas

protective tariff *noun* a tariff which tries to ban imports to stop them competing with local products

provisions *noun* money that is set aside in a firm's accounts for an anticipated expenditure, as opposed to 'contingent liability' which is something which may or may not occur, but for which provision still has to be made in the accounts

proxy *noun* a document which gives someone the power to act on behalf of someone else

PRP *abbreviation* performance-related pay

PRT *abbreviation* petroleum revenue tax

PSBR *abbreviation* Public Sector Borrowing Requirement

PSDR *abbreviation* Public-Sector Debt Repayment

PSNCR *abbreviation* Public-Sector Net Cash Requirement

public choice theory, public choice *noun* the economic theory relating to how much choice the public has in the economic decisions taken by a government. The public does not have a single preference, but many different preferences which can not all be reflected in a government's economic policy.

public company *noun* same as **public limited company**

public debt *noun* the national debt, plus other debts for which the central government is ultimately responsible, such as the debts of nationalised industries

public expenditure *noun* the spending of money by the local or central government

Public Expenditure Survey Committee *noun* a UK government committee, composed of members from various departments and chaired by the Treasury, which examines and plans proposed public expenditure. Abbreviation **PESC**

public finance *noun* the raising of money by governments (by taxes or borrowing) and the spending of it

public good *noun* a good which can be supplied to everyone, and of which the supply does not diminish as they are being consumed. If a good can be bought or sold, then it is a private good.

public interest *noun* the good of the public in general, as opposed to individuals or groups

public limited company *noun* a company in which the general public can invest and whose shares and loan stock can usually be bought and sold on the Stock Exchange. Abbreviation **Plc, PLC, plc**. Also called **public company**

public ownership *noun* a situation in which the government owns a business, i.e. where an industry is nationalised, or controls a body which provides public services

public sector *noun* one of the parts of the economy or the business organisation of a country made up of the government and local authorities, nationalised industries and public services. Also called **government sector**

Public Sector Borrowing Requirement *noun* ◊ **Public-Sector Net Cash Requirement**. Abbreviation **PSBR**

Public-Sector Debt Repayment *noun* the amount of public debt which the government can repay when the economy is in surplus (i.e. when there is no PSNCR). Abbreviation **PSDR**

Public-Sector Net Cash Requirement *noun* the amount of money which a government has to borrow to pay for its own spending (i.e. the difference between the government's expenditure and its income). It was formerly called the Public-Sector Borrowing Requirement. Abbreviation **PSNCR**

public spending *noun* spending by the government or by local authorities

public utilities *plural noun* companies (such as electricity, gas or transport) which provide a service used by the whole community

public works *noun* government spending on a country's infrastructure, such as roads, railways, airports, hospitals and schools

pump priming *noun* government investment in new projects which it hopes will benefit the economy

purchase tax *noun* a tax paid on things which are bought

purchasing power *noun* a quantity of goods which can be bought by a group of people, or with an amount of money

purchasing-power parity *noun* an exchange rate shown as the ratio of the purchasing power of one currency against the purchasing power of another, relating to a basket of goods. Abbreviation **PPP**

purchasing-power parity theory *noun* the theory that exchange rates are in equilibrium when the amount purchased by one currency equals the amount purchased by another; in theory, if one currency buys more than another, then it is advantageous to exchange the second currency for the first so as to increase purchasing power, with result that the exchange rate would fall because of the influence of the market; in reality, exchange rates tend to be influenced by market dealers more than by comparative purchasing power

pure competition *noun* a hypothetical model of a market where all products of a particular type are identical, where there is complete information about market conditions available to buyers and sellers and complete freedom for sellers to enter or leave the market

put option *noun* the right to sell shares at a certain price at a certain date (NOTE: The opposite is **call option**.)

pyramiding *noun* the action of building up a major group by acquiring controlling interests in many different companies, each larger than the original company

Q

QC *abbreviation* **1.** queen's counsel **2.** quality circle

qualification of accounts *noun* same as **auditors' qualification**

qualifying days *plural noun* working days, up to a maximum of 28 weeks, for which statutory sick pay can be claimed

quality circle *noun* a group of workers in a company who meet to discuss quality controls and working practices. Abbreviation **QC**

quality control *noun* the process of making sure that the quality of a product is good

quango *noun* same as **quasi-autonomous non-government organisation** (NOTE: The plural is **quangos**.)

quantity demanded *noun* the amount of a good or service which consumers ask to purchase over a given period

quantity discount *noun* a discount given to a customer who buys large quantities of goods

quantity of money *noun* the amount of money in circulation in a country at a certain time, i.e. the money supply

quantity supplied *noun* the amount of a good or service which producers offer to supply over a given period

quantity theory of money *noun* the theory that a relationship exists between the quantity of money in the economy and the level of prices. This is the theory that control of the money supply means control of inflation.

quartile *noun* one of three figures below which 25%, 50% or 75% of a total falls, or each of the four groups separated by these figures. The word is used in relation to a frequency distribution, such as the amount of turnover attributable to each customer. It is more common to refer to the upper and lower quartiles (below 25% and above 75%) than to other quartiles.

quasi-autonomous non-government organisation *noun* a group of people appointed by a government with powers to deal with certain problems (such as the Race Relations Board or ACAS). Also called **quango**

quasi-money *noun* same as **near money**

quasi-rent *noun* same as **economic rent**

question marks *plural noun* same as **problem children**

quick ratio *noun* same as **liquidity ratio**

quota *noun* a fixed amount of something which is allowed

quota sample *noun* a sample which is preselected on the basis of specific criteria in order to best represent the universe

quota system *noun* a system in which imports or supplies are regulated by fixing maximum amounts. If distribution is arranged through a quota system, this means that distribution is arranged by allowing each distributor only a certain number of items.

quotation *noun* an estimate of how much something will cost

quoted company *noun* a company whose shares can be bought or sold on the Stock Exchange

quote-driven system, quote-driven market *noun* a price system on a stock market in which marketmakers quote a price for a stock (as opposed to an order-driven system in which prices vary according to the level of orders)

R

Ramsey, Frank (1903–1930) British philosopher based at the University of Cambridge who wrote on probability and taxation

Ramsey model *noun* a model applying calculus of variations to economics

Ramsey pricing *noun* a pricing rule by which price rises or increased taxes should be made on those goods for which there is the greatest demand, and not on those which are particularly price-sensitive. Also called **inverse elasticity rule**

R&D *abbreviation* research and development

random sample *noun* a sample for testing taken without any selection

random variable *noun* a variable whose value is the result of a random phenomenon, used in measuring interest within a random experiment

random walk *noun* the situation in which a variable changes in a way which is not dependent on previous changes. In sampling, it is a technique which allows for random selection within certain parameters set up by a non-random technique. It is also used to describe movements in share prices which cannot be forecast.

range *noun* a scale of items from a low point to a high one ■ *verb* to vary on a scale from a low point to a high one

range of a good *noun* the distance which customers are prepared to travel to buy a particular good or service

rank correlation *noun* the ratio between two variables shown by their order of rank, rather than by value

RAR *abbreviation* risk-adjusted return on capital

ratchet effect *noun* the effect of the highest previous variable on the current variable, as when wage demands are based on the previous highest wage offered. This is apparent when incomes rise, but when they fall, individuals have difficulty is getting accustomed to the fall and tend to continue spending at the same level.

rateable value *noun* formerly, the value of a commercial property as a basis for calculating local taxes

rate of exchange *noun* same as **exchange rate**

rate of inflation *noun* same as **inflation rate**

rate of interest *noun* same as **interest rate**

rate of production *noun* the speed at which items are made. Also called **production rate**

rate of return *noun* the amount of interest or dividend which comes from an investment, shown as a percentage of the money invested

rate-of-return regulation *noun* a regulation which prevents firms from earning a high rate of return, especially in the case of utilities

rate of technical substitution *noun* the increased production of one commodity which is achieved by reducing production of another. Abbreviation **RTS**

rate of unemployment *noun* same as **unemployment rate**

rates *plural noun* local UK taxes on property, formerly on all, now only on business premises

rate support grant *noun* an amount of money given by central government to a local authority to be spent in addition to money raised by the rates

ratio *noun* the proportion or quantity of something compared to something else. It is the figure which results from dividing one number by another.

rational behaviour, rational expectations *noun* the assumption that economic agents act rationally and must predict future trends on the basis of accurate information

rationalisation, rationalization *noun* the streamlining of something, making it more efficient (NOTE: The term is also used in a cynical way as a euphemism for mass redundancies.)

rational number *noun* a number which can be written as the ratio of two whole numbers. 0.333 can be written as the rational number 1/3.

rationing *noun* government action to allocate a product which is in short supply, rather than to allow market forces, such as price, to affect the distribution

Rawls, John (1921–2002) US mathematician and economist whose theories were based on the idea of a social contract, that basic social goods such as income, wealth, self-respect should be distributed equally through the population

Rawlsian social welfare *noun* the theory that social welfare should be based on the requirements of the poorest individuals in a population, and that the aim of welfare should be to make them better off. Social inequality is only acceptable in that it encourages the less well off to work harder to improve their position.

raw materials *plural noun* substances which have not been manufactured (such as wool, wood or sand)

RDA *abbreviation* Regional Development Agency

RDG *abbreviation* regional development grant

Reaganomics *plural noun* the policies of US President Ronald Reagan in the 1980s, which reduced taxes and social security support and increased the national budget deficit. By cutting taxes the Reagan administration hoped to increase employment, productivity and output, thus avoiding the need to increase the government deficit by borrowing.

real balance *noun* money supply divided by prices, as shown in a price index. This shows the amount of a good or service which could be bought with a certain amount of money.

real balance effect *noun* same as **Pigou effect**

real business cycle theory *noun* the theory that changes in the business cycle are the result of random shocks, such as a war or natural calamity, and not by the process of supply and demand

real earnings *plural noun* income which is available for spending after tax and other contributions have been deducted, corrected for inflation. Also called **real income, real wages**

real exchange rate *noun* an exchange rate shown in constant terms after taking inflation into account

real GDP *noun* GDP which has been adjusted for inflation

real GNP *noun* GNP which has been adjusted for inflation

real growth *noun* growth in an economy which is higher than the rate of inflation

real income, real wages *noun* same as **real earnings**

real interest rate *noun* the interest rate after taking inflation into account

real value *noun* the value of an investment which is kept the same (by index-linking, for example)

receiver *noun* a person appointed by a debenture holder to liquidate the assets of a company on his or her behalf

receivership *noun* the situation of being put into the hands of a receiver

recession *noun* a fall in trade or in the economy of a country. There are various ways of deciding if a recession is taking place: the usual one is when the GNP falls for two consecutive quarters.

recessionary gap *noun* the amount by which equilibrium GDP falls short of full-employment GDP. This leads to lower prices and the government has to take fiscal measures to correct the problem.

recipient country *noun* a poor country which receives aid from a richer country (the donor)

reciprocal *adjective* applying from one country or person or company to another and vice versa

reciprocal demand *noun* the demand of one country for goods from another, and vice versa. According to J. S. Mill, terms of trade between two countries are established according to the level of demand for each other's goods (this is called the equation of international demand).

reciprocal holdings *plural noun* a situation in which two companies own shares in each other to prevent takeover bids

reciprocal trade *noun* trade between two countries

reciprocity *noun* an agreement between two countries to give each other similar terms of trade, which are not applied to other countries. It implies that the two countries treat each other's citizens as they would their own.

recognised investment exchange *noun* a stock exchange, futures exchange or commodity exchange recognised by the FSA. Abbreviation **RIE**

recognised professional body *noun* a professional body which is in charge of the regulation of the conduct of its members and is recognised by the FSA. Abbreviation **RPB**

recognition lag *noun* the time it takes for policymakers to recognise the existence of a boom or a slump, or to recognise that an economic shock has taken place

recommendation *noun* a type of EU legislation which has no binding force

recommended retail price *noun* the price which a manufacturer suggests a product should be sold at on the retail market, though often reduced by the retailer. Abbreviation **RRP**. Also called **administered price, manufacturer's recommended price**

recovery *noun* **1.** the regaining of something apparently lost **2.** the movement upwards of shares or of the economy

recovery share *noun* a share which is likely to go up in value because the company's performance is improving

recursive model *noun* a model in which the current values of a variable affect the current values of another, while the previous values of the second variable have already affected the current values of the first

recycling *noun* the processing of waste material so that it can be used again, especially common in dealing with waste glass, paper or metal

redeem *verb* **1.** to buy back an item given as security on a loan **2.** to exchange something such as a security or voucher for money

redeemable security *noun* a financial security which can be redeemed at its face value at a certain date in the future

redemption date *noun* the date on which something such as a loan is due to be repaid

redemption value *noun* the value of a security when redeemed

redemption yield *noun* the yield on a security including interest and its redemption value

redeployment of labour *noun* the moving of workers from one place of work to another or from one job to another

rediscount *verb* to discount a bill of exchange which has already been discounted by a commercial bank

redistribution of income *noun* the principle that a government should aim to take wealth from the rich and give it to the poor. It is achieved by taxing the rich and giving welfare payments to the poor.

redlining *noun* the illegal practice of discriminating against prospective borrowers because of the area of the town in which they live

reduced form *noun* a form of an equation where endogenous variables are only shown as functions of exogenous variables

reducing balance depreciation *noun* a method of depreciating assets, in which the asset is depreciated at a constant percentage of its cost each year

redundancy *noun* the dismissal of a person whose skills are no longer needed

redundancy payment *noun* a payment made to a worker to compensate for losing his or her job

reflate *verb* to stimulate an economy

reflation *noun* the act of stimulating the economy by increasing the money supply or by reducing taxes

reflationary policy *noun* a policy which aims to stimulate economic activity. Such a policy can be fiscal, by reducing the level of taxation, or monetary such as increasing government spending.

refusal to supply *noun* the action of producers who refuse to supply an agent with a product, either because they do not want to supply agents who stock the products of a rival firm, because they are not sure that the agent can handle the product properly or because they do not believe the agent can pay for the product

regional aid *noun* aid to a certain region which has economic problems, given by a central government or a regional authority such as the EU

Regional Development Agency *noun* a government body dealing with the economic development of a certain region. There are several of them in different parts of the UK, and in many other countries such as Australia or Canada. Abbreviation **RDA**

regional development grant *noun* a grant given to encourage a business to establish itself in a certain part of the country. Abbreviation **RDG**

regional policy *noun* the policy of a central government towards the regions of the country, by which it hopes to encourage economic development and raise the standard of living in certain deprived regions

regional selective assistance aid given to assisted areas under EU legislation. Abbreviation **RSA**

registered company *noun* a company which has been officially set up and registered with the Registrar of Companies

registered unemployed *plural noun* people who have no jobs, are registered for unemployment benefit and are actively looking for work

Registrar of Companies *noun* a government official whose duty is to ensure that companies are properly registered, and that, when registered, they file accounts and other information correctly. The Registrar of Companies is in charge of the Companies Registration Office or Companies House.

Registrar of Friendly Societies *noun* formerly, a government official whose duty was to oversee the running of friendly societies. In the UK, this duty is now carried out by the FSA, but it still exists in many other countries.

regression analysis, regression model *noun* a method of discovering the relationship between one variable and any number of other variables giving a coefficient by which forecasts can be made. The technique is used by statisticians to forecast the way in which something will behave.

regressive taxation *noun* a taxation system in which tax gets proportionately less as income rises. This includes single sum taxes, such as a poll tax, which form a smaller proportion of an individual's income as his or her income rises. Compare **progressive taxation**

regulation *noun* **1.** the act of making sure that something will work well, especially the control of services such as transport or financial services by a central government **2.** a rule or law to make sure that something will work well **3.** a rule laid down by the Council of Ministers or Commission of the European Union which is of general application, binding in its entirety and applies directly to all member states

Regulation S-X *noun* the rule of the US Securities and Exchange Commission which regulates annual reports from companies

regulator *noun* a person who sees that members of an industry follow government regulations

regulatory agency *noun* an organisation which sees that members of an industry follow government regulations

regulatory capture *noun* the general trend for independent regulators to side with the interests of the industry they are supposed to regulate rather than with the interests of the general public or the consumers whom they are supposed to protect

reinsurance *noun* insurance where a second insurer (the reinsurer) agrees to cover part of the risk insured by the first insurer

relative dispersion *noun* same as **coefficient of variation**

relative-income hypothesis *noun* the theory that people are more interested in keeping their living standards up to a level which is relative to the standards of people around them or to the standard they enjoyed previously rather than looking for an absolute increase in income. This hypothesis was superseded by the permanent-income hypothesis of Milton Friedman.

relative prices *plural noun* prices of goods or services or factors of production, seen in relation to each other. They figure in indifference curves and isocost curves.

relativities *plural noun* comparisons between the salaries of different groups of workers in different firms

renewable energy *noun* energy from the sun, wind, waves, tides or geothermal deposits or from burning waste, none of which uses up fossil fuel reserves

renewable resources *plural noun* resources such as forests which can be replaced by natural environmental processes in a reasonable short period of time

rent *noun* an amount of money paid to use an office or house or factory for a period of time ■ *verb* to pay money to use something for a period of time

rent control *noun* the regulation of rents by the government

rent gradient *noun* the rent of buildings or land shown as a proportion of the distance they are situated from a town centre. Traditionally, rents go down the further you are from a city centre, but with the decline of inner city areas and the rise in importance of suburbs this may no long hold true.

rentier *noun* a person whose income derives from rents or interest, and who does not earn an income from employment

rent review *noun* an increase in rents which is carried out during the term of a lease. Most leases allow for rents to be reviewed every three or five years.

rent seeking *noun* the act of trying to improve personal income at the expense of someone else, rather than by increased work or productivity

repeated game *noun* a game where the same players play more than once, and so gradually learn their opponents' strategies

replacement cost *noun* the cost of purchasing an item to replace an existing asset. Also called **cost of replacement**

replacement cost accounting *noun* a method of accounting in which assets are valued at the amount it would cost to replace them, rather than at the original cost. Also called **current cost accounting**. Compare **historical cost accounting**

replacement cost depreciation *noun* depreciation based on the actual cost of replacing the asset in the current year

replacement investment *noun* investment in new assets to replace old ones

replacement rate *noun* the proportion of an organisation's workforce which is replaced every year

replacement ratio *noun* the ratio between the total income of an unemployed person (including benefits and allowing for rent) and the income he or she should earn if employed. If the ratio is high, then it acts as a disincentive to seeking employment.

repo *noun* same as **repurchase agreement** (NOTE: The plural is **repos**.)

repo interest rate *noun* the interest charged by a central bank to purchasers of Treasury bills at discount

representative firm *noun* a theoretical firm which is taken to be the average for an industry

repressed inflation *noun* a situation in which there is excess demand for goods and services which could lead to inflation if prices were not controlled. The effect of this is to keep the goods in short supply and encourage a black market.

repurchase agreement *noun* an agreement by which a bank agrees to buy something and sell it back later (in effect, giving a cash loan to the seller). This is used especially to raise short-term finance.

required reserves *plural noun* reserves which a US bank is required to hold in cash in its vaults or as deposit with the Federal Reserve. Compare **excess reserves**

resale price maintenance *noun* a system in which the price for an item is fixed by the manufacturer and the retailer is not allowed to sell it for a lower price. Abbreviation **RPM**

Resale Prices Acts 1964, 1976 *plural noun* UK Acts of Parliament which prevent suppliers from imposing resale price maintenance. Under these acts, it is unlawful for a supplier of goods to make it a condition of supply that its goods will not be sold below a specified price, or to notify dealers of a price stated or calculated to be understood as a minimum price.

research and development *noun* scientific investigation which leads to making new products or improving existing products. Accounting standards divide research costs into (i) applied research, which is the cost of research leading to a specific aim, and (ii) basic, or pure, research, which is research carried out without a specific aim in mind: these costs are written off in the year in which they are incurred. Development costs are the costs of making the commercial products based on the research and may be deferred and matched against future revenues. Abbreviation **R&D**

reserve asset ratio *noun* liquid assets shown as a percentage of liabilities. Also called **reserve ratio**

reserve base *noun* the total of all the reserves in a central banking system

reserve currency *noun* a strong currency used in international finance, held by other countries to support their own weaker currencies

reserve ratio *noun* same as **reserve asset ratio**

reserve requirements *plural noun* the proportion of bank deposits which a bank is required by law to keep in cash or on deposit with a central bank

reserves *plural noun* cash which a bank holds in its vaults or, in the USA, on deposit with the Federal Reserve

reserve tranche *noun* a part (25%) of the quota available to any IMF member which can be drawn on demand without the IMF imposing any conditions

residual *adjective* remaining after everything else has gone

residual unemployment *noun* unemployment among people who are not capable of doing the work available even in times of full employment

resource allocation *noun* the allocation of scarce resources (i.e. factors of production) to certain sectors of the economy which can utilise them most efficiently

resources *plural noun* inputs, such as the factors of production, which can be used effectively to produce a good or service. Natural resources are those resources which exist in the form of raw materials; human resources are the workforce considered as a factor of production.

restraint of trade *noun* a situation in which a worker is not allowed to use his or her knowledge in another company on changing jobs

Restrictive Practices Court *noun* formerly, a UK tribunal which oversaw competition policy. It is now replaced by the Competition Commission. Abbreviation **RPC**

restrictive trade agreement *noun* an agreement between different producers on prices and discounts which has the effect of removing competition from a market

Restrictive Trade Practices Acts 1956, 1968, 1976 *plural noun* former UK legislation which regulated competition, now replaced by Competition Act 1998

retail *noun* the sale of small quantities of goods to ordinary customers ■ *adverb* in small quantities to ordinary customers ■ *verb* to sell small quantities of goods to ordinary customers

retail banking *noun* normal banking services provided for customers by the main high street banks (as opposed to wholesale banking)

retailer *noun* a person who runs a retail business, or a retail,business itself, which sells goods direct to the public

retailer number *noun* the number of the retailer, printed at the top of the report slip when depositing credit card payments

retail investor *noun* a private investor, as opposed to an institutional investor

retail outlet *noun* a shop which sells goods to the general public

retail price *noun* the price at which the retailer sells to the final consumer

retail price index, retail prices index *noun* an index showing how prices of consumer goods have increased or decreased over a period of time. In the UK, the RPI is calculated on a series of essential goods and services. It includes both VAT and mortgage interest. The US equivalent is the Consumer Price Index. Abbreviation **RPI**

retained earnings, retained income, retained profit, retentions *plural noun* profit which is not paid to the shareholders in the form of dividends, but is kept to be used for future development of the business

return on capital employed, return on assets, return on equity *noun* profit shown as a percentage of the total capital invested in a business. Abbreviation **ROCE, ROA, ROE**

return on investment *noun* the relationship between profit and money invested in a project or company, usually expressed as a percentage. Abbreviation **ROI**

returns to scale *plural noun* the relationship between output and the factors of production which go into its production. If a factor of production increases and output increases less in proportion, this is called decreasing returns to scale; if output increases in exact proportion, this is called constant returns to scale and if output increases more than the input this is called increasing returns to scale.

revaluation, revaluing *noun* **1.** a method of calculating the depreciation of assets, by which the asset is depreciated by the difference in its value at the end of the year over its value at the beginning of the year (used only for small items, and under historical cost principles) **2.** the increasing of the value of a currency

revealed preference *noun* the theory that demand can be calculated from the preferences of customers. These depend on information about the customers' spending patterns faced with varying income or prices, together with the assumption that customers will act rationally when making the decision to purchase .

revenue *noun* money received by a firm

revenue-neutral policy *noun* a policy which has no effect on overall government revenue

revenue reserves *plural noun* retained earnings which are shown in the company's balance sheet as part of the shareholders' funds and are set aside to use to continue to pay dividends even if the company makes a loss. Also called **company reserves**

reverse takeover *noun* a takeover in which the company that has been taken over ends up running the company which has bought it

reverse yield gap *noun* the situation in which the returns on gilt edged securities (i.e. government stock) are higher than on equities (ordinary shares). This can occur during periods of high inflation because equities are supposed to provide a hedge against inflation; under normal conditions the yield on equities is usually higher than that of gilts to compensate for the risk involved.

revolving loans, revolving credit *plural noun* a system where someone can borrow money at any time up to an agreed amount, and continue to borrow while still paying off the original loan. Also called **open-ended credit**

Ricardian equivalence *noun* Ricardo's tentative theory that private individuals see the effect of government borrowing as a question of future taxation, which therefore has the same effect as if the government were to impose taxes instead of borrowing

Ricardo, David (1772–1823) successful English stockbroker who retired to write on economics, in particular on the theory of the distribution of goods to various classes of society, basing himself mainly on agricultural produce. He showed that increasing factors of production led to increased output until it reached a certain level, after which output fell proportionately (the law of diminishing returns). He also elaborated the theory of comparative costs as the basis for international trade (that goods will only be sold abroad if they are cheaper or need fewer units of a factor of production to produce than locally produced goods).

RIE *abbreviation* recognised investment exchange

rights issue *noun* the giving of shareholders the right to buy new shares at a lower price (NOTE: The US term is **rights offering**.)

risk *noun* possible harm or chance of danger

risk-adjusted return on capital *noun* comparisons of returns on different investments, which take risk into account, so that the return on safer investments is rated more highly. Abbreviation **RAR**

risk analysis *noun* an analysis of how much can be lost and gained through various marketing strategies

risk aversion *noun* a situation in which a higher value is given to something which is more certain than another. When investing in equities, the investor will expect a lower return in exchange for lower risk, while riskier investments will give higher returns.

risk capital *noun* same as **venture capital**

risk premium *noun* an extra payment (increased dividend or higher than usual profits) associated with more risky investments

ROA *abbreviation* return on assets

ROCE *abbreviation* return on capital employed

ROE *abbreviation* return on equity

ROI *abbreviation* return on investment

rolling account, rolling settlement *noun* a US system in which there are no fixed account days, but stock exchange transactions are paid at a fixed period after each transaction has taken place (as opposed to the British system, where an account day is fixed each month)

rollover *noun* extension of credit or of the period of a loan, though not necessarily on the same terms as previously

root *noun* a fractional power of a number

rounding *noun* the action of showing figures with fewer decimal places than they should have, to give a whole unit result. Normally figures below .5 are rounded down to the nearest whole figure below, and figures above .5 are rounded up.

rounding error *noun* an error which occurs when figures are rounded up or down

royalties, royalty *noun* money paid to an inventor, writer or the owner of land for the right to use his or her property. It is usually a certain percentage of sales, or a certain amount per sale.

RPB *abbreviation* recognised professional body

RPC *abbreviation* Restrictive Practices Court

RPI *abbreviation* retail price index

RPM *abbreviation* resale price maintenance

RRP *abbreviation* recommended retail price

RSA *abbreviation* regional selective assistance

RTS *abbreviation* rate of technical substitution

rule of thumb *noun* an easily remembered way of doing a simple calculation, such as calculating that a pound is half a kilo

rules of origin *plural noun* same as **local content rule**

runaway inflation *noun* same as **galloping inflation**

running costs *plural noun* same as **operating costs**

running yield *noun* the yield on fixed interest securities, where the interest is shown as a percentage of the price paid

Rybczynski theorem *noun* a theory developed by the Polish-British economist Tadeusz Rybczynski (1923–98) that when considering an economy with two factors of production contributing to two goods, with constant returns to scale, if the input of one factor is increased the output of the good which uses that factor will increase while the output of the other good which uses the other (constant) factor will decrease

S

sacking *noun* the dismissal of a worker from a job

saddle point *noun* a position of partially unstable equilibrium, i.e. an equilibrium which is stable at some points and unstable at others

safety margin *noun* an amount of time or space allowed for something to be safe

salary *noun* a payment for work made to an employee with a contract of employment, usually made monthly and paid directly into the employee's bank account or by cheque

sale and lease-back *noun* the situation in which a company sells a property to raise cash and then leases it back from the purchaser

sales mix profit variance *noun* the difference in profit from budget caused by selling a non-standard mix of products

sales promotion and merchandising *noun* promotional and sales techniques aimed at short-term increases in sales, such as free gifts, competitions and price discounts

sales revenue *noun* US income from sales of goods or services (NOTE: The UK term is **turnover**.)

sales tax *noun* a tax which is paid on each item sold (and is collected when the purchase is made). Also called **turnover tax**

sales volume *noun* the amount of sales of goods or services by a company (NOTE: The UK term is **turnover**.)

sales volume profit variance *noun* the difference in profits from a budget caused by selling more or less than the forecast number of units, where it is assumed that sales price and production costs are as planned

salvage value *noun* the value of an asset if sold for scrap

sample *noun* a small group or portion taken to show what a larger group or product is like ■ *verb* to examine or use a small group or portion to show what the whole is like

Samuelson, Paul (1915–) US economist, Nobel prizewinner for Economics 1970. ◊ **Stolper-Samuelson theorem**

S&P *abbreviation* Standard and Poor's

S&P 500 *abbreviation* Standard and Poor's 500-stock index

satisficing *noun* a situation or policy of making satisfactory profits and maintaining an acceptable market share rather than of maximising profits at all costs

saturation point *noun* a point where there cannot be any further increase in sales of a product in a certain market

save-as-you-earn *noun* a UK scheme in which workers can save money regularly by having it deducted automatically from their wages and invested in National Savings. Abbreviation **SAYE**

savings *plural noun* money saved (i.e. not spent), including money in savings accounts and also money invested in securities

savings account *noun* a bank account where you can put money in regularly and which pays interest, often at a higher rate than a deposit account

savings and loan, savings and loan association *noun* in the USA, a financial association that accepts and pays interest on deposits from investors and lends money to people who are buying property. The loans are in the form of mortgages on the security of the property being bought. Due to deregulation of interest rates in 1980, many S&Ls found that they were forced to raise interest on deposits to current market rates in order to secure funds, while at the same time they still were charging low fixed-interest rates on the mortgages granted to borrowers. This created considerable problems and many S&Ls had to be rescued by the Federal government. Abbreviation **S&L**. Also called **thrift** (NOTE: The UK term is **building society**.)

savings bank *noun* a bank where investors can deposit small sums of money and receive interest on it

savings bond *noun* in the USA, a document showing that money has been invested in a government savings scheme. Interest on US savings bonds is tax exempt. (NOTE: The UK term is **savings certificate**.)

savings certificate *noun* a document showing that money has been invested in a government savings scheme. UK savings certificates give an interest which is not taxable. (NOTE: The US term is **savings bond**.)

savings function *noun* the relationship between an individual's total savings and his or her income

savings ratio *noun* the proportion of an individual's income which is saved

Say, Jean-Baptiste (1767–1832) French economist who developed the theory of the factors of production (land, labour and capital), and the theory of the market which was criticised by Keynes. He proposed that total demand in a market cannot be more or less than total supply – the basis of laissez-faire economics.

SAYE *abbreviation* save-as-you-earn

Say's law *noun* the theory that supply will create demand, or that products are paid for by other products. Supply-side economists believe that stimulating the supply will create a demand and lead to an increase in economic activity.

SBU *abbreviation* strategic business unit

scarce currency *noun* same as **hard currency**

scarcity *noun* a situation in which the demand for something exceeds the supply. This can apply to anything from consumer goods or to raw materials.

scarcity value *noun* the value of something which is worth a lot because it is rare and there is a large demand for it

scatter diagram *noun* a chart where points are plotted according to two sets of variables to see if a pattern exists

Schedule A *noun* the schedule to the Finance Acts under which tax is charged on income from land or buildings

Schedule B *noun* the schedule to the Finance Acts under which tax is charged on income from woodlands

Schedule C *noun* the schedule to the Finance Acts under which tax is charged on profits from government stock

Schedule D *noun* the schedule to the Finance Acts under which tax is charged on income from trades, professions, interest and other earnings which do not come from employment, divided into six categories (or cases)

Schedule E *noun* the schedule to the Finance Acts under which tax is charged on pensions, wages and salaries from employment (including directors' fees)

Schedule F *noun* the schedule to the Finance Acts under which tax is charged on income from dividends

scheme of arrangement *noun* an agreement between a company and its creditors whereby the creditors accept an agreed sum in settlement of their claim rather than force the company into insolvency. Also called **voluntary arrangement**

Schumpeter, Joseph (1883–1950) Austrian economist who emphasised the importance of entrepreneurship in driving forward economic change. ♦ **creative destruction**

screening *noun* the process or practice of considering a range of items or people and only selecting some

screwdriver operation *noun* a manufacturing operation in a country where there is no local content and all the materials and parts are imported and only put together in that country

scrip issue *noun* an issue of shares whereby a company transfers money from reserves to share capital and issues free extra shares to the shareholders. The value of the company remains the same, and the total market value of shareholders' shares remains the same, with the market price being adjusted to account for the new shares. Also called **free issue, capitalisation issue**

SDRs *abbreviation* special drawing rights

SEAQ *noun* a computerised information system giving details of current share prices and stock market transactions on the London Stock Exchange. Dealers list their offer and bid prices on SEAQ, and transactions are carried out on the basis of the information shown on the screen. Transactions are recorded on the SEAQ database in case of future disputes. Full form **Stock Exchange Automated Quotations system**

search unemployment *noun* same as **frictional unemployment**

seasonal unemployment *noun* unemployment which rises and falls according to the season

SEC *abbreviation* Securities and Exchange Commission

secondary action *noun* action by workers in a factory which is not directly connected with a strike, to prevent it from supplying a striking factory or receiving supplies from it

secondary bank *noun* a finance company which provides money for hire-purchase deals

secondary industry *noun* an industry which uses basic raw materials to produce manufactured goods

secondary market *noun* a market where existing securities are bought and sold again and again, as opposed to a primary market, where new issues are launched

secondary picketing *noun* the picketing by striking workers of a factory which is not the one with which they are in direct dispute, often to prevent it from supplying the striking factory or receiving supplies from it

secondary products *plural noun* products which have been processed from raw materials (as opposed to primary products)

secondary sector *noun* same as **industrial sector**

secondary strike *noun* a strike by workers in a factory which is not directly connected with an existing strike, to prevent it from supplying a striking factory or receiving supplies from it

second best *noun* the theory that when what is required for an optimum economic situation is not available, then aiming for a second-best solution may have important implications for trade policies and even government policies

secondhand *adjective, adverb* which has been owned by someone before

second-order conditions *plural noun* conditions for the value of a variable to be either maximum or minimum. Compare **first-order conditions**

secret reserves *plural noun* reserves which are illegally kept hidden in a company's balance sheet, as opposed to 'hidden reserves' which are simply not easy to identify

sector *noun* a part of the economy or the business organisation of a country. A country's economy is divided into the public sector (i.e. the government and local authorities), the foreign sector (i.e. companies or governments based outside the country) and the private sector, which itself is made up of the corporate sector (firms which trade), the personal sector (individuals and their income and expenditure) and the financial sector (banks and other institutions dealing in money).

secular stagnation *noun* a situation in which a country remains in the stagnation stage of a business cycle for a very long time. It can result from high taxes, hyperinflation, government regulations and corruption.

secular supply curve *noun* a curve which shows the relationship between the rate of labour force participation and real wages. It acts as an indicator of changes in a country's economy.

secular trend *noun* a change in the economy which takes place over a very long period of time, such as a century

secured loan *noun* a loan which is guaranteed by the borrower giving assets as security

securities *plural noun* **1.** investments in stocks, shares and money market instruments **2.** certificates to show that someone owns stocks or shares

Securities and Exchange Commission *noun* the official body which regulates the securities markets in the USA. It receives annual reports from companies, and these are regulated by Regulation S-X. Abbreviation **SEC**

Securities and Futures Authority *noun* in the UK, a self-regulatory organisation which regulates trading in shares and futures. It is now part of the FSA. Abbreviation **SFA**

Securities and Investments Board *noun* the former regulatory body which regulated the securities markets in the UK It has been superseded by the FSA. Abbreviation **SIB**

securitisation, securitization *noun* the process of making a loan or mortgage into a tradeable security by issuing a bill of exchange or other negotiable paper in place of the loan

security *noun* a stock, share or money market instrument

seigniorage *noun* same as **inflation tax**

Select Committee on Estimates *noun* a committee of the House of Commons which examines government public spending estimates to see if best value is being obtained

self-assessment *noun* a system where each taxpayer is required to fill in his or her tax return and calculate how much tax is owed for the period. Taxpayers in the UK are given a period of five months (6 April to 30 September) during which they can submit details of their income and allowances for the previous tax year (i.e. to 5 April) and get the local tax office to prepare their assessment for them. After that period, taxpayers must do the calculations themselves. Taxpayers may receive penalties in the form of fines, for late filing of tax returns.

self-employed *adjective* working for yourself and not being on the payroll of a company ■ *plural noun* those people working for themselves and not on the payroll of a company

self-financing *noun* the financing of development costs, purchase of capital assets and similar activities by a company from its own resources ■ *adjective* which finances development costs, purchase of capital assets and similar activities from its own resources

self-invested personal pension *noun* a form of personal pension plan where the individual member is able to direct the investment of the money he or she pays into the plan. Currently an individual can invest up to 17.5% of earnings up to the age of 35 and up to 40% of earnings if he or she is in the 61–74 age bracket. There is a maximum per annum contribution and the accumulated investments must be used to purchase an annuity before the member reaches the age of 75. Abbreviation **SIPP**

self-liquidating *adjective* referring to a loan which is liquidated in the course of time through the terms of the loan. This applies to loans such as bridging loans or hire-purchase agreements which are liquidated eventually as the capital is repaid.

self-regulating organisation *noun* same as **self-regulatory organisation**

self-regulation *noun* the regulation of an industry by itself, through a committee which issues a rulebook and makes sure that members of the industry follow the rules (as in the case of the regulation of the Stock Exchange by the Stock Exchange Council)

self-regulatory organisation *noun* an organisation which regulates the way in which its own members carry on their business, such as the Securities and Futures Authority (SFA). Abbreviation **SRO**

self-sufficiency *noun* the ability of a household or a country to exist on products produced by itself without the need to purchase supplies from elsewhere

seller's market *noun* a market where shares, commodities or products are sold at higher prices because there is less stock available than the buyers want (NOTE: The opposite is a **buyer's market**.)

selling costs, selling overhead *plural noun* an amount of money to be paid for expenditure such as advertising or reps' commissions which is involved in selling something

senior capital *noun* capital in the form of secured loans to a company. It is repaid before junior capital, such as equity capital, in the event of liquidation.

seniority practices *plural noun* the use of length of service as a criterion when making staff redundant

sensitivity analysis *noun* the analysis of the effect of changes in the estimated values used in a forecast on the final result of the forecast

separation of ownership from control *noun* a situation in which the owners of a business do not manage it or control it. This applies particularly in large publicly-owned companies where there are many shareholders, none of whom has a controlling interest. It can also apply to smaller family-owned companies where the business is run by managers. However, in the case of large companies important shareholders like investment trusts and pension funds can exert pressure on the management to run the company in a certain way. Also called **divorce of ownership from control**

sequestration *noun* the taking and keeping of property on the order of a court, especially seizing the property of someone who is in contempt of court

serial correlation *noun* the correlation between succeeding values of a variable. Also called **autocorrelation**

series *noun* a group of bonds or savings certificates issued over a period of time but all bearing the same interest (NOTE: The plural is **series**.)

SERPS *abbreviation* State Earnings-Related Pension Scheme

service *noun* a facility which provides help as opposed to goods

service contract *noun* a contract between a company and a director showing all the conditions of work

service industry *noun* an industry which does not produce raw materials or manufacture products but offers a service (such as banking, retailing or accountancy)

services *plural noun* **1.** the business of providing help in some form when it is needed (activities such as insurance or banking as opposed to the making or selling of goods) **2.** systems which provide members of the public with what they need, such as transport or hospitals

service sector *noun* the service industries taken as a whole

set-aside *noun* the use of a piece of formerly arable land for something else, such as allowing it to lie fallow, using it as woodland or for recreation

settlement *noun* the payment of an account; payment for shares bought, or delivery of share certificates

settlement day *noun* **1.** the day on which shares which have been bought must be paid for. On the London Stock Exchange the account period is three business days from the day of trade. **2.** in the USA, the day on which securities bought actually become the property of the purchaser

severance pay *noun* money paid as compensation to an employee who loses a job through no fault of his or her own

SFA *abbreviation* Securities and Futures Authority

shadow economy *noun* same as **black economy**

shadow price *noun* the price given to a good or service which has no market price. The value of air quality or pollution may have to be calculated as part of the environmental costs of making a product, even though there is no market price for them.

share *noun* one of many equal parts into which a company's capital is divided. The owners of shares are shareholders or, more formally, members. US English often used the word stock where UK English uses share.

share capital *noun* the value of the assets of a company held as shares, less its debts

share certificate *noun* a document proving that someone owns shares

shareholder *noun* a person who owns shares in a company. Shareholders are formally called members. (NOTE: The US term is **stockholder**.)

shareholders' equity *noun* same as **equity capital**

share index *noun* an index figure based on the current market price of certain selected shares on a stock exchange

share issue *noun* the selling of new shares in a company to the public

share of the market *noun* same as **market share**

share option *noun* the right to buy or sell shares at a certain price at a time in the future

share premium *noun* the amount to be paid above the nominal value of a share in order to buy it

share premium account *noun* a part of a company's reserves formed when the difference in share value is credited to the company's account when shares are issued at a price above par

share price *noun* the price of a share when traded on the Stock Exchange. This varies both with the quantity of shares traded and according to the demand for the shares.

share price index *noun* a figure based on the current market price of a certain group of shares on a stock exchange, such as the FT-Stock Exchange 100 Share Index

share register *noun* the list of shareholders in a company with their addresses

share split *noun* same as **bonus issue**

shark repellent *noun* action taken by a company to make itself less attractive to takeover bidders. Companies can take various courses of action to make themselves unattractive to raiders. The company's articles can be changed to make it necessary to have more than a simple majority of shares to acquire voting control; directors can be given contracts with golden parachute packages which would be extremely expensive to implement; the company can create vast amounts of debt and give cash to its shareholders as bonus payments.

shell company *noun* a company which does not trade, but exists only as a name with a quotation of the Stock Exchange. Shell companies are bought by private companies as a means of obtaining a quotation on the Stock Exchange without having to go through a flotation. (NOTE: The US term is **shell corporation**.)

Sherman Act 1890 *noun* the first anti-trust act in the USA, which prohibited monopolies and other constraints on trade

shift system, shift work *noun* a work system in a factory using shifts, i.e. with groups of workers who work for a period, and then are replaced by other groups

shock *noun* a sudden unforeseeable event, such as a war or natural calamity, which has an effect on a country's economy

shock effect *noun* the effect of a shock on an economy. It may not always be negative – the effect of the shock of a new technological breakthrough may be extremely beneficial.

shop price *noun* same as **retail price**

shop steward *noun* an elected trade union official who represents workers in day-to-day negotiations with the management

short-dated securities *plural noun* government stocks which mature in less than five years' time

short position *noun* a situation in which an investor sells short (i.e. sells forward shares which he or she does not own). Compare **long position**

short rate *noun* the rate of interest on short-dated securities. Compare **long rate**

short run *noun* a period of time which is so short that changes cannot be made to factors of production. This may vary from industry to industry. Compare **long run**

short-run cost-curve *noun* a curve showing the relationship between the cost of producing something and the actual output, given the firm's actual level of fixed assets. In this case it is not possible to adjust many of the inputs.

short-term interest rates *noun* interest rates which apply for a short period (i.e. less than 12 months)

short-termism *noun* the practice of taking a short-term view of the market, i.e. not planning for a long-term investment

short-time working *noun* reduction of the hours of work as an alternative to making workers redundant

shut-down price *noun* the price for a good or service which is so low that the firm has to shut down

SIB *abbreviation* Securities and Investments Board

SIC *abbreviation* Standard Industrial Classification

sickness benefit *noun* a payment made by the government or private insurance to someone who is ill and cannot work

side-payment *noun* a payment made by a party to an agreement to another firm as an inducement to join in the agreement

sight deposit *noun* a bank deposit which can be withdrawn on demand

signalling *noun* the action of indicating something which may have no particular value in itself but which the person signalling wants to make known. It could be advertising a product, indicating a price change, obtaining a diploma or some other action.

simple interest *noun* interest calculated on the capital only, and not added to it

simulation *noun* the imitation of a real-life situation for training purposes

simultaneous equations *plural noun* two or more equations relating to the same two or more variables

Single A *noun* ◊ **A**

single currency *noun* a currency which is used by two or more countries. The euro is a single currency for most of the member states of the European Union.

Single European Act 1986 *noun* a rewriting of the basic European Community treaties, with the aim of creating a single European market by 1992

single European market *noun* same as **Internal Market**

single market *noun* a group of countries which trade together having reduced or removed all trade barriers between them; specifically, the EU Internal Market

sinking fund *noun* a fund built up out of amounts of money put aside regularly to meet a future need, such as the repayment of a loan

SIPP *abbreviation* self-invested personal pension

size distribution of firms *noun* the way in which firms of different sizes are represented in a certain industry. ♦ **concentration ratio**

skill *noun* the ability to do something because of training or natural ability

skimming price *noun* a high price which is fixed for a new product in order to achieve high short-term profits. The high price reflects the customer's appreciation of the added value of the new product, and will be reduced in due course as the product becomes established on the market.

slowdown *noun* a general reduction in a country's economic activity

slump *noun* **1.** a sudden and severe reduction in value **2.** a period of economic collapse with high unemployment and loss of trade. The world economic crisis of 1929–33 is known as the Slump. ∎ *verb* to reduce in value suddenly and severely

slumpflation *noun* situation in which a country experiences high inflation, high unemployment and below zero growth rates all at the same time

Slutsky equation *noun* an equation developed by the Russian mathematician Eugene Slutsky (1880–1948) which shows how a change in demand caused by a change in price can be divided into a substitution effect and a income effect

Slutsky theorem *noun* the theory that if a statistic converges almost surely or in probability to some constant, then any continuous function of that statistic also converges in the same manner to some function of that constant

small and medium-sized enterprises *plural noun* companies with a turnover of less than £11.2m and fewer than 250 employees. Abbreviation **SMEs**

small company *noun* a company with at least two of the following characteristics: turnover of less than £2.0m; fewer than 50 staff; net assets of less than £0.975m. Small companies are allowed to file modified accounts with Companies House.

SME *abbreviation* small and medium-sized enterprises

Smith, Adam (1723–1790) Scottish economist whose main work (the *Wealth of Nations* 1776) emphasised the importance of labour and the concept that the market was the driving force behind economic activity

Smithsonian Agreement 1971 *noun* an agreement between members of the IMF to try to reestablish a system of pegged exchange rates. It is so-called because the meeting was held in the Smithsonian Institute in Washington, DC.

Smithsonian parities *plural noun* the system of exchange rate parities agreed under the Smithsonian Agreement, by which the dollar was devalued and the dollar price of gold fixed. The parities only lasted a short time.

social accounting *noun* a method of presenting a country's national accounts on a per-sector basis, showing the trade achieved by each sector of the economy

social benefits *plural noun* benefits which come to the consumer as private benefits, as opposed to social costs

social capital *noun* the productive assets of a whole economy, including the infrastructure and the skills of the working population

Social Chapter *noun* a protocol to the Maastricht Treaty which commits signatory states to the promotion of employment, improved working conditions, dialogue between management and labour, development of human resources and the fight against exclusion

Social Charter *noun* same as **European Social Charter**

social costs *plural noun* costs which come to the consumer as private costs, as opposed to social benefits

socialism *noun* the idea that in a state the means of production, distribution and exchange should be controlled by the people, that the people should be cared for by the state and that wealth should be shared equally

social opportunity cost *noun* the opportunity cost to the society of making a certain good or service, at the expense of using the factor of production for a different good or service

social overhead capital *noun* same as **infrastructure**

social product *noun* same as **public good**

social security benefits *plural noun* money from contributions paid to the National Insurance scheme, provided by the government to people who need it. There are many benefits, such as those for single-parent families, disabled people and pensioners.

social services *plural noun* the department of a local or national government which provides services, such as health care, advice ormoney, for people who need help

social time preference rate, social time preference *noun* a lower discount rate applied to a long-term public-sector investment project, because society as a whole discounts long-term projects less than individuals do. Compare **private time preference rate**

social welfare *noun* the welfare of the society as a whole. It can be seen either as a general theoretical principle which applies to all members of society taken together as a group or, alternatively, it can be seen as the total of all satisfied preferences of individual members of the society.

social welfare function *noun* the way in which social welfare is constructed and relates between various members of society. It enables a choice to be made between different economic decisions on the basis of the welfare they bring to different individuals.

socio-economic groups *plural noun* groups in society divided according to income and position The UK socio-economic groups are: (1) senior managers, administrators, civil servants and professional people; (2) middle-ranking managers, administrators, civil servants and professional people; (3) junior managers, clerical staff; (4) workers with special skills and qualifications; (5) unskilled workers and manual workers; (6) pensioners, the unemployed and casual manual workers

soft currency *noun* the currency of a country with a weak economy, which is cheap to buy and difficult to exchange for other currencies (NOTE: The opposite is **hard currency**.)

soft landing *noun* a change in economic strategy to counteract inflation, which does not cause unemployment or a fall in the standard of living, and has only minor effects on the bulk of the population

soft loan *noun* a loan (from a company to an employee or from a government to a new business or to another government) at a very low rate of interest or with no interest payable at all

sole proprietor, sole trader *noun* a person who runs a business by himself or herself but has not registered it as a company

Solow economic growth model *noun* a theoretical growth model developed by Robert Solow (1924–), Nobel Prize for Economics 1987, which examines the problems of technological change in an economy; technological change and population growth together offset diminishing returns which occur as more capital is employed. Compare **Harrod-Domar growth model**

solvency *noun* the situation of being able to pay all your debts on the due date (NOTE: The opposite is **insolvency**.)

source and application of funds statement *noun* a statement in a company's annual accounts, showing where new funds came from during the year, and how they were used

sourcing *noun* the process of finding suppliers of goods or services. ♦ **outsourcing**

special deposits *noun* large sums of money which commercial banks have to deposit with the Bank of England

special drawing rights *plural noun* the unit of account used by the International Monetary Fund, allocated to each member country for use in loans and other international operations. Their value is calculated daily on the weighted values of a group of currencies shown in dollars. Abbreviation **SDRs**

specialisation, specialization *noun* the concentration on the production of one type of good or service, leaving others to provide the rest. This allows specialist producers to be more efficient and to use scarce factors of production more efficiently.

specie *plural noun* money in the form of coins

specie point *noun* formerly, the exchange rate point for a currency on the gold standard at which it became profitable to use gold instead of another currency

specific tax *noun* a tax which is levied at a certain rate on each unit of the good or service sold which is levied on the value of the good or service. Compare **ad valorem tax**

speculation *noun* a deal which it is hoped will produce a profit

speculative boom *noun* a boom caused by investors who put money into risky investments which produce higher than normal returns

speculative bubble *noun* same as **bubble**

speculative demand for money *noun* the need for money in liquid form in case an opportunity for quick profit occurs

speculative motive *noun* the motive for people or firms to hold money in the form of investments because they hope to make a capital gain, as opposed to the 'precautionary motive' where they hold money in case of emergencies, or the 'transactions motive' where they hold money to use for some definite transaction in the future

speculative unemployment *noun* a form of unemployment in which workers reduce the hours they work because the pay is too low and wait until pay rates rise again before taking up full employment

speculator *noun* a person who buys goods, shares or foreign currency in the hope that they will rise in value and so he or she will be able to sell at a considerable profit

spillover *noun* the connection between one part of an economy and another. This can either be financial, where one firm's actions have a financial effect on another firm, or non-financial where the firm's actions have an effect on another firm to which no value can be applied, as in the case of pollution.

split-capital trust, split-level investment trust *noun* an investment trust with two categories of shares: income shares which receive income from the investments, but do not benefit from the rise in their capital value; and capital shares, which increase in value as the value of the investments rises, but do not receive any income

spot market *noun* the market for buying commodities or financial instruments for immediate delivery

spread *noun* **1.** a range or variety **2.** (*on the Stock Exchange*) the difference between buying and selling prices (i.e. between the bid and offer prices)

squeeze *noun* a means of government control carried out by reducing amounts of money available ■ *verb* to reduce something adversely

SRO *abbreviation* self-regulatory organisation

SSP *abbreviation* statutory sick pay

stabilisation, stabilization *noun* the process of making something stable, as the preventing of sudden changes in prices,

stabilisation policy *noun* same as **demand management**

Stackelberg duopoly *noun* a duopoly where one firm is the leader, whose strategies influence the other firm, which is the follower. It was proposed by the German economist Heinrich von Stackelberg (1904–46).

stag *noun* a person who subscribes for a large quantity of a new issue of shares hoping to sell them immediately to make a profit

stages of economic growth *plural noun* the various stages through which an economy passes over a long period of time, from a feudal society with little or no technological development to a rich sophisticated technological economy

stagflation *noun* inflation coupled with stagnation of an economy

stagnation *noun* a situation in which an economy does not increase and makes no progress

stakeholder *noun* **1.** a person who has a stake in a business, such as a shareholder, an employee or a supplier **2.** a person who has a stake in society (NOTE: A stakeholder may be an employee, customer, supplier, partner, or even the local community within which an organisation operates.)

stamp duty *noun* a tax on legal documents such as the sale or purchase of shares or the conveyance of a property to a new owner

Standard and Poor's *noun* a US corporation which rates bonds according to the credit-worthiness of the organizations issuing them. Its ratings run from AAA to D, and any organisation with a rating of below BBB is considered doubtful. Standard and Poor's also issues several stock market indices including the S&P 500, the S&P SmallCap and S&P MidCap. Abbreviation **S&P**

Standard and Poor's Composite Index, **Standard and Poor's 500-stock index** *noun* an index of 500 popular US stocks

standard deviation *noun* the measure of how much a variable changes from its mean

standard error *noun* the extent to which chance affects the accuracy of a sample

standard hour *noun* a unit of time used to establish the normal time which a job or task is expected to take, and used later to compare with the actual time taken

Standard Industrial Classification *noun* an international scheme for classifying industries into 92 groups according to their products (such as poultry framing (No. 1240), plumbing (45330), hairdressing (93020), photography (74810)). It is used for statistical purposes and to make international comparisons more meaningful. Abbreviation **SIC**

standard of living *noun* the quality of personal home life (such as amount of food or clothes bought, and size of family car.)

standby arrangement *noun* a plan for what should be done if an emergency happens, especially the holding of money in reserve in the International Monetary Fund for use by a country in financial difficulties

standby credit *noun* credit which is available and which can be drawn on if a country needs it, especially credit guaranteed by a lender (a group of banks or the IMF in the case of a member country), usually in dollars

standing order *noun* an order written by a customer asking a bank to pay money regularly to an account

staple commodity *noun* a basic food or raw material which is most important in a country's economy

staple product *noun* a product, such as milk or bread, which is important to the individual consumer but of which the consumption does not rise and fall when incomes rise and fall

star *noun* a product which has a high market share and a high growth rate. It will need cash to finance its growth, but eventually should become a cash cow.

state bank *noun* in the USA, a commercial bank licensed by the authorities of a state, and not necessarily a member of the Federal Reserve System (as opposed to a national bank)

State Earnings-Related Pension Scheme *noun* in the UK, a state pension which is additional to the basic retirement pension and is based on average earnings over a worker's career. It is being renamed the State Second Pension. Abbreviation **SERPS**

state enterprise *noun* a state-controlled company

state member bank *noun* a US state bank which has elected to join the Federal Reserve System

state ownership *noun* the situation in which an industry is nationalised

state planning *noun* same as **central planning**. compare **command economy**

State Second Pension *noun* ◊ **State Earnings-Related Pension Scheme**

stationary state *noun* a theoretical state of an economy which consumes exactly what it produces and replaces what it consumes at the end of the relevant period

statistical discrepancy *noun* the amount by which sets of figures differ

statistical inference *noun* a method of getting information about a population by taking a sample group and analysing it

statistics *plural noun* figures showing facts (NOTE: takes a plural verb) ■ *noun* the study of facts in the form of figures (NOTE: takes a singular verb)

statute law *noun* an established written law, especially an Act of Parliament

statutory sick pay *noun* state pay made by an employer to a worker who is sick. The payments are claimed back by the employer against his or her NI contributions. SSP is paid for working days, called qualifying days, up to a maximum of 28 weeks. Abbreviation **SSP**

steady-state growth *noun* the situation in which each sector of an economy grows at the its own rate each year, as when population grows at 2.5% but national income at 2%. Compare **balanced growth**

stealth tax *noun* a tax which is not obvious to the people paying it

sterilisation *noun* a method by which a central bank can prevent surpluses or deficits in the balance of payments from affecting money supply This is achieved by either selling or buying foreign currency to offset the effect of the surplus or deficit.

sterling *noun* the standard currency used in the UK The official term for the UK currency is pound sterling

sterling M3 *noun* ◊ **£M3**

sticky wages *plural noun* wages which do not change when market conditions change. Workers do not want to earn less in real terms than before, or do not want any wage increase to be less than the rise in the rate of inflation.

stochastic *adjective* which happens randomly or by chance

stochastic process *noun* a process of which the outcome appears to be unpredictable

stock *noun* **1.** the quantity of goods for sale or kept available for use **2.** the total number of shares issued by a company **3.** a share of capital held by an individual investor ■ *adjective* kept for sale all the time ■ *verb* to keep goods for sale

stock appreciation *noun* increase in the value of stock held by a firm caused by an increase in prices

stockbroker *noun* a person who buys or sells shares for clients

stock control *noun* the system of checking that there is not too much stock in a warehouse but just enough to meet requirements (NOTE: The US term is **inventory control**.)

stock dividend *noun US* same as **bonus issue**

stock exchange, Stock Exchange *noun* the place where stocks and shares are bought and sold. If no location is specified, it is usually understood in the UK as the London Stock Exchange. Also called **stock market**

Stock Exchange Automated Quotations System *noun* full form of **SEAQ**

stock option *noun* an option given to an employee to buy stock of the company at a lower price than the current market price, at some time in the future

stockpile *noun* a large quantity of supplies kept by a country or a company in case of need ■ *verb* to keep supplies n case of need

stockpiling *noun* the action of keeping supplies in case of need

stock split *noun US* same as **bonus issue**

stock turn, stock turnround, stock turnover *noun* the total value of stock sold in a year divided by the average value of goods in stock

stock valuation *noun* the estimating of the value of stock at the end of an accounting period

Stolper, Wolfgang (1912–2002) Austrian-born economist whose work included a theory (with Paul Samuelson) used to explain the effect of international trade on wages

Stolper-Samuelson theorem *noun* a theory to explain the effect of international trade in an economy with two factors of production and two goods. The factor which is most available and is used in the country's exports, provides the most profits; the scarce factor which is used in imports gives a reduced profit; the result is to encourage protection of the country's manufacturing sector against imports.

stop-go cycle *noun* a government's economic policy which leads to short periods of expansion followed by short periods of credit squeeze

store of value *noun* money kept as a hedge against the risk of a fall in prices

straight line depreciation *noun* depreciation calculated by dividing the cost of an asset, less its residual value, by the number of years it is likely to be used. Various methods of depreciating assets are used: under the straight line method, the asset is depreciated at a constant percentage of its cost each year while with the reducing balance method the asset is depreciated at a higher rate in the early years and at a lower rate later.

strategic business unit *noun* a part or division of a large company which forms its own business strategy. Abbreviation **SBU**

strategy *noun* a plan of future action (NOTE: The plural is **strategies**.)

stratified sample *noun* a framework for the selection of a sample that ensures that it adequately represents the population or universe

strike *noun* an act of stopping work by workers, because of lack of agreement with management or because of orders from a union ■ *verb* to go on strike (NOTE: **striking – struck**)

striking price, strike price *noun* the price at which a new offer of shares is offered for sale

structural adjustment *noun* adjustment made to the economy of a country

structural budget deficit *noun* the deficit in national accounts (i.e. the government's borrowing requirement) calculated after taking account of where the economy is placed in the business cycle

structural form *noun* the reduced form of an economic system which has been restructured in order to impose a view suggested by a particular economic theory

structural unemployment *noun* unemployment caused by the changing structure of an industry or the economy

stylised fact *noun* an observation about the real world which is based on assumptions rather than on information

subsidiarity *noun* the principle that decisions should be taken at the lower possible effective level, so within the EU major decisions would be taken at governmental level, and not at the level of the Commission

subsidiary company *noun* a company which is more than 50% owned by a holding company, and where the holding company controls the board of directors

subsidy *noun* an amount of money given to help a firm which is not profitable

subsistence *noun* the minimum amount of food, money, housing and other factors which a person needs

subsistence theory of wages *noun* the theory that the average level of wages is related to the wage necessary to provide each worker with a subsistence level of existence

subsistence wages *plural noun* the lowest level of wages which allows workers to live. According to the iron law of wages, as the population increases, so wages tend to fall to the subsistence level.

substitute *noun* a person or thing that takes the place of another ■ *adjective* taking the place of another person or thing ■ *verb* to takes the place of someone or something else, or to put one person or thing in the place of another

substitute product, substitute good *noun* a product which may be bought instead of another when the price of the latter changes or if it becomes unavailable. An increase in the price of one will cause an increase in the demand for the other. This is the opposite of complementary products where the demand for one increases as the price of the other falls.

substitution effect *noun* the extent to which consumers will change from one product to another when the price of the former rises

sub-underwriter *noun* ◊ **underwriter**

sufficient condition *noun* a condition which is enough to guarantee a result. Compare **necessary condition**

sunk costs *plural noun* expenditure on factors which cannot be used for another purpose or cannot be recovered if the firm is shut down. Such expenditure might include advertising or building costs.

sunspot theory *noun* the theory of the 19th century economist, W. S. Jevons, that business cycles are related to sunspot cycles

superneutrality of money *noun* a situation in which the growth of money supply has no influence on the real growth of output in an economy. Compare **neutrality of money**

supernormal profit *noun* a profit earned by a business through having a monopoly

supplementary benefit *noun* formerly, a payment from the UK government to people with very low incomes. It was replaced by Income Support.

supplier *noun* a person or company that supplies or sells goods or services. Also called **producer**

supply *noun* the quantity of a good or service which is needed and is available for sale ■ *verb* to provide a purchaser with a good or service

supply and demand *noun* the amount of a product which is available and the amount which is wanted by customers

Supply Bill *noun* a bill presented to Parliament to provide money for government requirements

supply curve *noun* a graph which shows the relationship between the price of a product or of a factor of production and amount of a product supplied during a period

supply shock *noun* a sudden rise in productivity which gives higher output and profits without inflation

supply-side economics *noun* an economic theory that governments should encourage producers and suppliers of goods by cutting taxes, increasing subsidies and similar measures rather than encourage demand by making more money available in the economy (NOTE: takes a singular verb)

supply-side policies *plural noun* policies which aim to stimulate the working of an economy by means such as encouraging production and reducing regulations

support price *noun* a price (in the EU) at which a government will buy agricultural produce to stop the price falling

support ratio *noun* same as **dependency ratio**

surcharge *noun* an extra charge, especially an extra duty charged on imported goods to discourage their importation and encourage local manufacture

surplus *noun* an amount of something which is more than is needed

surplus value *noun* the value of what workers produce in excess of what they consume or what they need to live on. According to Karl Marx, this excess is the basis of profit to the capitalist employer, but is eventually partly paid back to the state in the form of tax.

survivor principle, survivor technique *noun* the theory that those firms with the lowest costs will survive in a market at the expense of the firms with higher costs

sustainable *adjective* **1.** which does not create conditions which bring it to an end **2.** which does not deplete or damage natural resources irreparably and which leaves the environment in good order for future generations

sustainable development *noun* a development which balances the satisfaction of people's immediate interests and the protection of future generations' interests

sustainable growth *noun* growth in an economy which is based on renewable resources and does not use up non-renewable resources

sustainable yield *noun* the greatest productivity which can be yielded from a renewable resource without depleting the supply in a given area

swap *noun* an arrangement between central banks to allow each other credit in their respective currencies so as to make currency transactions easier ■ *verb* to exchange something

sweated labour *noun* people who work hard for very little money

syndicate *noun* a group of underwriters on the Lloyd's insurance market, made up of active underwriters who arrange the business and non-working underwriters (called names) who stand surety for any insurance claims which may arise

synergy *noun* a situation of producing greater effects by joining forces than by acting separately

Taft-Hartley Act 1947 *noun* a US act which limited the rights of trade unions, banned closed shops and restricted the opportunity of unions to strike

take-off *noun* the next-to-last stage in the economic development of a country where it becomes capable of prolonged growth in per capita income

takeover *noun* the act of buying a controlling interest in a business by buying more than 50% of its shares. Compare **acquisition**

takeover bid *noun* an offer to buy all or a majority of shares in a company so as to control it

Takeover Code *noun* a code of practice which regulates how takeovers should take place. It is enforced by the Takeover Panel.

Takeover Panel *noun* the non-statutory body which examines takeovers and applies the City Code on Takeovers and Mergers. Also called **City Panel on Takeovers and Mergers**

tap issue *noun* an issue of government stock direct to the Bank of England for sale to investors. Government stocks are normally issued in tranches for sale by tender, but small amounts are kept as tap stock for direct sale to investors. The term is applied to any government stocks sold in this way.

tariff *noun* a tax to be paid on imported goods. Also called **customs tariff**. Compare **import levy, import tariffs**

tastes *plural noun* differences in consumer preferences which cannot otherwise be explained. Tastes vary according to factors such as age, sex, income and type of work.

tâtonnement process *noun* a process by which a perfect equilibrium can be reached, where buyers and sellers establish their prices separately and the prices gradually converge as supply and demand forces apply; tâtonnement is French for groping

tax *noun* money taken by the government or by an official body to pay for government services ■ *verb* to take money from the income of an individual or company, or when a good or service is used or bought, to pay for government services

taxable income *noun* income on which a person has to pay tax

tax and price index *noun* a figure which shows how much gross incomes have to change (usually to increase) so that taxpayers can enjoy the same level of disposable income in the face of increased retail prices and increased taxation

taxation *noun* the process or practice of charging taxes, or the degree to which something is taxed

tax avoidance *noun* the practice of trying (legally) to minimise the amount of tax to be paid

tax base *noun* the items which are taxed. The tax base for VAT does not include children's clothes or food; the tax base for corporation tax is all company profits.

tax burden *noun* the total amount of tax paid in a country, including income tax, corporation tax, VAT or sales tax

tax court *noun* in the USA, a court which deals with disputes between taxpayers and the Internal Revenue Service. The UK equivalent is a hearing before the Commissioners of Inland Revenue.

tax credit *noun* **1.** a sum of money which can be offset against tax **2.** a part of a dividend on which the company has already paid advance corporation tax which is deducted from the shareholder's income tax charge

tax declaration *noun* same as **tax return**

tax evasion *noun* the practice of trying illegally not to pay tax

tax exemption *noun* US a situation of being free from payment of tax

tax-exempt special savings account *noun* a discontinued type of account into which money could be placed to earn interest free of tax, provided it was left untouched for five years. Since 1999 the scheme has gradually been phased out but money in existing TESSAs can be reinvested in ISAs. Abbreviation **TESSA**

tax expenditure *noun* government expenditure which takes the place of tax. This includes such items as tax allowances for married couples and relief against capital gains tax. These allowances have the effect of increasing other taxes to allow the government to maintain its tax revenue.

tax haven *noun* a country where taxes are low, encouraging companies to set up their main offices there. Countries such as the Bahamas are tax havens.

tax holiday *noun* a period when a new company pays no tax

tax return *noun* a completed tax form, with details of income and allowances which is sent by a taxpayer to the Inland Revenue. Also called **tax declaration**

tax shelter *noun* a financial arrangement (such as a pension scheme) whereby investments can be made without tax

tax year *noun* the twelve-month period on which taxes are calculated. In the UK, the tax year runs from 6 April one year to 5 April the following year.

tax yield *noun* the amount of money raised by a tax, less the costs involved

T-bill *US* same as **Treasury bill** (*informal*)

technical progress *noun* advances in techniques which allow more outputs to be made from the same quantity of inputs, or to make different types of output from the same inputs

technological progress *noun* advances in techniques which lead to improved market share. Such techniques can be new machinery or improved education of workers.

technological unemployment *noun* unemployment caused by technical progress, in particular by the introduction of machines to take the place of workers

technology *noun* the application of human knowledge to create machines and methods which improve products and their production and marketing

technology gap *noun* the difference between two countries caused by different levels of technical progress

technology transfer *noun* the application of technology developed by one company in another company

tender *noun* an offer to do something for a certain price, especially an offer to buy a Treasury bill ■ *verb* to offer to do something for a certain price

tender issue *noun* an issue of Treasury bills for sale by tender

term assurance, term insurance *noun* a life assurance which covers a person's life for a period of time. At the end of the period, if the person is still alive he or she receives nothing from the insurance.

term loan *noun* a loan for a fixed period of time

terms of trade *plural noun* the difference between a country's exports and imports

term structure of interest rates *noun* interest rates seen in the context of the different maturity dates of the investments. This is only applicable to investments which have a fixed interest rate. Also called **yield to maturity**

tertiary industry *noun* an industry which does not produce raw materials or manufacture products but offers a service (such as banking, retailing or accountancy)

tertiary sector *noun* the sector of industry which includes all tertiary industries

TESSA *abbreviation* tax-exempt special savings account

test discount rate *noun* the rate of return necessary to justify investment on a large government-funded project

tests of significance *plural noun* tests to calculate the probability that a result is erroneous because of errors in sampling, or the probability that a hypothesis is validated

theory of the firm *noun* a group of theories concerned with firms, how they work in a market and how they differ from each other

Third World *noun* the countries of Africa, Asia and South America which do not have highly developed industries (*dated*)

3i *abbreviation* Investors in Industry

threshold *noun* a point at which something changes

threshold agreement *noun* a contract which says that if the cost of living goes up by more than a certain amount, pay will go up to match it

threshold price *noun* in the EU, the lowest price at which farm produce imported into the EU can be sold

thrift *noun* **1.** the practice of saving money by spending carefully **2.** *US* same as **savings and loan**

tied aid *noun* the financing of public sector capital projects in developing countries at a reduced rate. It is provided by the aid agencies of developed governments, and is offered on much better terms than normal aid.

tied loan *noun* a loan which involves a guarantee by the borrower to buy supplies from the lender

tie-in sales *plural noun* sales where a condition of the sale is that something else is also bought, as when a customer taking out insurance is forced to take further insurance to cover something else which he or she does not need. Such sales are usually prohibited, or at least severely restricted by law.

tight fiscal policy *noun* a government policy to restrict demand by increasing taxes

tight monetary policy *noun* a government policy to restrict money supply

tight money *noun* same as **dear money**

tight money policy *noun* same as **tight monetary policy**

time account *noun* same as **deposit account**

time deposit *noun* a deposit of money for a fixed period, during which it cannot be withdrawn

time inconsistency *noun* a change in policy which takes place after a certain amount of time, or policies taken at a certain time which conflict with previous policies

time lag *noun* a delay which takes place in the collection of economic data, or in taking policy decisions dependent on economic data

time preference *noun* the preference of consumers to purchase something immediately, instead of waiting until a later date. Also called **positive time preference**

times covered *plural noun* the number of times a dividend is covered by profits. Also called **dividend cover**

time series *noun* a series of values given to a variable at different times

time series analysis *noun* a method of assessing variations in data over regular periods of time, such as sales per month or per quarter, in order to try to identify the causes for the variations

time-series data *noun* data which is collected at regular intervals, i.e. each month, each quarter or each year

token money *noun* a form of money where the face value is higher than the cost of making it. Bank notes are token money, gold coins are not.

Tokyo round *noun* the seventh round of negotiations on international tariffs under the auspices of GATT, held from 1973–79. It cut international tariffs further and accorded preferential treatment to developing countries. ◆ **Kennedy round, Uruguay round**

tort *noun* a civil wrong done by one person to another and entitling the victim to claim damages

total cost *noun* all the cost of producing a certain amount of production, including fixed costs and variable costs

total domestic expenditure *noun* the total amount spent in a country, not excluding imports

total factor productivity *noun* the calculation of the relationship between output and all factors of production used to produce it

total quality management *noun* a management style which demands commitment to maintain and improve quality throughout the workforce (with emphasis on factors such as control of systems, quality and inspection of working practices). Abbreviation **TQM**

total revenue *noun* all income from all sources

total utility *noun* the whole satisfaction of each individual who consumes a certain quantity of a good or service

tournament theory *noun* the theory that each worker is motivated by the possibility of promotion as well as of extra pay, and this leads to competition between members of the workforce

TQM *abbreviation* total quality management

tracker fund *noun* a fund which tracks (i.e. follows closely) one of the stock market indices, such as the Footsie

trade *noun* the business of buying and selling ■ *verb* to carry on the business of buying and selling

trade association *noun* a group which links together companies in the same trade

trade balance *noun* the international trading position of a country in merchandise, excluding invisible trade. If exports are greater than imports there is a surplus (or favourable balance of trade). Also called **balance of trade**

trade barrier *noun* a control placed by a government to prevent imports coming into the country. Safety standards and tariffs are typical trade barriers. Also called **import restriction**

trade bill *noun* a bill of exchange between two companies which are trading partners. It is issued by one company and endorsed by the other. The person or company raising the bill is the drawer, the person or company who accepts it is the drawee. The seller can then sell the bill at a discount to raise cash.

trade creation *noun* the increase in international trade which follows from the reduction in trade barriers between countries

trade credit *noun* credit offered by one company when trading with another

trade cycle *noun* same as **business cycle**

trade deficit *noun* a situation in which a country imports more than it exports and so pays out more in foreign currency than it earns. Also called **balance of payments deficit, trade gap**

trade description *noun* a description of a product to attract customers

Trade Descriptions Act *noun* Acts of Parliament which limit the way in which products can be described so as to protect customers from wrong descriptions made by manufacturers

trade discount *noun* a reduction in price given to a customer in the same trade. Also known as 'trade terms'.

trade diversion *noun* the reduction in international trade with a country which is not a member of a group, caused when tariff barriers are reduced between members of the group and this has the effect of creating more trade within the group

trade gap *noun* same as **trade deficit**

trademark, trade name *noun* a particular name, design or logo which has been registered by the manufacturer and which cannot be used by other manufacturers. It is an intangible asset.

trade-off *noun* the exchange of one thing for another as part of a business deal (NOTE: The plural is **trade-offs**.)

Trades Union Congress *noun* an organisation linking all UK trade unions. Abbreviation **TUC** (NOTE: Although **Trades Union Congress** is the official name for the organisation, **trade union** is commoner than **trades union** in British English. The US term is **labor union**.)

trade union, trades union *noun* a workers' organisation which represents its members in discussions with employers about wages and conditions of employment

trade war *noun* a battle between countries to increase their trading positions, usually taking the form of import restrictions against foreign countries and increased subsidies for home industries

trade-weighted *adjective* compared to a basket of currencies of a country's major trading partners

trade-weighted index *noun* an index of the value of a currency calculated against a basket of currencies

trade-weighted value *noun* the value of a currency against that of a basket of other currencies

trading currency *noun* a currency, such as the dollar, which is used in international trade. Also called **vehicle currency**

trading profit *noun* a situation in which a company's gross receipts are more than its gross expenditure

trading stamp *noun* a special stamp given away by a shop, which the customer can collect and exchange later for goods

training *noun* the process of being taught how to do something, in particular instruction in particular skills

transaction *noun* a piece of buying or selling

transactions cost economics *noun* a form of economics which sees the firm as an economic entity, with its transactions being the reason for it to exist

transactions costs *plural noun* the costs involved in carrying out business transactions, including market research, invoicing and debt collection

transactions demand for money *noun* the need for firms or individuals to hold money in case some future business deal should materialise

transactions motive *noun* the motive for people or firms to hold money to use for some definite transaction in the future, as opposed to the speculative motive where they hold money in the form of investments because they hope to make a capital gain or the precautionary motive where they hold money to use in an emergency

transfer costs *plural noun* the costs of moving raw materials or finished goods from one place to another, including shipping, loading and harbour fees

transfer deed *noun* a legal document by which ownership of an asset, such as a house or a block of shares, is moved from one person to another

transfer earnings *plural noun* the amount which could be paid for a factor of production as it is currently being used to prevent it being used by someone else. Amounts paid above the level of transfer earnings are economic rent.

transfer payments *plural noun* payments which are not made for goods or services. These include pensions and money won by gambling.

transfer pricing *noun* prices used in a large organisation for selling goods or services between departments in the same organisation, and also in multinational corporations to transfer transactions from one country to another to avoid paying tax

transformation curve *noun* same as **production possibility boundary**

transitional unemployment *noun* **1.** a period when someone is out of work for a short time between two jobs **2.** unemployment caused by major economic change such as the introduction of new technology

transition economy *noun* an economy which is moving from a centrally planned state to a free market economy. Also called **economy in transition**

transitivity *noun* the way in which preferences are transferred logically. If product X is preferred to product Y and product Y is preferred to product Z, then it follows that product X is preferred to product Z.

transmission mechanism *noun* the ways in which changes in such things as prices, interest rates and incomes are covered in various sectors of an economy or in various countries of an economic group

transnational *noun* same as **multinational**

transnational corporation *noun* a large company which operates in various countries

Treasury *noun* **1.** the government department which deals with a country's finances. The term is used in both the UK and the USA. In most other countries, this department is called the Ministry of Finance. (NOTE: The term is used in both the UK and the USA; in most other countries this department is called the **Ministry of Finance**.) **2.** *US* same as **Treasury bill**

Treasury bill *noun* a short-term bill of exchange which does not give any interest and is sold by the government at a discount through the central bank. In the UK, the term varies from three to six months; in the USA, Treasury bills are for 91 or 182 days, or for 52 weeks. In the USA they are also called Treasuries or T-bills.

Treasury notes *plural noun* medium-term bonds issued by the US government

Treasury stocks *plural noun* bonds issued by the UK government. Also called **Exchequer stocks**

Treaty of Rome *noun* the treaty which established the European Economic Community and the European Atomic Energy Commission in 1957

trend *noun* the general way things are going

trickle-down *noun* the economic theory that the poorest members of society can be more easily helped by the effects of increased economic activity rather than by welfare payments from the government

trigonometric functions *plural noun* functions which are determined by the properties seen in right-angled triangles

triple A *noun* ◊ **A**

trough *noun* a low point (as in an economic cycle)

true and fair view *noun* the correct statement of a company's financial position as shown in its accounts and confirmed by the auditors

trust, trust company *noun* an organisation which supervises the financial affairs of private trusts, executes wills, and acts as a bank to a limited number of customers

trustee *noun* a person who has charge of money in trust

TUC *abbreviation* Trades Union Congress

turnkey operation *noun* a deal where a company takes all responsibility for constructing, fitting and staffing a building (such as a school, hospital or factory) so that it is completely ready for the purchaser to take over

turnover *noun* the amount of sales of goods or services by a company (NOTE: The US term is **sales volume**.)

turnover of labour *noun* same as **labour turnover**

turnover tax *noun* same as **sales tax**

turnpike theorem *noun* a form of optimal growth theory, put forward by Paul Samuelson, that the shortest route between two economic states may not be the quickest and that it may be better for a country to aim for a maximum growth rate even if it appears to go against the ratios of different production sectors which are considered desirable in the long term

two-part tariff *noun* a tariff by which consumers pay a certain rate for the first part of their consumption up to a certain level, and a lower rate after that

two-stage least squares *noun* a way of using simultaneous equations in econometric procedures by which right-hand variables are replaced by the result of their own equations. This gives a more accurate result than simply running the equations normally. The two stages referred to are firstly, the creation of new dependent variables to replace the originals, and secondly, regression calculated as normal but using the new variables. Abbreviation **2SLS**

two-tier board *noun* a system where a company has two boards of directors, an executive board which runs the company on a day-to-day basis and a supervisory board which monitors the results and deals with long-term planning

tying contract *noun* a contract under which a producer sells a product to a distributor on condition that the latter also buys another product

type I error *noun* an error found in decisions concerning hypotheses, when a correct hypothesis is not accepted, even if there is no good reason for not accepting it

type II error *noun* an error found in decisions concerning hypotheses, when a false hypothesis is accepted as being true when it should have been rejected

U

UBR *abbreviation* uniform business rate

UN *abbreviation* United Nations

unanticipated inflation *noun* a rate of inflation which has not been predicted by economists and which therefore comes as a surprise to business people, governments and workers

unbiased estimator *noun* the estimator with the smallest error

unbundling *noun* the process of separating companies from a conglomerate. The companies were independent in the past, and have been acquired by the conglomerate over a period of time.

uncalled capital *noun* capital which a company is authorised to raise and has been issued but for which payment has not yet been requested

uncertainty *noun* a situation in which the true facts are not known which makes it impossible to predict what will happen in the future; the decision-maker has to make difficult decisions. ♦ **fundamental uncertainty**

UNCTAD *abbreviation* United Nations Conference on Trade and Development

undated security *noun* a security with no maturity date

underdeveloped countries *plural noun* countries which are not fully industrialised

underemployment *noun* a situation in which workers in a company do not have enough work to do or are not used to their full capacity; they may therefore take up second jobs to fill their time and increase their earnings

underlying inflation rate *noun* the UK inflation rate which is calculated on a series of figures, including prices of consumer items; petrol, gas and electricity; and interest rates. The underlying inflation rate can be compared to that of other countries. Compare **headline inflation rate**

undersubscription *noun* a situation in which applications are not made for all the shares on offer in a share issue, and part of the issue remains with the underwriters

underutilised capacity *noun* a situation in which a company or factory operates at less than full capacity

undervalued currency *noun* a currency which is not valued highly enough

underwriter *noun* a person or company that underwrites a share issue or an insurance. When a major company flotation or share issue or loan is prepared, a group of companies (such as banks) will form a syndicate to underwrite the action. The syndicate will be organised by the lead underwriter (in the USA called the managing underwriter), together with a group of main underwriters. These in turn will ask others (sub-underwriters) to share in the underwriting.

underwriting *noun* the action of guaranteeing to purchase shares in a new issue if no one else purchases them

undistributable reserves *plural noun* same as **capital reserves**

undistributed profit *noun* profit which has not been distributed as dividends to shareholders but is retained in the business

UNDP *abbreviation* United Nations Development Programme

unearned income *noun* same as **investment income**

uneconomic *adjective* which does not make a commercial profit

unemployment *noun* a situation in which people have no jobs

unemployment benefit *noun* payment made to someone who is unemployed (NOTE: The US term is **unemployment compensation**.)

unemployment rate *noun* the number of people out of work, shown as a percentage of the total number of people available for work. Also called **rate of unemployment**

unfair dismissal *noun* the removing of someone from a job for reasons which are not legally fair (as when a female employee who has had maternity leave and wishes to return to work is refused a job by the company she was working for). Unfair dismissal cannot be claimed where a worker is dismissed for incapability, gross misconduct or in cases of genuine redundancy.

unfunded pension scheme *noun* a pension scheme which is not based on a pension fund, but where pensions are paid by the employer out of current income

uniform business rate *noun* a tax levied on business property which is the same percentage for the whole country. Abbreviation **UBR**

union/non-union wage differential *noun* the difference in wages earned by union members and non-union members in the same type of jobs. It is seen as a measure of the effectiveness of unions.

union shop *noun* US place of work where it is agreed that all workers must be workers of a union (NOTE: The UK term is **closed shop**.)

unitary taxation *noun* the taxation of a multinational firm in one country (the country of its bases) on all its operations. This avoids the possibility that firms may move transactions from one country to another to avoid paying tax.

unit banking *noun* the situation in which a state bank tends to have only one branch, operating under the umbrella of the Federal Reserve System. This is the system in the USA, while in the UK banks tend to operate a branch banking system with a few national banks, each with very many branches.

unit cost *noun* the cost of one item (i.e. total product costs divided by the number of units produced)

United Nations *plural noun* an international organisation including almost all sovereign states in the world, where member states are represented at meetings

United Nations Conference on Trade and Development
noun a permanent organisation of the United Nations General Assembly set up in 1964 to deal with issues concerning trade, investment and development. Its aims are to maximise opportunities for developing countries and to help them integrate into the world economy. Abbreviation **UNCTAD**

United Nations Development Programme *noun* the global
development network of the United Nations, which helps developing countries to knowledge, experience and resources through advice and aid provided by local experts. Abbreviation **UNDP**

unit of account *noun* a standard unit used in financial transactions among members of a group, such as SDRs in the IMF

unit trust *noun* an organisation which takes money from small investors and invests it in stocks and shares for them under a trust deed, the investment being in the form of shares (or units) in the trust. Unit trusts have to be authorised by the Department of Trade and Industry before they can offer units for sale to the public, although unauthorised private unit trusts exist. (NOTE: The US term is **mutual fund**.)

unlimited liability *noun* a situation in which a sole trader or each partner is responsible for all the firm's debts with no limit to the amount each may have to pay

Unlisted Securities Market *formerly.* the market for buying and
selling shares which were not listed on the main Stock Exchange. It has now been replaced by the Alternative Investment Market (AIM). Abbreviation **USM**

unrealised profit *noun* same as **paper profit**

unsecured loan *noun* a loan made with no security

upside potential *noun* the possibility for a share to increase in value (NOTE: The opposite is **downside risk**.)

urban economics *noun* the economics of urban areas. It deals with the growth of large urban areas and the problems they pose for such areas as transport, pollution and services.

Uruguay round *noun* the eighth round of negotiations on international tariffs under the auspices of GATT, held in 1986–94. It opened markets in agriculture and services, reduced government subsidies to local industries and protected intellectual copyrights. It also ended with the establishment of the

World Trade organisation as a successor to GATT. ⬧ **Kennedy round, Tokyo round**

U-shaped average cost curve *noun* a curve which shows how average costs vary with the amount of output. As output increases, so average costs fall, then they start to rise again because marginal costs increase as output increases. This gives a typical curve in the shape of a U.

USM *abbreviation* Unlisted Securities Market

usury *noun* the lending of money at very high interest

util *noun* a theoretical unit for measuring utility

utilitarianism *noun* a theory, propounded by Jeremy Bentham, that policies and institutions should be judged by how good they are for the people. His slogan was the greatest good of the greatest number.

utility *noun* **1.** one of the public utilities (companies, such as electricity, gas or transport, which provide a service used by the whole community) **2.** the usefulness of a product or service, the satisfaction which a consumer gets from a good or service he or she has bought, or the way in which a good or service contributes to a consumer's welfare

utility function *noun* a method of showing utility as a function of the consumption of goods and services by an individual. It increases with each unit consumed.

utility maximisation *noun* the action of individuals who make choices according to how they perceive the good which the choice will bring to them, especially in cases where the outcome of the choice is uncertain

utopian socialism *noun* an early form of socialism, in which services and goods are produced for the use of the community as a whole, derived from the writings of Robert Owen and Jean-Jacques Rousseau. It was an idealistic form of socialism and its members created ideal communities in Britain, the USA and other countries. It was approved of by Marx and Engels.

V

vacancy *noun* a job which is to be filled

vacancy rate *noun* the number of jobs which are available shown as a proportion of the total workforce

value *noun* the amount of money which something is worth ■ *verb* to assess the amount of money which something is worth

value added *noun* the amount added to the value of a product or service, being the difference between its cost and the amount received when it is sold (wages, taxes and similar factors are deducted from the added value to give the retained profit). Also called **net output**

Value Added Tax *noun* full form of **VAT**

value judgement *noun* a judgement based on an assertion of what is thought to be good or bad, rather than on a statement of fact

variable *noun* a thing which varies, especially a number which can take different values

variable cost *noun* money paid to produce a product which increases with the quantity made (such as direct labour costs and direct materials costs)

variable factor input *noun* an input of a factor of production which can be easily varied with the effect of increasing or reducing output

variable factor proportions *plural noun* the degree to which one factor of production can be substituted for another. If the proportion is high, then firms will switch from one factor to another according to whichever is cheapest.

variable rate *noun* a rate of interest on a loan which is not fixed, but can change with the current bank interest rates. Also called **floating rate**

variance *noun* a difference, especially that between what was planned and the actual results

VAT *noun* a tax paid by the consumer which represents the increased value of a product at each stage of its manufacture and distribution. Full form **Value Added Tax**

COMMENT: In the UK, VAT is organised by the Customs and Excise Department, and not by the Treasury. It is applied at each stage in the process of making or selling a product or service. Company 'A' charges VAT for their work, which is bought by Company 'B', and pays the VAT collected from 'B' to the Customs and Excise; Company 'B' can reclaim the VAT element in Company 'A''s invoice from the Customs and Excise, but will charge VAT on their work in their invoice to Company 'C'. Each company along the line charges VAT and pays it to the Customs and Excise, but claims back any VAT charged to them. The final consumer pays a price which includes VAT, and which is the final VAT revenue paid to the Customs and Excise. Any company or individual should register for VAT if their annual turnover or income is above a certain level

vault cash *noun* cash kept by a bank in its vaults, used for everyday business, and forming part of the bank's required reserves

VCT *abbreviation* venture capital trust

Veblen, Thorstein Bunde (1857–1929) *noun* US economist whose main concern was with the growth of large companies which could result in the position that the prosperity of a company need not coincide with the interests of the community at large; he invented the term conspicuous consumption to criticise the behaviour of wealthy individuals and firms

Veblen effect, Veblenian model *noun* a theory of buying behaviour proposed by Veblen, which explains much of consumption in terms of social influences or pressures rather than economic ones. ⟡ **conspicuous consumption**

vector *noun* a series of numbers arranged one after the other in a certain direction, either vertically or horizontally

vehicle currency *noun* same as **trading currency**

velocity of circulation *noun* the rate at which money circulates in the economy, usually calculated as the GNP shown as a percentage of the stock of money supply

venture capital *noun* capital for investment which may easily be lost in risky projects, but can also provide high returns. Also called **risk capital**

venture capital trust *noun* a trust which invests in smaller firms which need capital to grow. Money invested in a VCT must remain there for five years, and in return no capital gains are paid on £100,000 worth of VCT shares sold. Abbreviation **VCT**

VER *abbreviation* voluntary export restraint

vertical equity *noun* fairness in dealing with individuals with different incomes. This is the basis for progressive taxation.

vertical integration *noun* same as **backward integration**

vertical merger *noun* a merger of two firms which deal with different stages of the production or sale of the same product

visible *adjective* **1.** referring to real products which are imported or exported **2.** recorded or reflected in economic statistics

visible balance *noun* the balance of payments in visible trade, i.e. real goods, as opposed to services

visibles *plural noun* real products which are imported or exported, as opposed to services

visible trade *noun* the trade in real goods which are imported or exported

voluntary arrangement *noun* same as **scheme of arrangement**

World Trade organisation as a successor to GATT. ♦ **Kennedy round, Tokyo round**

U-shaped average cost curve *noun* a curve which shows how average costs vary with the amount of output. As output increases, so average costs fall, then they start to rise again because marginal costs increase as output increases. This gives a typical curve in the shape of a U.

USM *abbreviation* Unlisted Securities Market

usury *noun* the lending of money at very high interest

util *noun* a theoretical unit for measuring utility

utilitarianism *noun* a theory, propounded by Jeremy Bentham, that policies and institutions should be judged by how good they are for the people. His slogan was the greatest good of the greatest number.

utility *noun* **1.** one of the public utilities (companies, such as electricity, gas or transport, which provide a service used by the whole community) **2.** the usefulness of a product or service, the satisfaction which a consumer gets from a good or service he or she has bought, or the way in which a good or service contributes to a consumer's welfare

utility function *noun* a method of showing utility as a function of the consumption of goods and services by an individual. It increases with each unit consumed.

utility maximisation *noun* the action of individuals who make choices according to how they perceive the good which the choice will bring to them, especially in cases where the outcome of the choice is uncertain

utopian socialism *noun* an early form of socialism, in which services and goods are produced for the use of the community as a whole, derived from the writings of Robert Owen and Jean-Jacques Rousseau. It was an idealistic form of socialism and its members created ideal communities in Britain, the USA and other countries. It was approved of by Marx and Engels.

V

vacancy *noun* a job which is to be filled

vacancy rate *noun* the number of jobs which are available shown proportion of the total workforce

value *noun* the amount of money which something is worth ■ *verb* to ass the amount of money which something is worth

value added *noun* the amount added to the value of a product or servic being the difference between its cost and the amount received when it is so (wages, taxes and similar factors are deducted from the added value to gi the retained profit). Also called **net output**

Value Added Tax *noun* full form of **VAT**

value judgement *noun* a judgement based on an assertion of what i thought to be good or bad, rather than on a statement of fact

variable *noun* a thing which varies, especially a number which can take different values

variable cost *noun* money paid to produce a product which increase with the quantity made (such as direct labour costs and direct materials costs

variable factor input *noun* an input of a factor of production whic can be easily varied with the effect of increasing or reducing output

variable factor proportions *plural noun* the degree to which o factor of production can be substituted for another. If the proportion is hi then firms will switch from one factor to another according to whichever cheapest.

variable rate *noun* a rate of interest on a loan which is not fixed, but change with the current bank interest rates. Also called **floating rate**

variance *noun* a difference, especially that between what was planned the actual results

VAT *noun* a tax paid by the consumer which represents the increased v of a product at each stage of its manufacture and distribution. Full

Value Added Tax

COMMENT: In the UK, VAT is organised by the Customs and Ex Department, and not by the Treasury. It is applied at each stage in the proc of making or selling a product or service. Company 'A' charges VAT for work, which is bought by Company 'B', and pays the VAT collected from ' the Customs and Excise; Company 'B' can reclaim the VAT elemen Company 'A''s invoice from the Customs and Excise, but will charge VA their work in their invoice to Company 'C'. Each company along the

voluntary exchange *noun* trade between two firms or countries which can each refuse to trade with each other. In this case, both parties will benefit from trading. It can also be applied to the supply of public goods, on the assumption that the public must be allowed to decide what goods should be supplied. Because all of the parties to a voluntary exchange expect to gain from trade, institutions that make trading easier usually also improve social welfare.

voluntary export restraint *noun* an agreement by exporters not to export to a certain country, usually under threat of tariff barriers being imposed by that country. Abbreviation **VER**

voluntary unemployment *noun* unemployment which exists because people do not want to take existing work, either because they feel the wages are too low, or because they would get a better deal by living on government benefits

voting shares *plural noun* shares which give the holder the right to vote at company meetings

voucher *noun* a paper which is given instead of money

W

wage *noun* money paid (usually in cash each week) to a worker for work done (NOTE: **wages** is more usual when referring to money earned, but **wage** is used before other nouns)

COMMENT: The term 'wages' refers to weekly or hourly pay for workers, usually paid in cash. For employees paid by a monthly cheque, the term used is 'salary'.

wage drift *noun* the difference between wages and money actually earned, i.e. the situation in which a wage increase paid is greater than the officially negotiated one, the difference being made up with payments such as bonus and overtime payments. Also called **wages drift**

wage freeze *noun* a period when wages are not allowed to increase. Also called **freeze on wages, wages freeze**

wage indexation *noun* the linking of increases in wages to the percentage rise in the cost of living

wage-price spiral *noun* a situation in which price rises encourage higher wage demands which in turn make prices rise

wage rate *noun* the amount of money paid to a worker for an hour's work

wage restraint *noun* action to keep increases in wages under control

wage round *noun* a round of negotiations between representatives of employers and unions to determine the wage levels in an industry over the next period, usually for one year

wages *plural noun* workers' weekly or hourly pay, usually paid in cash. For workers paid by a monthly cheque, the term used is salary.

wages council *noun* an organisation made up of employer and employee representatives which fixes basic employment conditions in industries where places of work are too small or too scattered for trade unions to be established

wages drift *noun* same as **wage drift**

wages freeze *noun* same as **wage freeze**

wages policy *noun* a government's policy on what percentage increases should be paid to workers

wait unemployment *noun* same as **precautionary unemployment**

Wall Street *noun* **1.** a street in New York where the Stock Exchange is situated **2.** the US financial centre

Wall Street crash *noun* the crash of share prices on Wall Street in 1929, which started the Great Depression. The date is also called Black Tuesday.

Walras, Marie-Esprit-Léon (1834–1910) French economist and mathematician who developed the theory that for each product there is a demand which is dependent on price, and a supply price function which depends on the quantities produced. Theoretically, there should be a point of equilibrium where the demand price and supply price are the same.

Walras's law *noun* the law that the total value of goods demanded in an economy is equal to the total value of the goods supplied. It does not take into account the fact that people may save money.

wants *noun* the desire to purchase goods or services. This is a choice, and not a need.

warehouse capacity *noun* the space available in a warehouse

warrant *noun* an official document which allows someone to do something ■ *verb* to provide a warranty for a product

warranted growth rate *noun* the rate at which growth must increase if it is to be sustained, when firms believe growth will occur without any extra investment. ◆ **Harrod-Domar growth model**

warranty *noun* a legal document which promises that a machine will work properly and in which the producer agrees to compensate the buyer if the product is faulty or becomes faulty before a certain date

wasting asset *noun* an asset which becomes gradually less valuable as time goes by (such as a short lease on a property)

ways and means advances *plural noun* advances of money made by the Bank of England to the government

wealth *noun* the value of assets (other than cash and things such as machines) which are held by an individual, firm or country and which can be used to produce income. Wealth also includes human capital in the form of the resources provided by the workforce.

wealth effect *noun* the effect the amount of assets held by an individual has on his or her spending and saving patterns. It is assumed that if two individuals have the same income, the one with the most assets will spend most and save least.

wealth tax *noun* a tax on money, property or investments owned by individual taxpayers

wear and tear *noun* damage to equipment caused by use; fair wear and tear is a term used in insurance for acceptable damage caused by normal use

weighted average *noun* an average which is calculated taking several factors into account, giving some more value than others

welfare *noun* money paid by the government to people who need it

welfare criterion *noun* a criterion used to decide if a change in economic policy should be put into effect. Pareto stated that the criterion to be used was if the policy change resulted in increased welfare of someone and no decrease in welfare to others.

welfare economics *noun* the study of the way in which economic activity should result in increased welfare for the population. It concentrates on the objectives to be achieved in a welfare state.

welfare state *noun* a state which spends a large amount of money to make sure that its citizens all have adequate housing, education, public transport and health services

WFTC *abbreviation* working families tax credit

white knight *noun* a person or company that rescues a firm in financial difficulties, especially saving a firm from being taken over by an unacceptable purchaser

white noise *noun* a series of observations made over a period of time which are random and completely independent

White Paper *noun* a proposal from the UK government for a new law to be voted on in Parliament. Compare **Green Paper**

wholesale *adjective, adverb* buying goods from manufacturers and selling in large quantities to traders who then sell in smaller quantities to the general public

wholesale banking *noun* banking services between merchant banks and other financial institutions (as opposed to 'retail banking')

wholesale market *noun* the interbank money market, where banks and other financial institutions deal with each other

wholesale price *noun* the price of a product which is wholesale

wholesale price index *noun* an index showing the rises and falls of wholesale prices of manufactured goods. It usually moves about two months before a similar movement takes place on the Retail Price Index.

wholesaler *noun* a person or company that buys goods in bulk from manufacturers and sells them to retailers

Wicksell, Knut (1851–1926) Swedish economist whose interest in monetary theory showed that high interest rates occurred in conjunction with high prices

Wicksell effects *plural noun* the effect of a rise in wages rates and a fall in interest rates in raising the value of existing capital

wild cats *plural noun* same as **problem children**

wildcat strike *noun* a strike organised suddenly by workers without the approval of the main union office

windfall loss *noun* a sudden loss which is not expected

windfall profit *noun* a sudden profit which is not expected

windfall profits tax, **windfall tax** *noun* a tax on sudden profits

winding up *noun* the liquidation of a company

window dressing *noun* transactions shown in financial statements with the sole purpose of making a business seem better or more profitable or more efficient than it really is

wind up *verb* to put a company into liquidation

winner's curse *noun* the possibility that the company which wins a contract may in fact lose money on the work. This is especially likely if it made the lowest tender.

WIP *abbreviation* work in progress

withdrawal *noun* the removing of money from a bank account

withholding tax *noun US* a tax levied on interest or dividends before they are paid to the investor (usually applied to non-resident investors). Such tax may be reclaimed under a double taxation agreement.

with profits *adverb* guaranteeing the policyholder a share in the profits of the fund in which the premiums are invested

work *noun* things done using the hands or brain ■ *verb* to do things using the hands or brain

workable competition *noun* the theoretical consideration of competition which tries to give guidelines as to how competition policy should be applied

worker participation *noun* sharing by workers in management decisions

workfare *noun* a system where people have to do work for the community to qualify for welfare payments

working capital *noun* capital in the form of cash, stocks and debtors (less creditors) used by a company in its day-to-day operations (normally defined as the excess of current assets over current liabilities). Also called **circulating capital, floating capital, net current assets**

working families tax credit *noun* a benefit in the form of a credit which can be used to pay tax, accorded to working families on low incomes with one or more dependent children and few savings. Abbreviation **WFTC**

working population *noun* same as **labour force**

work in progress *noun* the value of service on a contract which has not been completed, or the value of goods being manufactured which are not complete at the end of an accounting period. Abbreviation **WIP** (NOTE: The US term is **work in process**.)

works committee, works council *noun* a committee of workers a' management which discusses the organisation of work in a factory

work-sharing *noun* a system where two or more part-timers sh* job, each doing part of the work

work-to-rule *noun* a period of working strictly according to the rules agreed between the union and management and therefore very slowly, as a protest

World Bank *noun* the central bank, controlled by the United Nations, whose funds come from the member states of the UN and which lends money to member states. The official title of the World Bank is the International Bank for Reconstruction and Development.

world economy *noun* the economy of the whole world, seen as a total

World Trade Organization *noun* an international organisation set up with the aim of reducing restrictions in trade between countries (replacing GATT). Abbreviation **WTO**

WTO *abbreviation* World Trade Organization

X Y Z

X-efficiency *noun* the situation of being as efficient as possible in using inputs to maximise production

X-inefficency *noun* the situation of not being as efficient as possible in using inputs to maximise production, a feature of larger organisations. It is the difference between the actual costs achieved and the costs which are theoretically achievable.

x-value *noun* same as **abscissa**

Yaoundé Convention *noun* an international agreement signed in 1964 to allow former French colonies to become associated to the European Community. It was replaced in 1974 by the Lomé Convention.

yardstick competition *noun* a method used by a regulator to judge the performance of a group of monopoly firms, as in the case of railway companies

Y-efficiency *noun* a measure of the efficiency of a firm in exploiting markets profitably. It can be the case that a firm does not exploit its market as profitably as it should because of the lack of competition.

yen *noun* the currency used in Japan (NOTE: It is usually written as ¥ before a figure: **¥2,700** (say two thousand seven hundred yen).)

yield *noun* an amount of money produced as a return on an investment, shown as a percentage of the money invested ■ *verb* to produce money as a return on an investment

COMMENT: To work out the yield on an investment, take the gross dividend per annum, multiply it by 100 and divide by the price you paid for it (in pence): an investment paying a dividend of 20p per share and costing £3.00, is yielding 6.66%.

yield curve *noun* a graph showing the yields on different types of investment. A negative yield curve is a situation in which the yield on a long-term investment is less than on a short-term investment, while a positive yield curve is a situation where the yield on a long-term investment is more than on a short-term investment.

yield gap *noun* the difference between the higher yield on equities (ordinary shares) and the lower yield on gilt-edged securities (i.e. government stock). If the returns on gilts are higher than on equities this is called the reverse yield gap.

yield to maturity *noun* same as **term structure of interest rates**

y-value *noun* same as **ordinate**

zero-coupon bond *noun* a bond which carries no interest, but which is issued at a discount and so provides a capital gain when it is redeemed at its face value

zero growth *noun* a situation in which there is no increase in economic activity, either because of economic stagnation or because of government policies to restrain growth

zero-rated *adjective* which has a VAT rate of 0%. In the UK, books and newspapers are zero-rated.

zero-sum game *noun* in game theory, a game where the players divide the total sum between them, some having less than others, but all adding up to 100%. Here there is no way in which players can agree to take more than 100%. Compare **negative-sum game, positive-sum game**

zoning *noun* the dividing of a town into different areas for planning purposes

63 3 260 11 3